Ordnance

North Devon,
Exmoor and the Quantocks
Landranger Guidebook

Compiled by Peter Titchmarsh, M.A., F.R.G.S.

JARROLD

How to use this Guide.

Space has not allowed us to include every place on Landranger Maps in the 'Places of Special Interest' section (pages 22-87). But the items have been selected to provide you with a varied and interesting companion during your travels around North Devon, Exmoor and the Quantocks. Places of exceptional interest have been highlighted by being printed in blue.

Each entry is identified first with the number of the Landranger map on which it appears (eg. 180, 181, etc). This is followed by two letters (eg. ST) and by a 4-figure reference number (eg. 07-37). The first two figures of this number are those which appear in blue along the north and south edges of Landranger maps; the other two appear in blue along the east and west edges.

Therefore to locate any place or feature referred to in this guide book on the relevant Landranger map, first read the two figures along the north or south edges of the map, then the two figures along the east or west edges. Trace the lines adjacent to each of the two sets of figures across the map face, and the point where they intersect will be the south-west corner of the grid square in which the place or feature lies. Thus the village of Monksilver falls in the grid square 07-37 on Landranger map 181.

The Key Maps on pages 4-7 identify the suggested starting points of our ten Tours and twelve Walks, and in the Tours and Walks sections, all places which also have a separate entry in the 'Places of Special Interest' section are in bold type. Each Tour and Walk is accompanied by a map, and there are cross references between Tours and Walks on both the maps and in the text.

Acknowledgements

We would like to thank Mr Reg Jones for his most interesting article on *Natural History*. We are also very grateful to the members of the Ramblers Association's three groups in West Somerset, North Devon and North West Devon for their help with the twelve *Walks*. This work included walking over the routes concerned and provision of the detailed directions for walkers which will be found in the guide.

First published 1985 by Ordnance Survey and Jarrold Colour Publications.
Reprinted 1989

Ordnance Survey
Romsey Road
Maybush
Southampton SO9 4DH

Jarrold Colour
Publications
Barrack Street
Norwich NR3 1TR

The contents of this publication are believed correct at the time of printing. Nevertheless, the Publishers cannot accept responsibility for errors and omissions, or for changes in details given.

Printed in Great Britain by Jarrold and Sons Ltd., Norwich. 289.

Contents

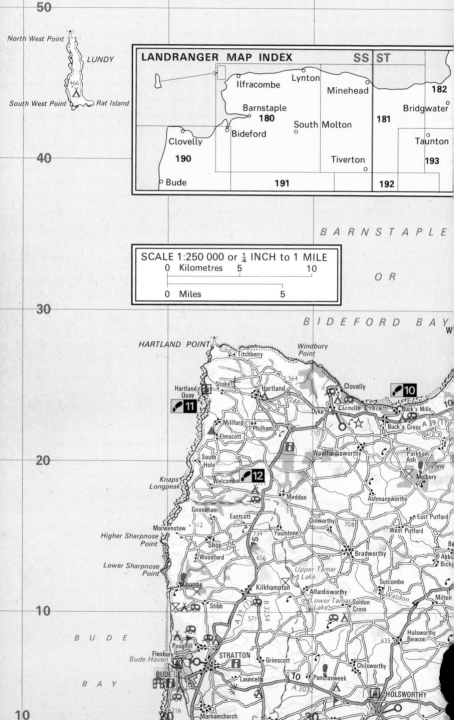

Key Map

50

40

30

20

10

10

SCALE 1:250 000 or ¼ INCH to 1 MILE

0   Kilometres   5   10

0   Miles   5

BARNSTAPLE

OR

BIDEFORD BAY

W

HARTLAND POINT
Titchberry

Windbury
Point

564

Clovelly

Hartland
Quay

Stoke

Hartland

B 3248

Clovelly Dykes

Buck's Mills

10

11

Dyke

Buck's Cross

A 39

Millford

Philham

710

Woolfardisworthy

Parkham
Ash

709

Elmscott

South
Hole

Melbury

Knaps
Longpeak

Welcombe

12

Ashmansworthy

Meddon

Gooseham

Eastcott

Dinworthy

708

East Putford

Morwenstow

512

Youlstone

West Putford

Higher Sharpnose
Point

734

Shop

Bradworthy

Ab

Lower Sharpnose
Point

Woodford

656

Upper Tamar
Lake

Sutcombe

R Waldon

Milton

Coombe

Kilkhampton

Alfardisworthy

Lower Tamar
Lake

Soldon
Cross

BUDE

Stibb

A 39

571

B 3254

Holsworthy
Beacon

635

Poughill

Flexbury

Bude Haven

STRATTON

Grimscott

Chilsworthy

BUDE

Launcells

10

Pancrasweek

HOLSWORTHY

BAY

216

20

Marhamchurch

30

531

Widemouth Bay

Bridgerule

Pyworthy

Hollacombe

SS

6
LYNTON
Lynn
1036.

9
Bull Point
Lee
675
Slade
ockham Bay
Point
451
Mortehoe
Woolacombe
654
36
Morte Bay
859
y Point
688
Pickwell
North
Buckland
Croyde
518
Knowle
Halsinger
Saunton
Braunton
Braunton
Burrows
Wrafton
Chivenor
rd
Bar

ILFRACOMBE
521
Hele
Berrynarbor
Combe Martin
Bay

Combe Martin
1145
10
Heale
899
Parracombe
Kentisbury
1106
Blackmoor Gate
1574

8
Kemacott
7
Martinhoe
Heddon s Mouth
Trentishoe
Woody
Bay
Barbrook
A 39
11
Shallowford
Furzeh

Pinkworthy
Pond 1598
9
Challacombe
B 3358

West
Down
Bittadon
Patchole
East Down
Arlington
Milltown
Muddiford
635
Loxhore
Knightacott
1079
Shoulsbarrow
Common
Leworthy
Bu
B 3226

Pipacott
Marwood
Prixford · 554
651
Shirwell
Bratton
Fleming
1618

Heanton
Punchardon
Ashford
dleigh
9
Stoke
Rivers
Gunn
868
Lydcott
Brayford
North
Heasley

BARNSTAPLE
Newport
Landkey
West
Buckland
Charles
East
Buckland
Heasley Mill
940
14
RIVER TAW
Fremington
B 3233
Bickington
Bishop's
Tawton
Swimbridge
732
Ne
Mo
N 361 (T)
RM

Yelland
Bickleton
Tawstock
12
Filleigh

Appledore
Instow
Horwood
Newton
Tracey
Herner
Cobbaton
Chittlehampton
478
B 3227
7
SOUTH
MOLTON
NORTHAM
Westleigh
10
BIDEFORD
Hiscott
Alverdiscott
Ensis
Chapleton
B 3226
George
Nympton
518
Alswear

East-the-
Water
343
Woodtown
Umberleigh
Clapworthy
567
Landcross
Littleham
Yarnscombe
Atherington
Warkleigh
Satterleigh
Chittlehamholt
Romansleigh
kland
wer
Monkleigh
8
Sherwood
Green
High
Bickington
Portsmouth
Arms·Sta.
King's
Nympton
753
Cadbury
Barton
Frithelstock
St Giles
in the Wood
Kingscott
Roborough
Northcote
Manor
King's Nympton
Sta.
Elstone
Chulmleigh
Cheldon
GREAT
TORRINGTON
B 3227
Little
Torrington
Langtree
661
Burrington
11
Chawleigh
Filleigh
625
Peters
Marland
Winswell
Beaford
B 3220
Riddlecombe
Ashreigney
Ashley
Eggesford
Sta.
Nymet
Rowland
Lapf
13
Merton
Huish
Dolton
Dowland
Hollacombe
Wembworthy
Coldridge
Shebbear
560
Petrockstowe
Meeth
454
Iddesleigh
Winkleigh
Brushford
East Leigh
R Torridge
Zeal
Monachoru
589
Buckland
Filleigh
Sheepwash
Monokehampton
Broadwoodkelly
Bondleigh
dford
lemoor
Black
Torrington
574
441
Highampton
Hatherleigh
B 3216
668
Bow
13
50
A 3072
632
Graddon
Moor
467
Lew
Honeychurch
Exbourne
70
A 3072
60
R Yeo

Introduction

This guide covers some of the most beautiful coast and countryside to be found in the West Country, and although not essential to its enjoyment, Landranger Maps 180 and 181, together with parts of Landranger Maps 190 and 182, could go hand-in-hand with the book, to provide a companion without equal. The area covered ranges from the gentle Black Down Hills, northwards across the rich Vale of Taunton Deane, to the long gorse- and bracken-covered ridge of the Quantocks. Not far to their west, beyond a lush farming valley through which a recently revived railway runs, are the Brendon Hills — an eastern extremity of Exmoor. There is wooded country stretching north from the Brendons to the coast, here enriched by the towns of Watchet and Minehead, with lovely Dunster not far away. To the south of the Brendon ridge, gently sloping country enfolds valleys among which will be found two sparkling reservoirs, bringing further interest to this tranquil and often undervalued landscape.

West, beyond the Brendons, lies the magic country of Exmoor, tamed by agriculture in parts, but still largely unspoilt. In the north it terminates mostly in high sea cliffs, while to the south and west it drops away gently into less dramatic but totally unspoilt farming country, among which will be found small towns like Bampton, Dulverton and South Molton, and a variety of modest villages, almost all of which are well worth exploring.

Beyond Exmoor's sea cliffs, the North Devon coast stretches westwards, with more cliff country punctuated in places by quiet coves and sandy beaches. Here will be found the resorts of Combe Martin and Ilfracombe, while beyond Bull Point, the coastline turns southwards and provides a series of splendid beaches, notably those at Woolacombe, Croyde and Saunton, and great craggy headlands like Morte Point and Baggy Point.

To the south again, lies the 'Land of the Two Rivers', the Taw and the Torridge. Here at the mouths of these two broad rivers, are the two fine old seaport towns of Barnstaple and Bideford, while their valleys head inland to embrace the hilly, wooded landscape, so wonderfully described by Henry Williamson, in his classic story, *Tarka the Otter*. To the north and west of this almost secret countryside run the great sea cliffs of north-west Devon, and among them, the north-facing coast shelters tiny Buck's Mills and steeply built Clovelly, one of Britain's loveliest coastal villages. Turning southwards at rugged Hartland Point, the tall cliffs then head southwards to the Cornish border, with a few minute beaches, only partly sheltered from the Atlantic's mighty forces.

This richly diverse landscape provides interest and amusement for every taste, from the bright attractions of Minehead and Ilfracombe, to the quietest coves and widest of beaches; from well visited towns and villages like Dunster or Clovelly to remote hamlets and villages lying well to the south of Exmoor; from fine country houses like Arlington Court or Knightshayes to cider mills or even a honey farm. But perhaps above all, it will be the memory of the fine open country of Exmoor and the Quantocks and the high sea cliffs bordering the Bristol Channel that will endure longest in the minds of those who come here.

We have devised a series of ten tours to guide you to the best features that this area has to offer. They are, like the guide as a whole, self-contained, but if you purchase the relevant Landranger map or maps you will be able to vary these tours to suit your own requirements. They have been designed primarily for motorists, but they are also suitable for cyclists, especially those classified as such.

Walkers would of course find these tours too long and too 'road-orientated', but to whet your appetite, we have also provided a series of twelve walks in widely varied countryside, and each of these links on to at least one of the tours. We cannot stress too strongly that your car is an ideal means to 'arrive' at an area, but to gain real enjoyment and satisfaction, it is infinitely preferable to explore the area on foot when you have arrived.

We do hope that you enjoy yourselves.

History Revealed...
A Short Survey of the Area's Past.

Although Neolithic (or Stone Age) farming communities had begun to settle in eastern and central Britain by the mid-fourth millennium BC, and had firmly established themselves on the upland ridges there by 2500 BC, there is little evidence to suggest that these Stone Age farmers made any impact in the area covered by this guide. It was possibly too far west and climatically inhospitable. However about 2000 BC the so-called 'Beaker Folk' moved westward from the Continent, heralding the Bronze Age, a culture that was to spread much further west than that of their Neolithic predecessors. This culture was characterised by worship at stone circles or henges, the most famous of which are at Stonehenge and Avebury. The only stone circles of any significance in our area are to be found on high Exmoor, to the south of **Porlock** Common, to the south of **Withypool** Hill, and on Almsworthy Common (181) (SS 84-41); but all three lack the drama of the great henge monuments. There are however many examples of Bronze Age burial mounds, or round barrows, to be found in the area, especially in the high country of the Quantocks, the Brendon Hills and the bleak western confines of Exmoor. **The Long Stone**, well to the north of Challacombe, is probably also of Bronze Age origin, and may once have been part of a series of stones put there for some ceremonial purpose.

A third wave of settlers, the Iron Age peoples, moved westward from the Continent between about 550 BC and AD 50. They organised themselves into larger and more cohesive groups, and were able to construct and maintain many large, well sited settlements, such as those at Shoulsbury (near **Challacombe**), **Countisbury**, **Dowsborough**, and **Norton**. They also started a process, to be continued later by the Romans and Anglo-Saxons, of extending their farming into the lower and more difficult valley country, and in some cases they incorporated great enclosures for their animals, like the ones at **Clovelly Dykes**.

The Romans landed in Britain in AD 43, and they advanced with considerable speed as far as the line that was to become the Foss Way, the great road that still runs almost all the way between Lincoln and Exeter. The country to its south and east was soon consolidated, and by AD 47 the legions were then able to move on to the task of pacifying the wilder parts of Britain to the north and west. The Dumnonii, the Iron Age tribe that inhabited Cornwall, Devon and western Somerset, well to the west of the Foss Way, appear to have been subdued by the Romans without much effort, and the only evidence of Roman military occupation is to be found at two small forts, at Old Barrow Hill, near **County Gate**, and on the cliffs to the north-west of **Martinhoe**. These were only occupied for a few years, and were probably part of a chain of signal stations and look-out posts built to control the Bristol Channel, on the north shore of which were the more warlike tribes inhabiting South Wales, the Silures. There is evidence of Roman mining activity near **Dulverton**, and of Roman settlement in the country between Wiveliscombe and Taunton, but this is not apparent to the visitor. It is also possible that a Roman road ran up from Exeter to the vicinity of Bideford (see **Ashreigney**), but this is still only a matter of conjecture.

It is not surprising that the next period of history has been called the 'Dark Ages', as our knowledge of what really took place in the centuries following the departure of the legions is still extremely scanty. **The Caratacus Stone**, near

The Caratacus Stone, near Winsford.

Winsford, was probably erected by some Celtic chief in the early years of the Dark Ages, but in the best tradition of the period its purpose is still far from clear. However it seems certain that the partly Romanised, largely Celtic inhabitants of our area were quickly overcome by Anglo-Saxons coming from the east, and that they moved to Cornwall, or were largely subjected by their conquerors. The Anglo-Saxons were, in their turn, subjected to the missionary activities of Irish and Welsh monks, who came over from the coast of south Wales, bringing their own particular brand of Christianity with them. The dedications of churches to these home-spun saints at **Braunton, Brendon, Chittlehampton, Porlock, Romansleigh** and **Watchet**, remind us of the lasting influence of these essentially simple men. At the same time, they must have been subject to violent raids by sea-borne Norsemen. One such raid was led by a certain 'Hubba the Dane', and there is a stone at Bloody Corner, between **Appledore** and **Northam**, marking the spot where he was buried, following the defeat of his band by Anglo-Saxons. St Decuman's Well at Watchet is believed to mark the spot where this unfortunate martyr was decapitated by a marauding Dane. Despite these legends, actual remains of Anglo-Saxon craftsmanship are not extensive in our area, but there is an interesting font to be seen at **Dolton**.

Norman work is to be found in many churches in the area, although none of this is up to the standard to be found further to the east, in Gloucestershire or Oxfordshire for instance. Some of the best examples are the doorways at **Buckland Brewer, East Worlington, Halse, High Bickington, Loxbeare, Parkham, Shebbear,** and **Woolfardisworthy**. There are also a multitude of Norman fonts, but there are no really outstanding specimens. The round-headed Norman arch gradually gave way to the pointed but still simple 'Early English' equivalent, and although this style predominated throughout most of the 13th century, examples are not often encountered in our area. However the emergence of English Gothic, heralding the 'Decorated' period, dates approximately from 1290 to 1350, and our 'Decorated' favourites in the area are the churches at **Clayhanger, Mortehoe, Tawstock** and **West Down**.

The late 14th, the whole of the 15th, and part of the 16th century was an age of considerable prosperity, with large landowners, wool merchants and clothiers making money in the area itself, and more wealth coming back from London as a result of successful West Countrymen's services to the state, or in the practice of law. It is interesting to note that no fewer than three Oxford colleges were founded by men from this area: Wadham (see **Knowstone**), Merton (see **Merton**), and Exeter College (see **Monkleigh**).

It was fortunate indeed that this prosperity coincided so closely with the final flowering of English Gothic, the style now known as 'Perpendicular'.

Cleeve Abbey.

There are a bewildering number of churches in our area, that were either entirely rebuilt in this era, or were radically altered and improved. Our favourites are perhaps **Bishops Lydeard, Bishop's Nympton, Chittlehampton, Kingston St Mary, North Molton, Old Cleeve,** and **Stoke**, but there are many others. Thanks to this coincidence of prosperity and piety the Perpendicular period was also a great time for the detailed improvement and enrichment of so many other churches. Our area is especially noted for its magnificent rood screens, fine examples of which may be seen at **Burrington, Carhampton, Chawleigh, Chulmleigh, Halse, Milverton, Minehead, Pilton,** and **Swimbridge**. Also to be found are many fascinating collections of bench-ends. These were carved largely in the 16th century, and it is interesting to note in some cases, the transition from a work of robust medieval flavour to finer, more delicate Renaissance craftsmanship. Some of our favourite bench-ends are at **Atherington, Bishops Lydeard, Braunton, Broomfield, Crowcombe, High Bickington, Kingston St Mary, Littleham, Stogumber** and **Sutcombe**.

Monastic remains in the area are limited, but the fine Cistercian **Cleeve Abbey** is both interesting and highly attractive. The only other abbey in the area was the Augustinian foundation at **Hartland**, but this is now an 18th and 19th century building. There were priories at Cannonsleigh, near **Burlescombe**, Barlynch, near **Dulverton**, and at **Pilton**, but little is to be seen of these. The ruins of the priory at Frithelstock are however of some interest.

Bridge and quaysides at Bideford.

All these monastic institutions were swept away by Henry VIII in the years immediately after 1539, but in the centuries that followed, our parish churches continued to reflect a strong religious tradition. Their content was often enriched in the 17th and 18th centuries with many splendid monuments. See especially **Goathurst, Holcombe Rogus, Molland, Pilton, Porlock, Stogumber, Tawstock** and **Watchet**.

In the 19th century, many churches were rebuilt or restored by Victorian architects, who were often brilliantly inspired by the past in cold academic terms, but who seldom had any regard for the patina of age and character that they so often swept away. It was not until the closing years of the 19th century that it became clear to William Morris, his friends and some of his contemporaries, that steps should be taken to reverse this trend, and where restoration has been carried out after this time an atmosphere of the past can often still be savoured. See especially **Cheldon, Church Stanton, Cruwys Morchard, Goathurst, Holcombe Rogus, King's Nympton, Molland, Satterleigh, Stawley, Sutcombe, Tawstock, West Putford, West Worlington, Winsford**, and especially **Parracombe Old Church**, which was saved due to a protest organised by John Ruskin.

The 20th century has not witnessed any great changes in the churches of the area, but there are a few worth visiting to appreciate what has been done. These include **Bicknoller**, with its 20th century glass; **Bishops Lydeard** and **West Bagborough**, both incorporating work by our favourite 20th century restorer, Sir Ninian Comper; **Dolton**, with its tablets by Laurence Whistler; and **Brushford** which has a chapel built by Sir Edwin Lutyens.

To return now to the secular front … the Normans built several castles in the area, and the most interesting survivors are **Dunster, Taunton** and **Tiverton**, all of which may be visited. The earthworks of other medieval castles may still be traced at **Bampton, Barnstaple, Nether Stowey** and Holwell, near **Parracombe**. In the centuries that followed, a series of busy market towns grew up, often in the shelter of these castles. Rivers were bridged, some with fine structures as at **Barnstaple, Bradford-on-Tone, Landacre** and **Bideford**, others by modest packhorse bridges, of which **Allerford, Bury, Horner, West Luccombe**, and **Winsford** are fine examples. **Tarr Steps** is a very special bridge, being similar to the clapper bridges of Dartmoor, but like them it is probably medieval, rather than prehistoric in origin.

Medieval manor houses include **Chambercombe** and **Gaulden**, both of which are open to the public, and **Nutcombe, Cothay**, and **Weare Gifford**. Fine Tudor manor houses include **Dodington, Cothelstone** and **Combe Sydenham**, each of which is open to the public, and also **Holcombe Court**

11

and **Nettlecombe Court**. The fortifications of these Tudor houses were only minimal, and this was a reflection upon the strong central control now imposed by Tudor monarchs upon a land that had previously suffered so many centuries of feudal unrest. However the Stuarts were not made of such strong stuff as their Tudor forebears, and in the middle years of the 17th century the country was torn apart by a bitter conflict between King and Parliament, the Civil War. While none of the major battles of this war took place in our area, there were many skirmishes here, including two encounters at **Great Torrington**, the second of which ended up with the accidental blowing-up of the church. However the focal point of the struggle for control of the west, was the castle at **Dunster**. This changed hands twice, being first besieged by the Royalists, and latterly by the Roundheads under Colonel (later Admiral) Blake.

The 17th and 18th centuries produced many fine houses in the area, including the Court House at **East Quantoxhead**, **Combe Florey**, **Barford Park**, and Castle Hill at **Filleigh**; and in the 19th century, **Arlington Court**, **Watermouth Castle**, and **Knightshayes**. In many cases parks were created, and most of the landscape, apart from the wilder hill and moor country, was now changing fast, with the acceleration of the enclosures. This was a movement that had been started in the 16th century, and which was largely completed by the beginning of the 19th, as a result of those sweeping changes in agricultural methods, now known collectively as the Agricultural Revolution. Fragmentary remains of earlier agricultural systems can still be seen at **Braunton Great Field**, and on the hillsides above **Combe Martin**.

The Industrial Revolution on the other hand did not have a great impact on our area, which has always remained a largely rural one, but the 18th and early 19th century did see the building of two canals, the **Grand Western** and the **Torrington Canal**, and mills were built at **Tiverton**, **Wellington** and **Uffculme**. However by the end of the 19th century the waterways were already in decline, and the railways had gained supremacy over them, with a network of lines carrying passengers and freight into most corners of the area, and with smaller mineral railways even pushing into the remote mining areas of the **Brendon Hills** and the country around **North Molton** and **Heasley Mill**.

The railways were also largely responsible for the growth of the area's greatest 'industry', the provision of holidays. Modest resorts like **Lynmouth** had already grown up as a result of the inability of the leisured classes to holiday on the Continent during the long wars with Napoleon, but it was the railway that led to the rapid growth of this activity in the latter half of the 19th century, and this movement was further stimulated by the publication of *Westward Ho!* in 1855, and above all, *Lorna Doone* in 1869, a book that has continued to hold the imagination of visitors until the present day.

Now many of the railways, including the delightful little **Lynton and Barnstaple Railway**, have been closed, and the roads, many of which started as turnpikes in the 18th century, have been improved out of all recognition. The M5 motorway provides easy, perhaps too easy, access to the area, and the road westwards from it, to Barnstaple and beyond, is now being much improved. All the main roads through the area are busy with traffic, especially in summer, but once away from these no doubt essential arteries, visitors will find that it is still possible to move quietly through most of its small towns, villages and beautiful countryside, and to appreciate the rich diversity of its past.

Watermouth Castle.

Natural History

by Reg Jones

North Devon, Exmoor and the Quantocks have much to offer the naturalist. There is an impressive rocky coast interrupted by flatter shores, while inland there are wild moors, together with woods and cultivated land usually bounded by lush hedgerows.

Exmoor — The Coast. The heart of the eastern part of the area is Exmoor, an upland plateau terminating on its northern face in the heathy-topped hog's-back cliffs which curve gradually towards the sea, before making their final abrupt and often spectacular descent. Often inaccessible, the cliffs, notably those between Heddon's Mouth and Woody Bay to the west of Lynmouth, harbour nesting sea birds (see **Walk 7**, page 120, and **Walk 8**, page 122). Herring gulls are present in good numbers along with a few pairs of great and lesser black-backed gulls. In the last twenty five years the number of fulmars has increased steadily, while more recently, since 1972, a sizeable colony of kittiwakes has become established. Adding to the interest, there are guillemots and razorbills on the rocky ledges, and at lower levels, a few shags and cormorants. The most convenient way to see these birds is by making a boat trip from nearby Lynmouth.

Exmoor — The Moorland. Although Exmoor is described as an upland plateau, it is far from flat. The ground is undulating and a special feature is the way it is cleft by steep sided valleys, often well wooded, which are referred to locally as *'combes'*. The underlying rocks are mainly of relatively soft sandstones and shales, lacking in lime, hence the number of lime kilns on the little beaches in the area, where lime was brought over from South Wales in small coasting vessels, and burnt before being taken inland for spreading on the fields. The climate is wet and often inhospitable. Consequently it is not surprising to find the untreated land at the higher levels to be wet, acidic and peaty, supporting only moorland vegetation.

The nature of this moorland varies.

Central Exmoor, an area almost coincident with the old 'forest', has the worst conditions and the vegetation is mainly purple moor grass with tracts of bog or mire whose surface is enlivened here and there by the nodding plumes of cotton grass or the golden starry-flowered bog asphodel. To the north and to the south, where the land is not so waterlogged, there is heather moorland with common heather, or ling, as the dominant plant, creating a purple-flowered carpet in August and September. Other familiar plants are present. In damper patches the pink-flowered cross-leaved heath occurs, while on the better drained slopes, bilberries or whortleberries are abundant. Where drier conditions prevail, as on the hog's-back cliffs, the vegetation

Bell Heather.

is more heath-like, the ling being accompanied by crimson bell heather and gorse, both the summer flowering western gorse and the taller spring flowering common gorse. Western gorse grows up to an altitude of around 375m, above which the ling persists, along with whortleberry. Unfortunately much of the drier moorland has been reclaimed, a process which has gone on for very many years.

Exmoor — The Combes. On the steep sides of the more sheltered combes, the soil is drier and more loamy. Such slopes are often clothed with woods of sessile oak, the trees being more robust at the foot, where the soil is deepest and the shelter greatest, but reduced to scrubby specimens towards the summit. Accompanying the oaks will be other species such as rowan and birch, while in the valley bottoms lowland trees may take over. Early in the year, there is a ground flora of primroses, bluebells and wood anemones, but in summer the moist, shady conditions are much appreciated by ferns and mosses, with bracken filling the more open spaces. A ramble around Dunkery Beacon and the woods near Horner Water (see Walk 3, page 112) will illustrate the changes in the vegetation, as one moves from the valleys to the heather-covered uplands. Those visitors who are particularly interested in natural history will profit from studying the displays and reference material on view at the field study centre at Malmsmead, near Brendon, which is run by the Exmoor Natural History Society (see page 60).

The Red Deer. Exmoor is renowned for its wildlife. Of the larger mammals, foxes and badgers are present in good numbers, but the area is particularly famous for its red deer. Few tourists see them because, feeding for the most part at night, they tend to lie up in the woods or in the bracken during the day. Dusk and early morning are the best times for observation as they then move to and from their resting places. Red deer are larger than other native species and the males or stags have pointed antlers of a distinctive pattern. Antlers are temporary horny structures which are shed each year in late April or early May, at which time the animals retire to the densest cover. The development of replacements is soon under way, the

new growth being covered initially by a soft thin skin, richly supplied with blood vessels, which is described as 'velvet'. By late summer, the growth is completed and the velvet withers and cracks, being removed by rubbing against trees. During September each fully grown stag, in prime condition, collects together a harem of hinds over which he exerts an aggressive dominance. He bellows vigorously and drives off other acquisitive males. This is in preparation for mating, usually in October, after which excitement declines and family groups tend to disperse. It is not until the following June that the hind drops her calf, often in bracken, where, clad in a dappled coat, it lies hidden and inconspicuous for the first few days of life.

Exmoor Ponies. While red deer may be difficult to locate, the Exmoor pony is more accommodating. Small parties roam the moorland throughout the year. They are extremely hardy and are said to be closer to the true native wild horse than any other breed. Small and deep chested pure-bred ponies are characterised by oatmeal-coloured muzzles, slightly hooded eyes and short, pointed ears. The colour may be bay, brown or dun and there are no white flashes. Over the years some cross-breeding has occurred, so that not all the animals on view are true Exmoors.

Birds of Exmoor. Away from the coast, there is an appreciable variety of birds. Dippers and grey wagtails haunt the sparkling streams and in the upper reaches of the moorland valleys there are some ring ouzels. In the wooded combes there is a good selection of woodland birds including redstarts, wood warblers and pied flycatchers. Of the birds of prey, the buzzard is often in view, soaring effortlessly overhead, mewing plaintively from time to time. The habitat which combines moorland with wooded farmland suits it well. Kestrels and sparrow hawks are also present as, in summer, is the merlin which can sometimes be seen flying low in headlong pursuit of small birds such as the meadow pipit. This is the commonest small bird on all types of moorland, but there are others: resident stonechats and summer visiting whinchats and wheatears. As in more northern lati-

Red Deer Stags.

tudes, the bubbling song of the curlew can be heard in spring over the open uplands and where there is sufficient heather, a small population of red grouse is present, although the black grouse is now probably extinct.

Exmoor Ponies.

The Quantocks. The high ridge known as the Quantocks is sometimes described as an outlier of Exmoor. There are many similarities. Those interested in natural history should visit Fyne Court, Broomfield (182) (ST 22-32), the headquarters of the Somerset Trust for Nature Conservation, where there are displays illustrating the main features of the area (see Broomfield, page 32, and Tour 1, page 88). A walk along the spine of the Quantocks from Lydeard Hill to Crowcombe Park Gate, or on our Walk 1, from Holford (see page 108), allows the visitor to have a bird's-eye view of the different habitats: upland heaths, deciduous and coniferous woodlands and cultivated land.

Braunton Burrows. Bideford Bay offers very different conditions from those further east. At low tide, to the north of the Taw and Torridge estuary, extensive lime-rich sandy flats are exposed, Saunton Sands, while on the adjacent shore is one of the largest sand dune systems in Britain, Braunton Burrows. Dunes form from sand, blown inland from the flats, which is consolidated by colonizing plants. The youngest dunes, nearest the sea, are bound together for the most part by marram grass along with such plants as sea holly and sea bindweed. Those dunes farther inland are populated by a much wider variety of species and at Braunton there is a full succession with the oldest dunes

being clothed in shrubby scrub. Between successive dunes are hollows or 'slacks' which are usually damp and they support a rich flora. Apart from familiar plants, like marsh orchids, which appear abundantly, there are rarities such as water germander. Along the southern part of the Burrows is a National Nature Reserve. Unrestricted access to the whole area is not possible since part is used for military training. Probably because of disturbance, there are fewer breeding birds here than might be expected, but in summer ringed plovers, oystercatchers, shelduck and wheatears are present.

The West Coast. In the west, from Hartland Point to the Cornish border, the cliffs take the full force of Atlantic storms. Subjected to this vigorous buffeting, a dramatic coastline has developed, with projecting buttresses and jagged offshore stacks. This is a wilder stretch than that from Hartland Point to Westward Ho! where the cliffs are more sheer with little foreshore. The rock differs from that in the east, being more unstable, and the flora and fauna is less rich. For example, apart from some fulmars and herring gulls, there are no significant colonies of seabirds.

Common Buzzard.

Leisure Activities ...
A Brief Summary

The area covered by this guide provides a bewildering variety of sport and leisure activities and we have listed some of those which we feel will be of particular interest to visitors.

Motoring. You will probably have arrived in your own car, but if you wish to hire a self-drive car or chauffeur-driven car, there is a wide choice available. Self-Drive cars are available from the following garages:

Taw Garages, Barnstaple, *Tel: (0271) 74173*
County Garage, Barnstaple, *Tel: (0271) 73232*
Premier Garage, Minehead, *Tel: (0643) 3458*
Huxtables Garage, Taunton, *Tel: (0823) 283344*
White Bros, Taunton, *Tel: (0823) 335481*
Ivor Pengelley, Tiverton, *Tel: (0884) 256419*
If alternative services are required, or if you require a chauffeur-driven car, use the local Yellow Pages, or Thompson Directory, as there are many other services available.

Bus. Local bus services can be fun if you are prepared to fit in with their schedules, which are normally governed by local transport needs. Timetables giving details of times and routes may be obtained from the Coach and Bus Station at Taunton *Tel: (0823) 772033*; the Bus Station in the Strand, at Barnstaple *Tel: (0271) 45444*, where runabout 'Explorer' tickets are available; Kingdom's Tours, Exeter Rd., Tiverton *Tel: (0884) 252373*; Sherrin's Coaches, Minehead *Tel: (0643) 4450*; Lovering's Blue Coaches at Ilfracombe *Tel: (0271) 63673*; and Filers Travel at Ilfracombe *Tel: (0271) 63819.*

Train. Details of British Rail's train services in the area may be obtained from the Railway Stations at Taunton *Tel: (0823) 283444*, and Barnstaple *Tel: (0271) 45991*, and details of the West Somerset Railway's services may be obtained from their Minehead Station *Tel: (0643) 4996*. The latter service is most useful, and there is a connecting bus service between its southern terminus at Bishops Lydeard and British Railways' Taunton Station. Unlike this privately run line, British Railways' trains will reach very few of the places mentioned in the guide, and they are probably more suitable for 'long-haul' routes either in or out of the area.

Caravanning and Camping. There are so many suitable sites in the area covered by this guide, that it would be impossible, in a publication of this nature, to provide a list that could be judged to be adequately representative. The invaluable annual 'newspaper', *The Exmoor Visitor*, provides a good list of sites located in and around the Exmoor National Park, and all the local Tourist Information Offices and National Park Information Offices can provide further help. The West Country Tourist Board publish a free annual booklet, *Camping and Caravan Parks in England's West Country*, and this is available from all Tourist Information Centres in the area. There are also a number of excellent countrywide booklets on sale nationally from January 1st each year. But if you wish to have the very best camping and/or caravan site information, you would be advised to join one of the national clubs covering these activities. These include: *The Camping and Caravanning Club, 11, Lower Grosvenor Place, London SW1W 0EY*, and *The Caravan Club, East Grinstead House, East Grinstead, West Sussex RH19 1UA.*

Cycling. This is a splendid way of looking around the area, and once off the main routes (which is the object of most of our listed tours) the little 'unclassified' roads (yellow on the Landranger map) are relatively peaceful. If you do not have your own machine, these can be hired from:

Tower View Cycles, *Tower View Estate, Sticklepath, Barnstaple,* Tel: *(0271) 78033*
P. G. Haynes, *5, Mart Road Trading Estate, Minehead,* Tel: *(0643) 5363/3461*
Taunton Holiday Cycle Hire, *St Quintin's Hotel & Caravan Park, Bathpool, Taunton,* Tel: *(0823) 259171*
Maynard's Cycle Shop, *25, Gold St., Tiverton,* Tel: *(0884) 253979*
If you still have difficulty in making arrangements, the very helpful *Cyclists Touring Club, 69 Meadrow, Godalming, Surrey GU7 3HS* Tel: *(048 68) 7217*, supply a useful list of Bicycle Hirers. Why not become a member?

Walking. This is the ideal way of exploring the area, and may be combined with any of the above means of transport. You will find twelve Walks described on pages 108-131, and we hope that these will provide a pleasant introduction to the pleasures of walking with map and guide in this wonderfully unspoilt countryside. Exmoor and the coast are the great walking areas, but do not miss out the Quantocks, as they offer a wide range of walking opportunities in a relatively compact area.

Stout shoes and waterproof clothing, including a windcheater or anorak, are desirable, and during the wetter part of the year, walking boots can widen the scope of your journeys, taking in more of those sodden fields and footpaths than might otherwise be possible. Small rucksacks are worth while, and while a compass is useful on any walk, it is recommended that one be taken if any moorland area is being tackled. It would also be advisable to take a small amount of food and a change of clothing if moorland walking is involved, as the weather can change remarkably quickly in this high country. But providing that you are adequately equipped, do not let this advice put you off any planned adventures.

Although there is a network of over 600 miles of clearly signed and colour-coded walks in the Exmoor National Park (see the National Park's *Waymarked Walks* publications), do not always expect to find well defined paths in other areas. If walking on non-waymarked paths, rights of way are clearly shown on both the Landranger map and on the Pathfinder extracts, but these may not show up too clearly on the ground. If in doubt, do try to ask locally regarding rights of way, and at all times do make sure that your dog is on a lead if livestock are anywhere near, and that all gates are left as you found them, which will normally be closed.

Horse Riding. Details of the very wide range of available riding facilities may be obtained from any of the Tourist or National Park Information Centres; and the *Somerset Tourist Office, County Hall, Taunton, TA1 4DY* publish a very useful list of riding establishments. All levels of skill are catered for, from the complete expert to the novice; and pony trekking is an ideal way to explore Exmoor

and the Quantocks. For the areas to the west and south-west, refer to the relevant local Tourist Information Centre.

The Best of the Beaches. This is a brief list starting from the east of the area, heading westwards: Map 181: Watchet, Blue Anchor Bay, Minehead; Map 180: Combe Martin, Ilfracombe, Woolacombe, Putsborough, Croyde Bay, Saunton, Instow, Westward Ho!; Map 190: Buck's Mills, Shipload Bay, Speke's Mill Mouth, Welcombe Mouth and Marsland Mouth.

Fun on the Water. This area has much to offer those who, in some way or other, love to 'mess about in boats'. There are many points along the coast where small boats may be launched, but if you are inexperienced in matters concerning the sea, do ask for local advice. Tides are strong in the Bristol Channel, and the influence of the Atlantic and its weather is never far away. Dinghy sailing is especially popular at Instow, in the relatively sheltered mouth of the Torridge. Details of the facilities available at the various reservoirs in the area may be obtained from *South West Water, Fisheries and Recreation Officer, Peninsula House, Rydon Lane, Exeter EX2 7HR,* and *Wessex Water, Fisheries and Recreation Officer, PO Box 9, King Square, Bridgwater, TA6 3EA.* Sailing on inland

Pony Trekking on Exmoor.

Horse-drawn barge on the Grand Western Canal, near Tiverton.

waters is largely a club activity, but short term membership is often available. There are clubs at Hawkridge Reservoir (182) (ST 20-36), Wimbleball Lake (181) (SS 97-30), and Tamar Lake (190) (SS 29-11). A further water amenity is the Grand Western Canal (Country Park), on which horse-drawn barge trips are available from the Wharf at Tiverton *(Tel: (0884) 253345)*. Licences to use non-powered craft may be obtained from the same loca-

tion. Although just out of the area covered by this guide, the St Quintin's Hotel and Caravan Park at Bathpool, on the A38 just to the east of Taunton (193) (ST 25-26), *Tel: (0823) 259171*, has rowing boats for hire, for use on the Bridgwater and Taunton Canal. Licences for the use of craft on this canal, and on any other British Waterways canal, may also be obtained from here.

Golf. There are ten courses in the area covered by this guide. They are: The Taunton & Pickeridge, 4 miles south of Taunton, *Tel: (082 342) 240. Map 193 (ST 24-18)*, Vivary Park Municipal, Taunton, *Tel: (0823) 289274/ 333875. Map 193 (ST 22-23)*, The Enmore Park, *Tel: (027867) 481. Map 182 (ST 24-35)*, The Minehead & West Somerset, *Tel: (0643) 2057. Map 181 (SS 99-46)*, The Tiverton, *Tel: (0884) 252187. Map 181 (SS 99-13)*, The Chulmleigh, *Tel: (0769) 80519. Map 180 (SS 68-14)*, The Ilfracombe, *Tel: (0271) 62176. Map 180 (SS 54-47)*, The Saunton, *Tel: (0271) 812436. Map 180 (SS 45-37)*, The Royal North Devon, Westward Ho!, *Tel: (02372) 73817. Map 180 (SS 44-30)*, and The Torrington, *Tel: (0805) 22229. Map 180 (SS 48-20)*.

Fishing. There are a wealth of fishing opportunities in the area covered by our map.

Dunster Castle.

Combe Sydenham Hall.

Much valuable information relating to river and reservoir fishing may be obtained from *South West Water, Fisheries and Recreation Officer, Peninsula House, Rydon Lane, Exeter EX2 7HR,* and *Wessex Water, Fisheries and Recreation Officer, PO Box 9, King Square, Bridgwater, TA6 3EA.* The latter organisation publishes a useful booklet, *Fishing and Recreation,* and this contains much useful information on all types of fishing, including a section on *Fishing in Coastal Waters.* Further information regarding trout farms in the area (some of which provide fishing) may be derived from our 'Places of Interest' section, under **Clatworthy Reservoir, Combe Sydenham, Exebridge, King's Nympton, Muddiford** and **Thornbury.** See also **Great Torrington** (for Darracot), **Hawkridge Reservoir, Tamar Lakes, Watersmeet, Wimbleball Lake** and **Wistlandpound Reservoir.** Sea fishing from boats may be arranged at Watchet and Porlock Weir, but for further information, consult the various National Park and Tourist Information Offices.

Sports Centres, and other sporting facilities. There are fine modern sports centres at Barnstaple, the North Devon Leisure Centre, *Tel: (0271) 73361;* at Wellington, the Wellington Sports Centre, *Tel: (082 347) 3010;* and there is a Sports Complex at Tiverton. Most towns have facilities for tennis, bowls and swimming, and Taunton is the home of Somerset County Cricket.

Places to Visit.... A summary list showing page number followed by map number and map reference.

Castles.
Dunster Castle (NT) (43) (181) (ST 99-43)
Taunton Castle (73) (193) (ST 22-24)
Tiverton Castle (74) (181) (SS 95-13)

Historic Houses, and Other Buildings.
Arlington Court (NT) (23) (180) (SS 61-40)
Barford Park (46) (182) (ST 23-35)
Blundell's Old School, Tiverton (NT) (74) (181) (SS 95-12)
Castle Hill (Filleigh) (47) (180) (SS 67-28)
Chambercombe Manor (34) (180) (SS 53-46)
Cleeve Abbey (38) (181) (ST 04-40)
Coldharbour Mill, Uffculme (76) (181) (SS 06-12)
Coleridge Cottage, Nether Stowey (NT) (63) (181) (ST 19-39)
Combe Sydenham Hall (39) (181) (ST 07-36)
Cothelstone Manor (39) (181) (ST 18-31)
Dodington Hall (42) (181) (ST 17-40)
Dunster Castle (NT) (43) (181) (SS 99-43)
Dunster Water Mill (44) (181) (SS 99-43)
Gaulden Manor (48) (181) (ST 11-31)
Hele Mill (51) (180) (SS 53-47)
Knightshayes Court (NT) (55) (181) (SS 96-15)
Tapeley Park (72) (180) (SS 47-29)
Wellington Monument (NT) (80) (180) (ST 13-17)

Gardens and Parks.
Arlington Court (NT) (23) (180) (SS 61-40)
Bicclescombe Park, Ilfracombe (54) (180) (SS 51-46)

Hele Mill.

Glen Lyn House Gardens, Lynmouth (60) (180) (SS 72-49)

Goodland Gardens, Taunton (74) (193) (ST 22-24)

Hestercombe (51) (193) (ST 24-28)

Hillsborough Pleasure Grounds, Ilfracombe (54) (180) (SS 53-47)

Hobby Drive, Clovelly (38) (190) (SS 33-23)

Knightshayes Court (NT) (55) (181) (SS 96-15)

Marwood Hill Garden (60) (180) (SS 54-37)

Middleham Memorial Gardens, Lynmouth (60) (180) (SS 72-49)

Rosemoor Gardens (67) (180) (SS 50-18)

Victoria Park, Bideford (28) (180) (SS 45-27)

Vivary Park, Taunton (74) (193) (ST 22-23)

Woodside Gardens, Pilton (65) (180) (56-34)

Wildlife Parks, Farm Parks, and Natural History Centres.

The Big Sheep, Abbotsham (22) (180) (SS 42-26)

Bodstone Barton Working Farm (39) (180) (SS 57-44)

Exmoor Bird Gardens, nr Blackmoor Gate (30) (180) (SS 65-40)

Exmoor Farm Animal Centre, nr Hunter's Inn (53) (180) (SS 66-48)

Exmoor Natural History Centre, Malmsmead (60) (180) (SS 79-47)

Milky Way (61) (190) (SS 32-22)

North Devon Farm Park (57) (180) (SS 61-30)

Quantock Visitor Centre, Fyne Court (32) (182) (ST 22-32)

Quince Honey Farm, South Molton (70) (180) (SS 71-25)

Somerset Farm Park, nr Bossington (30) (181) (SS 90-47)

Tropiquaria, Washford (77) (181) (ST 04-41)

Country Parks.

Combe Sydenham Country Park Trout Farm (39) (181) (ST 07-36)

At the Cobbaton Combat Vehicles Museum.

The Grand Western Canal Country Park (48) (181) (SS 98-12 etc)

Northam Burrows Country Park (63) (180) (SS 44-30)

Museums and Art Galleries.

Alscott Farm Museum, nr Shebbear (69) (190) (SS 46-11)

Burton Art Gallery, Bideford (28) (180) (SS 45-26)

Cobbaton Combat Vehicles Museum (38) (180) (SS 61-26)

Coldharbour Mill, Uffculme (76) (181) (ST 06-12)

Combe Martin Motor Cycle Collection (39) (180) (SS 58-46)

Croyde Gem Rock and Shell Museum (41) (180) (SS 44-39)

Great Torrington Museum (49) (180) (SS 49-19)

Hartland Quay Museum (50) (190) (SS 22-24)

Ilfracombe Museum (53) (180) (SS 51-47)

Lyn and Exmoor Museum, Lynton (60) (180) (SS 72-49)

Museum of North Devon, Barnstaple (26) (180) (SS 55-33)

North Devon Maritime Museum, Appledore (23) (180) (SS 46-30)

St Anne's Chapel Museum, Barnstaple (26) (180) (SS 56-33)

Somerset County Museum, Taunton (74) (193) (ST 22-24)

Somerset Military Museum, Taunton (74) (193) (ST 22-24)

Somerset & Dorset Railway Museum, Washford (77) (181) (ST 04-41)

Tiverton Museum (75) (181) (SS 95-12)

Watchet Museum (78) (181) (ST 07-43)

Factories, Factory Shops, etc.

Coldharbour Mill, Uffculme (76) (181) (SS 06-12)

Dartington Glass, Great Torrington (49) (180) (SS 49-19)

Fox Brothers, Wellington (79) (181) (ST 12-21)

Hancock's Devon Cider, Clapworthy (36) (180) (SS 67-24)

John Wood, Old Cleeve (65) (181) (ST 03-42)

Sheppy's Cider Farm, nr Bradford-on-Tone (30) (181) (ST 17-22)

Taunton Cider, Norton Fitzwarren (64) (181) (ST 19-25)

Wilscombe Design, Wiveliscombe (86) (181) (ST 08-27)

Craft Activities.

The number of potteries and other craft workshops in the area is considerable. To identify most of these please refer to the 'Places of Interest' section under the following headings: *Ashreigney, Beaford, Braunton, Brompton Regis, Hartland, Kingston St Mary, Simonsbath* and *Vellow*.

A Few Special Events.
First Thursday in May — May Fair at Great Torrington
July — Taunton Festival
September — The Exe River Struggle, at Tiverton.
Wednesday preceding 20th September — Barnstaple Three Day Fair
October — Taunton Carnival.
Last Thursday in October — October Fair at Bampton
For a list of other fascinating events, dates of which change annually, see the relevant leaflets which are available from the various Tourist Information Centres listed below.

The Somerset and Dorset Railway Museum, Washford.

Further Information.

Tourist Information Centres.
Barnstaple. *Tuly St. Tel: (0271) 47177*
Bideford. *The Quay.(Summer only) Tel: (023 72) 74591/77676*
Braunton. *The Car Park. Tel: (0271) 816400*
Combe Martin. *Sea Cottage, Cross St. (April-end Sept). Tel: (027 188) 3319/2692*
Dulverton. *Exmoor National Park Visitor Services, Exmoor House. Tel: (0398) 23665. For separate list of Exmoor National Park Information Centres, see block below*
Ilfracombe. *The Promenade. Tel: (0271) 63001*
Lynton. *Information Office, The Town Hall. Tel: (0598) 52225*
Minehead. *The Market House. Tel: (0643) 2624*
Porlock. *The Post Office. Personal callers only.*
South Molton. *Information Centre, 1, East St. Tel: (076 95) 2378/4122*
Taunton. *Information Centre, Central Library, Corporation St. Tel: (0823) 274785/270479*
Tiverton. *Phoenix Lane. (Summer only) Tel: (0884) 255827*
Watchet. *Swain St. (Tel. no. not known at time of printing)*
Wellington. *Squirrel Museum, Fore St. (Summer only) Tel: (082 347) 4747*
Woolacombe. *Hall '70, Beach Rd. Tel: (0271) 870533*

Exmoor National Park Information Centres.
Combe Martin. *Sea Cottage, Cross St. (April-end Sept). Tel: (027 188) 3319/2692*

County Gate, Countisbury. *Information Centre (April — end Sept). Tel: (05987) 321*
Dulverton. *Visitor Services. Tel: (0398) 23665*
Dunster. *Information Centre (April-end Oct). Tel: (064 382) 835*
Lynmouth. *Information Centre, The Esplanade (April-end Oct). Tel: (05985) 2509*

Other Useful Addresses, and/or Telephone Numbers.
West Country Tourist Board, *Trinity Court, Southernhay East, Exeter, EX1 1QS*
National Trust Regional Office (Devon). *Killerton House, Broadclyst, Exeter, EX5 3LE Tel: (0392) 881691*
National Trust Regional Office (Wessex, which includes Somerset). *Stourton, Warminster, Wilts, BA12 6QD Tel: (0747) 840224*
Devon Nature Conservation Trust. *Tel: (0392) 79244*
Somerset Nature Conservation Trust. *Tel: (082 345) 587*
R.A.C. 24 Hour Breakdown Service, Bristol. *Tel: (0272) 739311*
R.A.C. 24 Hour Breakdown Service, Plymouth. *Tel: (0752) 221411*
A.A. 24 Hour Breakdown Service, Exeter. *Tel: (0392) 412999*
Police, Barnstaple. *Tel: (0271) 73101*
Police, Exeter. *Tel: (0392) 52191*
Police, Minehead. *Tel: (0643) 3361*
Police, Taunton. *Tel: (0823) 337911*

Ordnance Survey Agents.
Pelikan Bookshop, Magdalene Lane, Taunton TA1 1SE *Tel: (0823) 335828*
Practical Optics, 56 Boutport St., Barnstaple EX31 1SH *Tel: (0271) 72681*

Places of Special Interest

Abbots Bickington (190) (SS 38-13) Here in high, remote country to the west of the infant Torridge, are a few houses and a minute 13th and 14th century church with a small spire. Although heavily restored by the Victorians, it retains several features of interest, including many medieval tiles (made at Barnstaple, and usually referred to as 'Barnstaple tiles'), and fragments of 14th and 15th century glass in the east window. Like Abbotsham (see below), this village formed part of the original endowment of Hartland Abbey, and the abbot used to hold a court here, the farm beside the church still being known as Court Barton.

Abbotsham (180) (SS 42-26) This village on high ground between Bideford and the sea, formed part of the original endowment of late 10th century Tavistock abbey, hence the name 'Abbot's Ham'. It has considerable modern development, but its church is well worth visiting. Although heavily restored in about 1870, this contains much of interest, including a fine series of 16th century

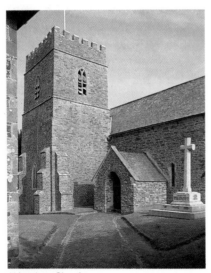

Abbotsham Church.

bench-ends with a wonderfully rich variety of carved figures and symbols. There is a fluted Norman font, and beautiful ceiled wagon-roofs to its nave, transept and chancel complete with carved angels. Do not miss the 18th century monument to John Willett, who lived at Combe, a fine early-17th century house well to the north of the village. One of his ancestors, woolstapler John Willett, has his initials and woolstapler's mark carved upon one of the bench ends.

Do not miss a visit to 'The Big Sheep' – a working farm with tourist attractions, including a modern sheep dairy, a restaurant and shop. This is directly accessible from the A39. *(Tel: 02372 72366.)*

Aisholt (181) (ST 19-35) Minute and very scattered village on the eastern slopes of the Quantocks, with its church on the edge of hanging woodlands above the little stream that feeds Hawkridge Reservoir. The little church is largely 15th century, and does not contain anything of great interest. It is on such a steep slope that its belfry is almost level with the churchyard. The poet Coleridge had hopes of settling in Aisholt at one time, but his wife Sara would have none of it. 'The situation is delicious', he wrote to a friend in about the year 1800, 'but Sara being Sara, and I being I, we must live in a town or else close to one, so that she may have neighbours and acquaintances'. About a century later another poet, Henry Newbolt (the writer of such heroic verses as *Drake's Drum*) often came to stay in a cottage here, and referred to Aisholt as 'that beloved valley'.

Walk west from here, up on to the crest of the Quantocks, at Wills Neck (ST 16-35), and return by way of wooded Cockercombe (ST 18-36). Alternatively walk to Aisholt from the car park by the Triscombe Stone (ST 16-36).

Allerford (181) (SS 90-47) Delightful hamlet, just off the busy A39, with a picturesque two-arch packhorse bridge over a little stream which flows into Porlock Bay just beyond Bossington. Both hamlets shelter beneath steep wooded slopes, and there are walks east along a quiet road to Selworthy village, or northward up through woods, and out on to the bare hillsides of Bossington Hill and Selworthy Beacon. There is also a walk north-west, through Bossington hamlet, to the shingly shore of Porlock Bay, behind which there is a path to Porlock Weir.

Alverdiscott (180) (SS 51-25) Minute village astride the B3232, Barnstaple to Great Torrington road. It is situated in high rolling countryside, and there are fine views from its largely 15th century church. This was over-restored in the early-19th century, but there are medieval tiles in the south porch, a pulpit with early Renaissance panels and a Norman font capped with a Jacobean font cover. Behind the organ there is a hauntingly beautiful effigy of a boy, who died in 1639 at the early age of ten. The boy clutches a prayer book and is dressed in handsome cavalier clothes. At least he missed the horrors of a civil war that was, within a year or two, to involve almost every family in the land. Also do not overlook the monument in the north aisle to Gilbert Hody, dated 1686.

Alwington (180) (SS 40-23) At the centre of this scattered parish a large handsomely pinnacled church stands almost alone, above the valley of the little River Yeo. This is a largely 15th century building, with ceiled wagon-roofs and arcading of Lundy granite. It contains a wealth of old woodwork, including a family pew made up of Jacobean panels brought from Portledge House (39-24), once the home of the Coffin family, and now a hotel. The pulpit and reredos are also made up of earlier materials; in this case, medieval bench-ends. Some of these bench-ends are still put to their original use, but they have been joined by much more recent reproductions. There are also some old Barnstaple tiles, and some pleasant wall monuments to members of the Coffin family, some of whose descendants, the Pine-Coffins, still live in the district.

Angersleigh (181) (ST 19-19) Quietly situated below the northern slopes of the Blackdown Hills, this small village has an extensively restored church with a 14th century tower. The carving of most of the woodwork within, was the work of A. E. Eastwood, who lived at nearby Leigh Court, a dignified early 19th century building, with a porch supported by Ionic columns.

Anstey Commons (181) (SS 85-29) East and West Anstey Commons are traversed by an attractive open road running westward from Dulverton, and on West Anstey Common, at 83-29, there is a massive thirteen-ton boulder beside the road, placed by his friends, in memory of Philip Froude Hancock (1865-1933). Being a hunting man Hancock knew and loved West Anstey, and he must have relished not only the open riding country of the Common itself, but also the splendid views to be had from it, both north to the central moorland, and south over the rolling hill country of central Devon. At 85-28 the Common is crossed by the Two Moors Way (see page 76), on its way north to Withypool, and beyond to the coast.

Appledore (180) (SS 46-30) This large, full of character, fishing village overlooks the broad tidal waters marking the union of the Taw and Torridge before they pour out to sea through a narrow channel into Bideford Bay. There are fine views across the water to Braunton Burrows, and over the wide sands to Instow. Appledore has been prosperous in recent years, with two of the West Country's most successful shipyards, but despite this, it has retained a delightfully relaxed manner, with a broad quay beside its road, overlooked by Georgian and early Victorian cottage terraces. One of the above shipyards, that belonging to J. Hinks & Son, may usually be visited during working hours. *(Tel: 02372 74231)*

Domesday Book (1086) records the fact that the Abbot of Caen in Normandy had a fishery in the nearby manor of Northam, and this probably refers to salmon fishing, which has certainly been carried on at Appledore for many hundreds of years. The church here was only built in 1838 and is not of great interest to visitors, but on no account should a visit to the little Maritime Museum in Odun Road be missed. Here will be found models in authentic

Appledore ... a view from Instow.

SCALE 1:25 000 or 2½ INCHES to 1 MILE

settings, with photographs and paintings illustrating the seafaring life and shipbuilding. There is also a tape-slide show daily, and a permanent exhibition mounted by the National Maritime Museum, illustrating the historic links between North Devon and North America. *(Tel: 02372 74852.)*

At Bloody Corner (SS 45-29), on the road southwards to Northam, there is a stone commemorating the supposed burial place of Hubba the Dane, leader of a band of sea-raiders, defeated by the Saxon defenders of Appledore.

Arlington (180) (SS 61-40) The church and a few houses are situated on the edge of Arlington Court's beautiful park. Apart from its tower the church was rebuilt in 1846, but it contains several monuments to the Chichester family. Do not miss the elegant late-18th century monument to Mary Anne Chichester, nor the typically poignant mid-19th century memorial to another Mary Anne, depicting an angel taking her skywards. However most will come here to look at the monument by John Piper to Miss Rosalie, the last of the Chichesters of Arlington, to whom we are in debt for her most generous gift to the National Trust (see below).

Arlington Court (NT) (180) (SS 61-40) The manor of Arlington passed to the Chichesters by marriage in the 14th century, and they remained as owners from that time until 1947, when Miss Rosalie Chichester gave the estate to the National Trust, only two years before she died. The present mansion was built in 1820-23 by a Barnstaple architect, one time pupil of Sir John Soane, Thomas Lee, who also designed the Wellington Monument (see page 80). Although it is not of outstanding architectural interest, Arlington Court is beautifully situated on the edge of the steep wooded park that Miss Chichester, a great lover of wild birds and animals, transformed into a 'nature reserve' long before this concept became fashionable. This work, between 1908 and 1947, included the building of an eight mile long, high iron fence, entirely surrounding the park.

The delightful interior of the house, which so beautifully reflects the tastes and strong personality of its last occupant, has a light, Edwardian flavour, and its contents include a fascinating collection of model ships, shells, snuff boxes, pewter and porcelain, most of which had been assembled by Miss Rosalie herself, an inveterate collector, and capable water-colourist. Do not miss the gorgeous red amber elephant, nor the silver model of *Gipsy*

SCALE 1:25 000 or 2½ INCHES to 1 MILE

Moth IV, the boat in which her nephew, Sir Francis, circumnavigated the world single-handed (see Shirwell, page 69). There is a fine collection of 19th century horse-drawn vehicles in the stables to the east of the church, and carriage rides may be taken in the park, where Shetland ponies and Jacob sheep may be seen grazing. Visitors are also able to follow a nature walk through the woods and beside the lake, with the help of an excellent leaflet. There is also a well stocked shop and a licensed restaurant. *(Tel: 07695 2120)*.

It is possible to walk south-east from here, to Bratton Fleming, and then north to Wistlandpound Reservoir, returning to Arlington on a relatively quiet road.

Ashford (180) (SS 53-35) This village stands on a steep hillside looking southwards out over the broad Taw estuary. Its church was rebuilt in 1854, but, like Alwington, it contains a fascinating collection of medieval woodwork, with bench-ends being re-used in the pulpit.

Ash Priors (181) (ST 15-29) Small village in low country to the south-west of the Quantocks. The largely 15th century church was heavily restored in 1874, but the tall tower with its projecting stair-turret is an attractive feature. Walk north from here to Combe Florey.

Ashreigney (180) (SS 62-13) This stands in high country between the Taw and Torridge valleys, and is not of great interest, its church having been heavily restored at the end of the 19th century. However there is a pleasant walk northwards, down through woods, over the little Mully Brook, and up to Burrington. Well to the west of Ashreigney, there is an interesting pottery at 15th century Higher Northcott Farmhouse (SS 59-14), which is probably best approached eastwards from the B3217, south of High Bickington *(Tel: Ashreigney 242)*.

Ashreigney may have been on the line of a Roman road running from Exeter towards Bideford, also passing north-westerly through Ebberly Hill (SS 57-19) and Gammaton Moor (SS 49-24). This looks likely from a study of *Landranger Map 180*, but apparently no proof of its existence has so far been uncovered.

Atherington (180) (SS 59-23) Delightful village set on a hill-top to the west of the Taw valley, with a welcoming village shop, and a collection of colour-washed cottages around a small sloping square, all dominated by a tall-towered church, itself a landmark for many miles around. There are splendid views north-eastwards from the churchyard, to the southern flanks of Exmoor, but it is the interior of the church that is of the greatest interest. This was restored by J. L. Pearson, the architect of Truro Cathedral, in 1884, but has been left comparatively unscathed. See especially Devon's sole remaining rood loft, complete with narrow winding stair, the work of two carvers from nearby Chittlehampton in about 1535. See also the beautiful series of elaborately crocketed bench-ends, the splendid roof, the window full of medieval glass in the north chancel aisle, and several monuments removed from Umberleigh (see page 76), which include the effigy of a 13th century knight, and a 16th century tomb chest with inlaid brass figures.

Tall-towered Atherington Church.

Baggy Point (180) (SS 41-40) Rugged National Trust headland, the sandstone cliffs of which are a haven for a wide variety of birds. The white post with climbing steps, on top of the Point, is a wreck post, and is used in coastguard training exercises. In the year 1799, HMS *Weazle* was wrecked on the rocks here with the loss of 106 lives.

This splendid area is best approached from the Croyde Bay car park (see page 41), although it is also possible to walk from the car park above Putsborough Sand. For further details, see the National Trust leaflet *Woolacombe to Croyde Bay*.

Bampton (181) (SS 95-22) Modest little town on the River Batherm, a short distance above its confluence with the Exe. Sheltering in prettily wooded country, Bampton seems remote from the

SCALE 1:25 000 or 2½ INCHES to 1 MILE

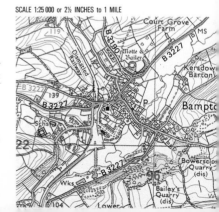

Bampton.

wilds of Exmoor, which are only a few miles to the north. It is a natural route centre and lies astride the still busy B3227, but the town's largely Georgian flavour still survives in its quieter corners. In medieval times it had a weekly market and two fairs each year, and its October Fair (held on the last Thursday in October) is still noted throughout the West Country for its sale of Exmoor ponies, and its colourful stalls and other amusements.

The large church is mainly 13th and 15th century in origin, but its interior was ruthlessly scraped and re-pointed by over-enthusiastic Victorian 'restorers', and little flavour of the past remains. However do not overlook the 15th century wagon-roof, and the screen to the tower room, nor the base of a Saxon cross in the south porch. The north-eastern end of the town is overlooked by the earthworks of a medieval 'motte and bailey' castle, but regrettably this is not of great interest.

On the A396, about two miles south-west of the town, there is an attractive early iron chain bridge carrying a minor road westward over the Exe. This relatively quiet road then leads through deep woodlands (93-20), and makes a very pleasant walk, running westwards, up the valley of the little Iron Mill Stream as far as Spurway Mill (89-20), a distance of about four miles. Another walk from Bampton is north-west up over the fields to Exbridge, passing a farm called Coldharbour (94-23), and making use of a public road in its latter stages.

Barford Park (182) (ST 23-35) See Enmore, pages 45-46.

Barnstaple (180) (SS 56-33) A busy but delightful old town at the head of the lovely Taw estuary, crossed here by a fine sixteen-arch bridge. There has been much development here in recent times, but much of the largely Georgian centre is unspoilt and retains a 'country-town' flavour so often lacking in larger towns further east.

It was granted borough and market-town rights as early as the tenth century, and was given a mint, the earliest coins from which date from 979. Domesday Book (1086) records that Barnstaple was one of only four boroughs in Devon, and by this time the Norman **Castle (1)** had almost certainly been built. The mound of this can still be seen to the east of the **Civic Centre (2)**, at the busy corner of Castle Street and North Walk. By the mid-12th century, the town had been encircled by a wall, but the last remains of this feature, the north and west gates, were demolished in the mid-19th century. For most of its history Barnstaple has been Devon's third most prosperous town (after Exeter and

Plymouth), and from earliest times until the present day, it has been a great market centre, also holding an important annual fair for three days in September (always beginning on the Wednesday preceding the 20th September). In the Middle Ages it was a considerable port, and was noted for its ship building, wool trading and cloth manufacture. Due to silting up of the Taw estuary, much of Barnstaple's foreign and coastal trade passed to Bideford, which stands at the mouth of the much faster flowing, and therefore less silt-laden Torridge; and its cloth manufacture was eventually lost to the mills of places like the Stroud valley in Gloucestershire.

Decline was however a slow process and the merchants of Barnstaple were still prosperous enough in the early-17th century to build the delightful little stone arcade on the town quay, and to rebuild it again in 1708. Standing between Castle Street and the river, it is still known as **Queen Anne's Walk (3)**, and has a statue of Queen Anne upon its portico. This was used as a business exchange and still incorporates the *'Tome Stone'*, a stone table upon which money was placed by the merchants, thus sealing the transaction that they had just completed by word of mouth alone.

Despite this decline the town was still prosperous enough in the late 18th and early-19th centuries to continue its growth, and there is a wealth of Georgian buildings still to be seen largely in the heart of the town. However by the middle of the 19th century, although ship-building had not entirely ceased, Barnstaple found itself relying more and more on its position as a market town and agricultural centre, and it is due to this fact that so much of its character has been retained. This is typified by two marvellous 19th century survivals: **Butcher's Row (4)**, a fascinating street with identical booth-like shops, most of which are still used by butchers; and nearby, the long covered **Pannier Market (5)**, which, with its glass roof supported on cast-iron pillars, is alive with activity each Tuesday and Friday, when a bewildering variety of produce is on sale. Do not miss this lively reminder of the not so distant days when farmers and their wives used to bring produce in from the surrounding countryside in panniers loaded on their horses and mules.

To the east of Butcher's Row, and away from the bustle of Barnstaple's lively main streets, is the old, tranquil heart of the town which contains the

Beside the Taw, at Barnstaple.

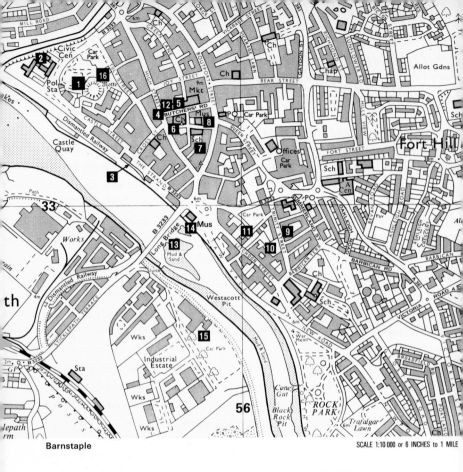

Barnstaple

SCALE 1:10 000 or 6 INCHES to 1 MILE

1 Barnstaple Castle
2 Civic Centre
3 Queen Anne's Walk
4 Butcher's Row
5 Pannier Market
6 Church of St Peter

7 Horwood's Almshouses and School
8 St Anne's Chapel
9 Salem Almshouses
10 Penrose Almshouses
11 Brannam's Potteries

12 Guildhall
13 Long Bridge
14 Museum of North Devon
15 North Devon Leisure Centre
16 Tourist Information Centre

Church of St Peter (6), looking out across a quiet alley-way to St Anne's Chapel (see below), and to the quaint 17th century *Horwood's Almshouses and School (7)*. The church has its origins in the 13th century, but its lead covered broach spire was only added in the 17th century. Heavily restored by the notable architect, Gilbert Scott in the 1870s, it has a rather dark interior, but there are several 17th century monuments worth seeing. The 14th century *St Anne's Chapel (8)* was originally a chantry chapel, but it was subsequently used for four hundred years as a Grammar School. Librettist John Gay, born in Barnstaple in 1685 and best known for his *Beggar's Opera*, was a pupil here. This building now houses a re-creation of the old school room with its original unique oak furniture, as it must have been in Gay's time here. The museum in the crypt is devoted to the history of schooling in Devon and in Britain as a whole. (Tel: 0271 46747.)

Other places worth looking at in Barnstaple include two other sets of almshouses, *Salem Almshouses (9)* in Trinity Street, and the 17th century *Penrose Almshouses (10)* in Litchdon

Street. In this latter street will also be found the showrooms of the thriving *Brannam's Potteries (11)*, where the famous *Royal Barum Ware* is made, and well worth visiting. This also brings to mind Barnstaple's medieval past when it was renowned for the making of floor tiles. Many of these so-called 'Barnstaple Tiles' can still be seen in the churches of North Devon, especially in those to the south and west of Barnstaple itself.

At the junction of Butcher's Row and the High Street is the late Georgian *Guildhall (12)*, which has a collection of plates and seals on display, while on the opposite side of the road is the attractive 15th century *Three Tuns Tavern*, which is enriched with fine panelling and fireplaces. Near the town end of the fine, sixteen-arch *Long Bridge (13)*, looking out over the busy Square, is the *Museum of North Devon (14)*, with many interesting displays interpreting the natural and human history of North Devon, including a 'Victorian Fernery'. Upstream from the bridge, on the far side, is the fine modern *North Devon Leisure Centre (15)*. (Tel: Barnstaple 73361)

These then are some of Barnstaple's best known

26

points of interest, but in your walk around the town do not overlook the wealth of 18th and early 19th century buildings that contribute so much to Barnstaple's pleasant 'West Country' flavour. Further advice may be obtained from the **Tourist Information Centre (16)**, in Tuly Street, near the castle mound. *(Tel: Barnstaple 47177.)*

(Also see Pilton, page 65)

Bathealton (181) (ST 07-24) Small village in a quiet setting beside a stream, with a church rebuilt in the 19th century, and well to its west, a prehistoric settlement (ST 05-24) overlooking the Tone valley. There is a pleasant bridleway north-west from Greenvale Farm, and an open road through woodlands, east and south towards Langford Budville (ST 11-22).

Beaford (180) (SS 55-14) This village sits comfortably astride the B3220 in quiet country above the deep Torridge valley. Its largely 15th century church has a dumpy tower topped by a small spire, but its interior has been over-restored. However do not miss the wagon-roof to the aisle, nor the Norman font ornamented with cable moulding. A charming, but rather depressing inscription on one of the 17th century wall tablets reads, *'We spring like flowers for a daye's delight at noone we flourish and we fade at night'*. Near the church is 'The Beaford Centre', which was established here in 1966, by the Dartington Hall Trust, to stimulate interest and enthusiasm in the arts over a wide area of the rural West Country. This is a base for activities that range from music and poetry to the theatre, but does not provide facilities for casual visitors to Beaford. At the Old Parsonage, on the B3220, half a mile to the north of the village, will be found the Beaford Pottery *(Tel: Beaford 306)*.

There is an excellent circular walk from Beaford, running down to the Torridge valley, along the wooded banks of the river past Beaford Bridge, and finally returning to the village.

Berrynarbor (180) (SS 56-46) Prettily sited on the slopes of a steep valley, less than a mile inland from the coast, Berrynarbor takes its name from the former lord of the manor, Berry de Narbert. The best feature is the handsome 15th century red sandstone tower of its church. Its interior is enriched by an arcade of white Beer stone, from the quarries set amongst the steep cliffs of Beer in far off South Devon, and almost certainly brought

Berrynarbor.

around the hazardous Cornish coast. There is a Norman font, but see especially the attractive monuments to Richard Berry (1645) and to Jane Spence (1815), both fine examples of the mason's art. There is also a monument to Bishop Jewell, the famous Elizabethan cleric who was born at Bowden Farm, about a mile to the south (SS 56-45), and who eventually became Bishop of Salisbury.

Watermouth Castle (SS 55-47), a Gothick building overlooking the coast to the north, was built in 1825, and now houses a wide variety of attractions for family holidaymakers, including among others, Mechanical Music Demonstrations, Model Railway, Smugglers' Dungeon, Pets' Corner, etc.

Bicknoller (181) (ST 11-39) Small village below the western slopes of the Quantocks, and mercifully just far enough away from the busy A358. Church and cottages make a pleasant group, and this cannot have changed much since the poet Coleridge and his friends used to walk over the Quantock ridge from his home at Nether Stowey to take refreshment at Bicknoller's inn before returning. In the churchyard there is an old cross and the village stocks are close by. The handsome, largely Perpendicular church, has a beautiful rood screen and a set of carved medieval bench-ends, with a few modern additions. 15th century carvings on the nave capitals and elsewhere are well worth lingering over, and Christopher Webb's glass in the east and north windows restores our faith in 20th century craftsmanship. In the church hangs a framed rubbing of a delightful verse taken from a monument on the outer south wall of the porch. It reads:

O who would trust this world
or prize what's in it
That gives and takes and chops
and changes ev'ry minit

On the Quantock slopes, well to the east of the church, there are the circular earthworks of a prehistoric 'hill-slope enclosure', known as Trendle Ring, which was probably used for the protection of stock. It is possible to walk from Bicknoller, up on to the Quantock ridge at Bicknoller Post, from whence there is a bewildering choice of routes *(see Landranger Map 181, or Pathfinder Map ST 04/14).*

Bideford (180) (SS 44-26) Built on a hillside sloping down to its long tree-lined quay on the River Torridge, Bideford is a busy, cheerful town, and one of the most attractive in the West Country. Compared to Barnstaple it was rather a late starter. It was given to the Grenvilles by William II, and remained their property until 1744. It had attained borough status by the early 13th century, and in 1271 Richard de Grenville was granted the right to hold a weekly market and a five day annual fair. It was about this time that the original bridge across the Torridge was built. This has had a long history of repairs and widening (the most recent being in 1968, when it had to be closed for three months).

It was in 1573, due to the efforts of the famous Sir Richard Grenville, that the town received a charter of incorporation from Queen Elizabeth I, which may be seen in the Courtroom of the Town Hall, along with a similar charter granted by James I. A few years later, in 1591, it was with a crew of Bideford men that Sir Richard fought the Spaniards in the Azores, in his equally famous ship, the *Revenge*. Due largely to Sir Richard's colonisation of Carolina and Virginia, Bideford's trade with

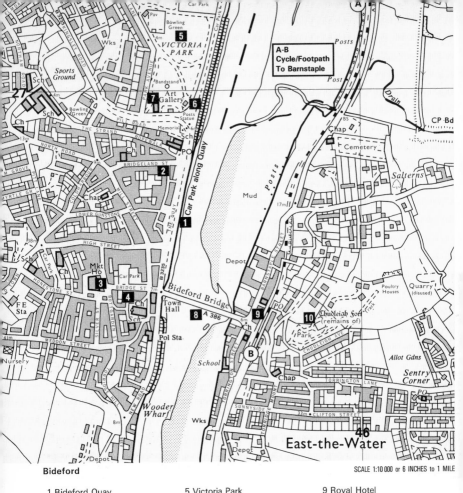

Bideford

SCALE 1:10 000 or 6 INCHES to 1 MILE

1 Bideford Quay	5 Victoria Park	9 Royal Hotel
2 Bridgeland Street	6 Tourist Information Centre	10 Chudleigh Fort
3 Pannier Market	7 Burton Art Gallery	
4 Church of St Mary	8 Bideford Bridge	

North America grew to very significant proportions, and it was only after the loss of these and all our other North American colonies, that it started to go into decline.

This decline continued into the early 19th century, when most international trade shifted to Bristol, Liverpool and London, but the swiftly flowing Torridge, unlike the more sluggish Taw at Barnstaple, prevented the silting up of *Bideford Quay (1)*. Due to this good fortune, Bideford's port has continued to attract some traffic, and small coasters and timber ships from as far as the Baltic may still be seen alongside its quays. It is from here that the supply ship *Oldenburg* leaves regularly for Lundy Island (see Lundy, page 58-59).

Apart from its bridge and quaysides, Bideford has pleasant streets sloping up from the Quay and parallel with it, with cheerful shops and elegant houses, especially in *Bridgeland Street (2)*. Its attractive *Pannier Market (3)* at the head of Bridge Street and second only in importance to Barnstaple's, is still held each Saturday.

The Church of St Mary (4) was entirely rebuilt in 1864, but it contains an excellent Norman font complete with ropework moulding and carved

panels, and a 16th century monument to Sir Thomas Graynfyldd, with an armoured Sir Thomas on a tomb-chest behind a fine stone screen.

It is also possible to visit the North Devon Maritime Museum at Appledore (see page 23), by way of a long path, largely beside the Torridge, a distance of about three miles. In its early stages this path passes the attractively laid out *Victoria Park (5)*. Here will be found the so-called 'Armada Guns'; although these are no doubt of great antiquity, their origin is uncertain. On the Quay, near the entrance to Victoria Park, there is a *Tourist Information Centre (6)*, and the Park is also the site of the *Burton Art Gallery (7)*, which contains a pleasant collection of paintings, and which also frequently houses special travelling exhibitions.

Across the long, twenty-four-arch *Bideford Bridge (8)*, is Bideford's suburb, East-the-Water, and here, overlooking the bridge is the *Royal Hotel (9)*, which incorporates the remains of a 17th century merchant's house, with two fine plaster ceilings and a very grand staircase. On a hill behind the Royal Hotel is *Chudleigh Fort (10)*, built in the Civil War by Major General Chudleigh when Bideford and Barnstaple declared for Parliament against

28

the King. Its grounds are now a public park.

Bishops Lydeard (181) (ST 16-29) A long village, not far from the south-western slopes of the Quantocks, and now happily well removed from the busy A358. There were red sandstone quarries near here, and this warm, mellow stone is much in evidence at Bishops Lydeard, both in the church and in the village's domestic buildings. The church is largely Perpendicular, and its tower is a particularly fine example of this late flowering Gothic style. The interior contains a fine rood screen, and a wonderful set of early 16th century bench-ends, with their many subjects including a stag, a ship, and a windmill. There is also an octagonal font, a good Jacobean pulpit, and a brass depicting Nicholas Grobham (1585) and his wife at prayer. The interior has been further enhanced by the work of one of our favourite 20th century restorers, Sir Ninian Comper, who decorated the chancel in 1923.

Mellow stone at Bishops Lydeard.

In the churchyard will be found a medieval cross, with a figure carved upon its shaft, and in the village there is an attractive set of almshouses, founded in 1616 by Sir Richard Grobham, a descendant of Nicholas Grobham, who is depicted on the brass in the church. Do not miss the Fives Tower, a late-18th century building in the car park of the Lethbridge Arms Inn. The game of fives was once very popular in this part of Somerset, and was usually played against church towers; but this tower was built especially for the game.

To the south-west of the village, beyond the A358, is Bishops Lydeard Station, the present southern terminus of the revived line between here and Minehead, operated by the West Somerset Railway (see page 82). Do try to make use of this most attractive facility, which is further enhanced by a connecting bus service between here and British Rail's Taunton Station.

Bishop's Nympton (180) (SS 75-23) Pleasant village with many thatched cottages bordering its long, sloping street. It is situated in high, rolling country between the valley of the Yeo and that of the charmingly named Crooked Oak stream, and was once part of the Bishop of Exeter's estate, hence the name *Bishop's*. The church dates from the early 16th century, and has a very handsome

Perpendicular tower, but its interior was unfortunately over-restored by the Victorians, and lacks any great feeling for its medieval past. However it has retained its original ceiled wagon-roof to the nave, and there is a fine wall monument built into the north wall, a tomb chest that probably also served as an Easter sepulchre, rather like the one to be found at Heanton Punchardon (see page 50). This is thought to be the tomb of Sir Lewis Pollard, an outstanding lawyer in his day, who was Justice of the Common Pleas between 1514 and 1526.

It is possible to walk south-west from here, over the fields to Mariansleigh, and to loop round through Alswear and Radley, to return to the starting point at Bishop's Nympton.

Bishop's Tawton (180) (SS 56-30) Long village in the Taw valley, beside the busy A377, and now almost a suburb of Barnstaple. However it has a number of attractive old thatched cottages, a pleasant inn, the Chichester Arms, and delightful views across the river to Tawstock Court and its church. Bishop's Tawton was one of the most important properties of the Bishops of Exeter, and until the time of Henry VIII, the farmhouse next to the church was one of the bishop's palaces. Although the present building has medieval origins, do not be confused by the castellations, which were almost certainly added in the late 18th century.

The church has a medieval stone spire, a very rare feature in Devon, where most of the spires are much later in date. Unfortunately the chancel, vestry and porch were rebuilt by the Victorians, but the interior contains a 15th century ceiled wagon-roof in the nave, and several pleasant monuments to members of the Chichester family, who had lived at Hall, now a 19th century neo-Elizabethan mansion, further up the valley to the south-east (SS 58-27). See also the monument to the infant daughter of Charles Dart, who died in 1652, and who is represented by a sad little figure wrapped in swaddling clothes, on a cushion.

There is a pleasant walk east and north-east from here, up Sentry Lane, and across fields parallel with, and partly beside a small tributary of the Taw, to Landkey. It is also possible to walk eastwards, up on to Codden Beacon on Codden Hill, the highest point in the district, and one from which there are fine views.

Bittadon (180) (SS 54-41) Minute village across a deep valley, to the east of the B3230, with an attractive walk north-eastwards, over to Berry Down where there is a scattered group of no fewer than nine Bronze Age round barrows or tumuli (SS 56-43). The church was re-built in the 1880s, and is not of great interest to visitors, apart perhaps from the late 17th century wall monument to Edward Pointz.

The Black Down Hills (181) (193) (ST 14-16 etc.) A pleasantly wooded range of hills lying to the south of the Vale of Taunton Deane, and never rising over a thousand feet. Only the western half of these hills are covered in this guide. The northern edge is much steeper than the south, which slopes off gently down to the wooded Culm valley. The best known features are the tall obelisk of the Wellington Monument (see page 80) and Castle Neroche (193) (ST 27-15), a massive Norman earthwork, probably based upon an Iron Age settlement. There is a Forestry Commission car park, picnic site and waymarked forest trail at Castle Neroche, and on a fine day it is claimed that no fewer than five counties may be seen from here. Castle Neroche is outside the area covered by this guide, but is well worth visiting. Read more about the Black Down Hills in Ronald Webber's excellent book, *The Devon and Somerset Blackdowns.*

Blackmoor Gate (180) (SS 64-43) This is a well known western 'gateway' to Exmoor, and prominent road junction. At South Stowford (SS 65-40), off the B3226, about two miles to the south, will be found the **Exmoor Bird Gardens and Children's Zoo**. Here in well landscaped gardens, penguins, waterfowl and peacocks mix with visitors, and there is a variety of other foreign birds and other friendly animals to be seen. There are tea-rooms and picnic areas. *(Tel: (059 83) 352 for opening times.)*

Blue Anchor (181) (ST 02-43) This small resort has a long open beach, backed in part by attractive cliffs and a multitude of caravans. There are fine views westward along the wide curve of Blue Anchor Bay, and alabaster rocks above the shore to the east. There is a useful little station here, on the West Somerset Railway (see page 82). Use the coastal path to walk west to Dunster and Minehead, or east to Watchet.

Bossington (181) (SS 89-47) Pretty hamlet with thatched, colour-washed cottages, and walnut trees shadowing a little stream, soon to flow over a pebbly beach into Porlock Bay. The hamlet shelters beneath the steep, wooded slopes of Bossington Hill, and there are walks up over here to Selworthy Beacon, or north to Hurlstone Point, as well as a coast path to Porlock and beyond to Porlock Weir. While in Bossington, do not miss a visit to the Somerset Farm Park, in the hamlet of Lynch just to its south. Here will be found many breeds of old English farm animals, and one of the country's largest private agricultural museums. There are demonstrations of driving and working Exmoor ponies and heavy horses, and in the farmyard there is also an early 16th century chapel with a pleasantly unspoilt interior. *(Tel: 0643 862816.)*

Bradford-on-Tone (181) (ST 17-22) Modest village just to the north of the A38, and mercifully well removed from the M5 motorway. The church is largely Perpendicular, and has a stout west tower with its stair-turret in the centre of one of its sides, rather than at one of the corners which is the more normal pattern. The north chapel was added in the 19th century, and the only item in the interior of real interest is the handsome 18th century pulpit. The pleasant two-arched bridge over the little River Tone at the north end of the village, dates back to the 15th century. There is a footpath, north-east from here, beside the Tone to Norton Fitzwarren.

At Three Bridges Farm, on the A38, there is a cider mill and museum, called **'Sheppy's'**, where visitors may wander around the orchards, press room, museum, and shop. The Sheppy family started brewing commercially in 1925, and since that time they have won over two hundred awards for their 'pure Somerset cider'. *(Tel: (082 346) 233 for details.)*

Bradworthy (190) (SS 32-13) A large, windswept village grouped around a wide square, more Cornish in flavour than Devonian, with a few genuine country flavour shops. The handsome church tower looks out over the Bradworthy Hotel and across the square, and raises hopes of an equally attractive interior. However this is in fact unexceptional, apart from the monument to Anne and Susannah Nicholls, the rather draughty late 17th century pulpit, and the medieval Barnstaple tiles.

Bratton Fleming (180) (SS 64-37) Straggling village in high country not far to the west of Exmoor, with a long sloping street and a pleasant inn serving bar snacks and beer from the wood, the White Hart. The church was rebuilt in the mid-19th century, and is not of great interest to visitors, although the view westwards from its tower is well worthwhile if access can be gained. The long-dismantled Lynton and Barnstaple Railway (see page 60) once ran down the valley below here, and there is a pleasant walk crossing this, passing Smythapark (SS 62-38) and over to Loxhore, from whence it is possible to walk north to Arlington Court (SS 60-40).

Braunton (180) (SS 48-36) This claims to be the largest village in England (population over 4000), and has grown to this size as a dormitory suburb of Barnstaple. It has busy shops astride the A361 and B3231 and a multitude of housing estates beyond them. However the older part of the village, at its northern end, in a valley overlooked by a ruined Perpendicular chapel, is reasonably attractive. The church, like those at Barnstaple and Swimbridge, has a crooked lead-covered spire, and it also has a pretty stream flowing beside its churchyard. It is dedicated to St Brannoc, a saint who crossed over from Wales in the 9th century, and who is reputed to be buried here. He dreamed that he should build his first English church where he first met a sow with her litter, and the realisation of this dream is commemorated on a carved roof boss above the north door of the church, depicting the sow and her piglets. The present church dates from the 13th century, but is now a very high and wide, largely Perpendicular building, the contents of which are full of interest. See especially the fine, richly carved 16th century bench-ends, the various medieval roofs, the Norman font, the carved panels in the chancel, and the Jacobean pulpit and reading desk. See also the brass in the Lady Chapel of Lady Elizabeth Bowcer, which is a palimpsest, this being a re-used brass, with part of the figure of a knight on the reverse. (There was a thriving trade in these 'second-hand' brasses in medieval times, many of them being imported into England from Flanders.) Below the nearby Church House, and opposite the Black Horse, is Braunton's interesting little museum. In the summer months there is a Tourist Information Centre at the main car park. *(Tel: 0271 816400.)*

To the south-west of the village lies **Braunton Great Field** (SS 47-35), a remarkable survival of a system of agriculture first practised in Anglo-Saxon times, when most land was farmed in strips in large open fields. Originally there were at least 700 strips at Braunton, but due to consolidation over the years, the number has been reduced to only a few, and most of the remaining ones are now of course much wider than the Saxon originals.

Beyond the Great Field, is **Braunton Marsh,** a wonderfully atmospheric, flat green area, intersected by small reed-lined drainage channels, and once a great favourite with the writer Henry Williamson, the author of *Tarka the Otter*, some of whose exploits took place here (see also Weare Giffard, page 79). Beyond this again are the **Braunton Burrows,** a wonderful desert landscape with dunes, some rising to over 70 feet. Beyond the dunes is the great expanse of **Saunton Sands** stretching southwards for almost three miles, from Saunton to Airy Point, where the recently joined Taw and the Torridge flow into the sea. Marsh, dunes and sands all provide fine bird-watching opportunities. There are Ministry of Defence firing ranges in this area and visitors must keep clear of some parts if red flags are flying. Also please respect the requirements of the Nature Conservancy Council, which is responsible for maintaining a Nature Reserve here.

It is also possible to walk along the north shore of the Taw estuary to Barnstaple, following the course of a dismantled railway line.

Brayford (180) (SS 68-34) Small village in the deep valley of the River Bray, and only two miles beyond the western fringes of Exmoor. The 16th century antiquary, John Leland, mentions in his famous *Itinerary*, 'a poore Village caullid Brayforde', but like most travellers in Tudor times, he was not a great lover of the wilder and more remote places he visited.

The church of All Saints, High Bray, is perched on steep hillsides above the village, and there are fine views from here, up the valley towards Exmoor. It is a largely Perpendicular building, but was much restored in the 1870s. The interior is not of great interest to visitors, but it does contain a Norman font, and part of a 15th century rood screen, which has been moved into the tower arch. There is a pleasant walk south from the church, along quiet Barton Lane, and down through woods to Newtown Bridge (SS 69-32).

Brendon (180) (SS 76-47) Prettily scattered along the wooded East Lyn valley with its scree-covered slopes with high moorland country above it on almost every side, Brendon village has one or two shops, an inn and a hotel. St Brendan's church overlooks the valley about a mile to the west, and was rebuilt in 1738. It was further 'restored' in the 19th century, but its contents include an interesting Norman font, and there is a pretty sundial over the porch dated 1707.

There is a path from here, down beside the East Lyn River to Watersmeet, and beyond to Lynmouth (see **Walk 6** for details of its latter stages). Also walk south from Brendon, up over Exmoor to Dry Bridge, on the B3223 (SS 76-45).

Brendon Common (180) (SS 76-44) Here are great open stretches of moorland country, some of the best that Exmoor has to offer. This is on both sides of the B3223, where there are at least three good car parks (in the vicinity of Dry Bridge and Farley Hill). Gorse, bracken, heather and the occasional thorn tree cover the hillsides, with small streams and bogs in the valleys below. Wild ponies may usually be seen in this area, and it is possible to walk eastwards to the valley of the Badgworthy Water,

to explore the 'Doone Country', and to link with our **Walk 5**, page 116.

The Brendon Hills (181) (ST 00-35 etc.) These hills are an eastern outlier of Exmoor, but lie mostly within the borders of the Exmoor National Park. There are fine wooded views to north and south of the long road running from east to west along a whaleback ridge from Elworthy (ST 08-34) to Wheddon Cross (SS 92-38). There are extensive Forestry Commission woodlands covering the slopes to the north of this road, with car parks and picnic sites at Chargot (SS 97-35), and Kennisham (SS 96-35), and a further site at Croydon Hill (SS 97-41), on a minor road south from Dunster, which is also on our **Walk 2**, page 110. There are fine views from the lawns outside the hospitable Ralegh's Cross Inn (ST 03-34), which has a restaurant and also serves good bar food.

Iron ore was almost certainly extracted from these hills by the Romans, and there is evidence that in Elizabethan times ore was mined by specially imported Germans. However it was in the latter half of the 19th century that ore was taken in great quantities for use in the smelters of South Wales. The West Somerset Mineral Railway was built especially for this purpose, and it ran first along the ridge, from Goosemoor (SS 95-35) eastwards to Ralegh's Cross Station (ST 02-34), before going down a steep incline in Eastern Wood, a short distance to the north of the station, to connect with the lower section heading down the valley of the Washford River to the harbour at Watchet. By 1883 mining here had become uneconomic and the mines were abandoned. Attempts were made to reopen some of them in the early 20th century, but conditions proved this impractical, and now only a few signs of past endeavours remain.

Bridge Reeve (180) (SS 66-13) Quiet hamlet beside the River Taw, just to the west of the A377, Barnstaple to Exeter road, and two miles west of Chulmleigh. An old chapel here has been converted into a craft shop (Chapel Craft) specialising in engraved glass and unusual wooden items. *(Tel: Chulmleigh 80884 for opening times.)* There is a pleasant woodland walk south-west from nearby Kersham Bridge, beside a small stream to Hollocombe (Map 191) (SS 63-11). *(If possible use Pathfinder Map SS 61/71.)*

Brompton Ralph (181) (ST 08-32) Small village on the steep south-eastern slopes of the Brendon Hills. The church has a tall Perpendicular tower (a landmark for many miles around), with a correspondingly tall tower arch within. Its interior was ruthlessly restored in the 1880s, but the Jacobean altar rail and the restored rood screen make a visit here worthwhile. Willett's Tower on a wooded hill across the valley to the north-east, is a folly built in 1820 to resemble a church tower. There is no public right of way to it.

The best walk from Brompton Ralph is southwards, down the wooded valley known as Combe Bottom (ST 08-30), to Wiveliscombe.

Brompton Regis (181) (SS 95-31) Small village in hilly country to the south-west of the Brendon Hills, and to the immediate west of Wimbleball Lake (see page 83), a large reservoir built in the 1970s. The

Brompton Regis.

village, which was a market town in medieval times, is built around the four sides of its churchyard, with shops, inn and cottages making an attractive group. There is a pottery at Hiccombe House, just to the south of the village on the road to Hartford *(Tel: Brompton Regis 228)*, and a variety of timber items are made at Pulhams Mill Studio, on the road to Wimbleball Lake *(Tel: Brompton Regis 366)*.

The church dates back to the 13th century and is complete with its original dumpy west tower. The interior was restored in 1853, when its 15th century fan vaulted screen was unfortunately ripped out and sold (those over-enthusiastic Victorians again!). Do not overlook the 16th century Dyke brass with its verse recalling the death of a young girl of nineteen:

Reader, it is worth thy pains to know
Who was interred here below.
Here lies good nature, pity, wit,
Though small in volume yet most fairly writ.
She died young, and so oft-times tis seen
The fruit God loves He's pleased to pluck it
green.

The best walk from here is south to Hartford, below the Wimbleball Dam, and then down the wooded Haddeo valley to Bury (SS 94-27). It is also possible to walk north over more open country to Gupworthy (SS 96-35).

Broomfield (182) (ST 22-32) The little church is in a well-shaded and beautifully quiet setting on the eastern edge of the Quantocks. The west tower and the chancel date from the early 14th century and most of the rest is about two hundred years younger. The interior is unspoilt by restoration and contains a wealth of interesting features. See especially the fine set of benches and bench-ends (probably by the same craftsman who made the bench-ends at Kingston St Mary and Crowcombe), the early 16th century wagon roofs, the old stone floors, and in the tower floor, the headless brass of Richard Silverton, a chaplain who died in 1443, and who according to an inscription *'sumptuously repaired and magnificently decorated'* the church.

The nearby Fyne Court, a 17th century building, was burnt down in 1898, but the surviving buildings and surrounding woodlands are leased to the Somerset Trust for Nature Conservation, which has developed it as a **Visitor Centre for the Quantocks.** Here is a most interesting 'Interpretation Centre' relating to the Quantocks, a well-stocked shop, and a series of delightful woodland walks in

the twenty-six acre grounds. *(Tel: Kingston St Mary 587 for opening details.)*

There is a triangular-shaped Iron Age settlement, Ruborough Camp, in woodlands to the north (ST 22-33), but this is not accessible to the public.

Brushford (181) (SS 92-25) Small village just to the west of the Barle valley, and about two miles southeast of Dulverton. Here is a comfortable hotel much loved by sportsmen, the Caernarvon Arms, with intriguing signs of a dismantled railway close by. The church has a stout west tower, and some excellent late Perpendicular windows. Inside will be found a fine Norman font of dark Purbeck marble, and two very different treasures, both from France. In the south chancel window there is some early 16th century French stained glass, while in the north chapel, built only in 1926 by the outstanding architect of his time, Sir Edwin Lutyens, there is the dignified effigy of Colonel Aubrey Herbert, the work of a Paris craftsman.

Brushford Church.

There is a pleasant walk from Brushford along the east bank of the Barle to Dulverton.

Buckland Brewer (180) (SS 41-20) Hill-top village between the valleys of the Yeo and the Duntz, with fine views out over the surrounding countryside. It is known that the church tower was rebuilt as long ago as 1399, after being struck by lightning, and this rebuild has survived until today. The rest of the church was reconstructed in 1879-80, but by this time Norman work was very much admired, and the beautiful Norman south door with its rows of birds' and humans' heads was retained. See also the interesting 17th and 18th century monuments (especially that to Anthony Dennys, dated 1641, with his wife and children at prayer), and the Norman image niche in the wall above the font. Do not miss a visit to the warm and welcoming Coach and Horses, a pleasant inn with a little restaurant at its rear.

Buck's Mills (190) (SS 35-23) Delightful little fishing hamlet, with a flavour of southern Cornwall, rather than northern Devon. Here are pretty thatched cottages overlooking a rock strewn, shingly beach, with some sand. It is approached down an attractive tree-shaded road leading off the A39, at Buck's Cross, and is the starting point for **Walk 6**. There is an old lime kiln close to the shore, and limestone was once brought over here from South Wales, and taken to the farms inland after being burned in the kiln. It is possible to walk some distance along the often rocky shore, but do not attempt this at times when the tide may be rising. There is space for only about fifty cars in the village car park.

Bulkworthy (190) (SS 39-14) Minute village in the valley of the upper Torridge, with a small church, which was built in the early 15th century by Sir William Hankford, Chief Justice of the King's Bench in the reign of Henry V (see also Monkleigh, page 62). Sir William's family took their name from Hankford (SS 38-14), a farm well to the north-west of the village. The church, with its little bellcote, was heavily restored in 1873, when some of the bench-ends were used to make up a new pulpit. The hamlet of Haytown (SS 38-14) lies just above the infant Torridge, and has some picturesque cottages and a Georgian chapel. There is an attractive road north from here, to Woolfardisworthy, passing Melbury Woods (see page 60), where there is a Forestry Commission Picnic Site and Forest Trail, near the cross roads at Powler's Piece (SS 37-18).

Burlescombe (181) (ST 07-16) Small village just to the north of the M5 motorway, looking out from its low hillside setting, over broad valley country through which runs the Grand Western Canal. The tower of the 15th century red sandstone church stands out well above the village, and is very prominent from the M5. The north aisle contains two fine 17th century monuments to members of the Ayshford family, and there is a rood screen which must be contemporary with the Perpendicular (15th century) rebuilding of the church. Beyond the neighbouring hamlet of Westleigh (much disturbed by the busy main railway line), there is a bridge over the Grand Western Canal (see page 48), carrying a road past Canonsleigh Farm, which incorporates the remains of an Augustinian nunnery founded by the redoubtable Maud, Countess of Devon in 1284.

Take the small road south-west from Westleigh and re-cross the reed-bordered canal at Ayshford (ST 04-15), where the bridge is close to a farm, which was once the manor of the Ayshfords, and which has its own **private** 15th century chapel.

Burrington (180) (SS 63-16) Compact village in high country to the west of the Taw valley, with painted, thatched cottages and hospitable inn, all close to a large oak tree. There are pleasing views out over the rolling plateau country between Taw and Torridge, north-east to Exmoor and southwards to Dartmoor. The church was rebuilt in the early 16th century and is a fine example of the Perpendicular style. The south aisle has a wagon-roof, with angels and other decoration, and handsome granite arcading. The outstandingly beautiful, vaulted rood screen is contemporary with the rebuilding of the church, and itself makes a visit to Burrington well

Burrington Church.

worthwhile. However do not overlook the other interesting features which include a south door with its original Perpendicular tracery, a Norman font and Jacobean altar rails.

Walk south from here along the road, to the vicinity of Winswood (SS 64-15), and then southwest through Eggesford Forest to Ashreigney.

Bury (181) (SS 94-27) A delightful hamlet set in the deep wooded valley of the little River Haddeo, which is here spanned by a narrow and very beautiful three-arch bridge (too narrow for vehicles). There is a ford beside the bridge, but it is only passable when the river is low, and as it is only two miles below the dam forming Wimbleball Lake, the volume of flow is not easy to predict. Half a mile to

Bridge and ford, at Bury.

the south-west, on a steep hill overlooking the confluence of the Barle and Haddeo rivers, are the motte and bailey earthworks of Bury Castle. This was strategically well sited, but its origins appear to be very uncertain. Was it possibly an Iron Age settlement, later used by the Normans for at least a short time?

There is a fine walk from Bury, up through woodlands beside the River Haddeo, to the Wimbleball Dam, and Brompton Regis. A return can be made over the hills, passing by Haddon Farm (SS 95-28).

Calverleigh (181) (SS 92-14) 15th century Calverleigh church is set in woodlands just to the south of

THE CARATACUS STONE

the A361, in a valley about two miles north-west of Tiverton. Although over-restored by the Victorians, it retains its original south aisle wagon-roof, and there is some medieval stained glass, which was brought here from St Tremeur in far off Brittany in 1887. There is also a medieval rood screen and a quaint and unusual 17th century monument to Mary Coleman, with her kneeling figure backed by no fewer than three medallions depicting her face.

The Caratacus Stone (181) (SS 89-33) This is situated on the moorland country of Winsford Hill, to the immediate east of the Spire Cross crossroads. It stands about three feet out of the ground and leans over rather drunkenly beneath a small stone shelter. It is inscribed CARATACI NEPUS (the descendant of Caratacus) and was probably erected by a Celtic chief during the Dark Ages, at some time after the departure of the Roman legions from Britain. Let it be quite clear that the sculptor has carved Carataci, and that Caractacus would, in this context, be a mis-spelling.

There is a delightful local legend that tells of a carter who tried to move the stone to get at treasure said to be buried beneath it, and who was crushed to death when the stone fell on him. 'Now', the tale relates, 'the ghost of the carter and his team of horses haunts the spot on the darkest of nights'.

Carhampton (181) (ST 00-42) This large village is much disturbed by traffic on the busy A39, but it has an attractively painted inn, the Butcher's Arms, and a church, which despite heavy handed 'restoration' by the Victorians is well worth visiting. This has a red sandstone tower, which was rebuilt in 1870, but the rest retains its 15th century Perpendicular features. Inside will be found a magnificent late medieval rood screen, intricately carved, and painted in a way that must have been familiar to the parishioners when it was first installed, but which today's visitors might possibly prefer to see in bare wood. See also the beautifully lettered brass, and the dignified pulpit, both from the 18th century. The painter Joseph Mallord Turner is believed to have set up his easel and canvas on the small hill to the north of the village (ST 00-43) when he painted his well known picture of Dunster Castle.

Walk westwards, up a track and bridleway, across Dunster Park to Dunster village, or south-west, up over Withycombe Hill (ST 00-41), to Luxborough.

The Chains (180) (SS 73-42 etc.) This high plateau country on the north western side of Exmoor, is some of the bleakest moorland to be found in southern Britain, and its rain-soaked bogs give birth to the Exe, the Barle and the Hoaroak Water. It is an area that should only be explored by the experienced walker, but here will be found the very essence of Exmoor. The writer Henry Williamson found inspiration at the Chains, and he tells of summer days when he would lie with finger tips touching the grass, drawing strength from the very earth itself. Inevitably he wrote of Tarka coming here, in his immortal story, *Tarka the Otter*.

Challacombe (180) (SS 69-40) There is an inn and a shop in this small village which is tucked away in a valley on the south-western fringes of Exmoor, and part of which lies astride the B3358. The name

Challacombe means 'Cold Valley' and on all but the sunniest of days, this appears to be a fair description of its setting. The church, which lies well to the west of the village, was entirely rebuilt in 1850, and is not of great interest to visitors. Shoulsbury Castle, well to the south-east of the village (SS 70-39) is an extensive earthwork of uncertain origins, but local legend tells of King Alfred holding it against the Danes; a rather unlikely story. However there are fine views westward from here out over the rolling, wooded hills of north Devon, and Shoulsbury must have provided its occupants with an excellent strategic site.

There are opportunities for fine walks northward from the B3358, from points west and east of Challacombe, out over some of the highest parts of Exmoor (see Chapman Barrows, below, and The Long Stone, page 57).

Chambercombe Manor (180) (SS 52-47) A delightful manor farmhouse, situated in a quiet valley behind Ilfracombe. It contains an interesting collection of period furniture and china, a 15th century private chapel and a 'haunted room'. The house is set amongst lovely informal gardens, with ponds and waterfowl, and there is a restaurant serving coffee, lunches and teas. *(Tel: Ilfracombe (0271) 62624.)*

Chapman Barrows (180) (SS69-43) Here on a high ridge in moorland country between Parracombe and Challacombe is a group of no fewer than nine Bronze Age round barrows. Five of these form a line, which has been the parish boundary between the above two villages for many hundreds of years. The Long Stone (see page 57) is situated some 450 metres to the south-east. To visit the barrows walk north from a point on the B3358, less than a mile west of Challacombe, or south-east from Parracombe.

Charles (180) (SS 68-32) Here is a church and a few houses just above the deep wooded valley of the Bray, which is itself much scarred by extensive quarrying nearby. Apart from the outer shell of its tower, the church was rebuilt in 1875, and is not of great interest to visitors. R. D. Blackmore's grandfather was the incumbent of Charles, and the novelist is believed to have written much of *Lorna Doone* here, while staying at the rectory with his uncle.

Walk south-east from here, to Newtown Bridge, over the River Bray, and then northwards up a small road, known as Barton Lane, to Brayford church, at High Bray.

Chawleigh (180) (SS 71-12) Situated in high rolling country about mid-way between Exmoor and Dartmoor, and just to the south of the deep, wooded valley of the Little Dart River, the modest village of Chawleigh was a borough in the 15th century, but despite this it never appears to have been of great significance. The handsome church of St James is a largely 15th century building, with a fine rood screen and graceful granite arcading. The barrel roof of the chancel has cross-ribbing enhanced by no fewer than 120 floral bosses, and light flows into the building through generously proportioned, clear-glazed windows. At Stone Barton (SS 71-13), northwards beyond the Little Dart River, there are

Chawleigh. . .one of Devon's hidden gems.

the earthworks of 13th century Stone Castle, built by the delightfully named Isabella de Fortibus, Countess of Devon. There is a local legend that tells of a pauper of nearby Chulmleigh, who was so desperate that he decided to drown his seven children. They were however saved from this fate by Countess Isabel, and brought up, at her own expense, at Stone Castle.

Cheldon (180) (SS 73-13) Here is a small church and one or two houses, in a quiet setting just to the north of the deep, wooded valley of the Little Dart River. The largely 15th century church must have been remote enough to have escaped the more enthusiastic attentions of the Victorian 'restorers', and has a delightfully unspoilt interior. There are medieval tiles, 15th century bench-ends, and, from the 18th century, pulpit, text-boards, altar-rails, and two unusual painted ironwork gates. The origin of the two ladies in high relief plaster is obscure, but their hair and dress style appears to be Georgian.

Wooded countryside above the Little Dart Valley, near Cheldon.

Walk south from here to Cheldon Bridge on the Little Dart, and follow its north bank westwards, through woodlands, to Leigh Bridge (SS 72-13), before returning to Cheldon by road.

Cheriton (180) (SS 73-46) Small hamlet above the

Hoaroak Water valley, and the original site of St Brendan's church, which was 'moved' to a point mid-way between here and Brendon (SS 74-47) in the 18th century. There is a path, south-west from here and then south, linking on to the Two Moors Way, near Roborough Castle earthworks.

Chipstable (181) (ST 04-27) Small village enfolded in the wooded foothills of the Brendons, at the head of a little stream which flows into the headwaters of the River Tone. The church was rebuilt in 1869 by well-meaning, but heavy-handed London architect, Benjamin Ferrey, although, as was so often the case, he fortunately allowed the medieval tower to remain. Other survivals include some 16th century bench-ends, and the earlier arcading, with angels on the capitals.

Walk south-east over hill slopes, by Marshes Farm, to the River Tone, and then up a tree-lined path beside this little river, as far as Washbattle Bridge. To enjoy this delightfully unspoilt walking area to the full, use Pathfinder Map ST 02/12.

Chittlehamholt (180) (SS 64-20) This place name appears to mean 'wood of the dwellers in the valley', and indicates that it was a hamlet clearing in the forest, made by people from the parent village of Chittlehampton, about three miles to the north (see below). Chittlehamholt is situated on a high spit of land between the Taw and its tributary the Mole, less than two miles north of their union, and the area is well wooded still, thanks partly to the activities of the Forestry Commission. Enquire locally if there is a permitted forest path heading west and north towards the hamlet of Warkleigh (SS 64-22). The church at Chittlehamholt was built in 1838, and is not of great interest to visitors.

Chittlehampton (180) (SS 63-25) A large village centred upon its fine, wide sloping square, overlooked on three sides by trim thatched cottages, and on the fourth, by a large Perpendicular church. The 115-foot high church tower is claimed to be the finest in Devon, with the strength common to many in the county, but also with a delicacy of detail seldom found beyond the western borders of Somerset. The handsome south porch is approached up a path sheltered by pollarded limes, and there are pleasant views southwards, out over the square, to the wooded countryside lying between the Taw and Mole valleys.

The spacious interior of the church has suffered at the hands of the Victorians, and has indifferent benches, glossy tiles, and scraped and heavily pointed walls; all very much in contrast with the unspoilt charm of the porch and the medieval south door that it shelters. However do not miss the 15th century stone pulpit, the 17th century Giffard monument, and the remains of St Urith's shrine in the chancel.

It is to St Urith that we owe the surviving splendours of Chittlehampton. She was born at nearby Stowford in the 8th century, and suffered martyrdom at the hands of a gang of unruly Chittlehamptonians, who cut the unfortunate young lady to pieces with scythes, as they apparently did not agree with her particular religious views. From the time of her death until the Reformation, Chittlehampton was a renowned place of pilgrimage, and the visiting pilgrims must have largely financed the building of this splendid church.

When in Chittlehampton, do not miss a visit to the Pewter Craft Shop in the Square, where a variety of hand-worked pewter and other local crafts are on show.

Thatched cottages and fine medieval tower, at Chittlehampton.

Chulmleigh (180) (SS 68-14) This delightful small town above the wooded valley of the Little Dart River was once a thriving market town, and was made a borough in 1253. From this time onwards it was prosperous with its weekly market, its woollen industry and three annual cattle fairs. However by the end of the 18th century the woollen industry had moved away to the east and the north, the new turnpike roads were built in the nearby valleys and passed the town by, and with the coming of the railways, trade in cattle and sheep moved to new markets in the vicinity of stations, like Eggesford.

While these moves have not been to the financial advantage of the town, Chulmleigh's unique flavour of the past has been greatly enhanced by its isolation over the years. This isolation has now been partly overcome by modern road transport, but the 18th and early 19th century charm of its little hilly streets remains largely unspoilt. See especially the

17th century Barnstaple Inn, and of course the large 15th century church of St Mary Magdalen, with its fine west tower, rebuilt in 1881, and its outstanding, fifty-one foot long rood screen, surmounted by four

Church and War Memorial at Chulmleigh.

delightful little 17th century figures of the Evangelists, each equipped with a book and quill pen. See also the handsome wagon-roof to the nave, with its supporting angels and carved bosses, and the strange little Norman carving of the crucifix in the south porch.

Churchstanton (181) (ST 19-14) This consists of only a church and one or two houses, and is situated on the southern side of the Black Down Hills. The church is largely late 14th century Perpendicular, although the west tower is considerably older. The interior is full of character, with a handsomely carved south aisle arcade, and there are early 19th century box pews, and a west gallery of about the same date, which has been made up of medieval bench-ends.

There is a pleasant walk across country, north to Burnworthy, then west to Clayhidon, and returning to Churchstanton on quiet roads on the south side of the infant River Culm.

Clapworthy (180) (SS 67-24) Here in the lovely Bray valley, on the B3226, three miles to the west of South Molton, is an old mill, making 'Hancock's Devon Cider'. Five generations of the Hancock family have been making cider for at least a hundred years. There is a 'Colour Photograph Exhibition' on cider making, a craft centre, and a shop selling cider, scrumpy, honey and clotted cream (Tel: South Molton 2678).

Clatworthy (181) (ST 05-30) This overlooks a thickly wooded valley containing the headwaters of the River Tone, which has been dammed here to form the Clatworthy Reservoir (see below). Clatworthy itself is little more than a collection of cottages overlooked by a small church with Norman origins. When we last called here it was still lit by oil lamps, but this attractive feature may now have

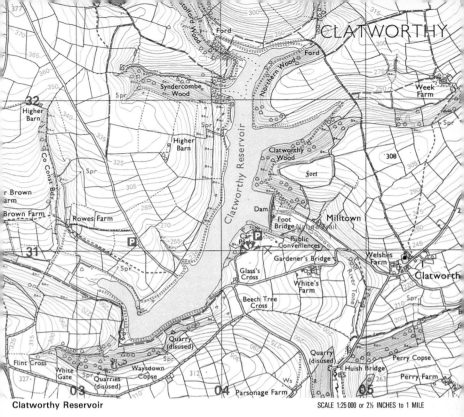

Clatworthy Reservoir

SCALE 1:25 000 or 2½ INCHES to 1 MILE

been replaced. Much restoration was carried out here in 1865, but the simple interior still retains a flavour of quieter, simpler times. It is hoped that the interesting carved roof bosses in the wagon roof of the south porch, in a bad condition when we last called here, have now been restored.

Clatworthy Reservoir (181) (ST 03-30) 130 acre reservoir in a fold of the southern slopes of the Brendon Hills, formed by a high dam across the infant River Tone. There is a car park close to the dam, with fine views northwards out over wooded and gorse covered slopes above the water's edge. There is also an adjoining picnic site, toilets and an interesting nature trail, which is well described in a

Clatworthy Reservoir ... in a southern fold of the Brendon Hills.

specially prepared leaflet. It is possible to fish here for brown and rainbow trout, and self-issue bank fishing permits are available at the angler's shelter. *(For boat fishing and other details tel: 0984 23549.)* The car park shown on the west side of the reservoir is only a small one, and is intended primarily for the use of anglers. To the immediate north of the dam there are the triangular-shaped earthworks of Clatworthy Castle, an Iron Age settlement with some of its banks rising fifteen feet above their accompanying ditch. Clatworthy Reservoir is on **Tour 2**, page 90.

Clayhanger (181) (ST 02-22) Here is just a church and a few houses, situated in rolling wooded country to the south of the B3227 Taunton to Bampton road. The church was over-restored in the late 19th century and partly rebuilt. However there are some attractive 16th century bench-ends in the best Devonshire tradition, and a marble monument to Richard Nutcombe, Sheriff of Devon in 1715, which should not be missed, particularly the inscription thereon, proclaiming that 'in an age both in principles and practice corrupt, (he) kept his faith entire and his morals untainted'. There is a pleasant walk, north-west from here, past 15th century Nutcombe Manor, home of the Nutcombe family for many hundreds of years, to Denscombe Mill, returning south and east on a quiet road, past Bulcombe.

Clayhidon (181) (ST 16-15) This consists of a small 15th century church, a few houses and an inn called the Half Moon, all above a valley with a stream running south from the Black Down Hills to join the headwaters of the River Culm. There is a plaque in a nearby lane recording the fact that a certain William Blackmore, a local land surveyor, was murdered there on 6th February 1853. Read the full story in Ronald Webber's book, *The Devon and Somerset Blackdowns*. There is a pleasant, but rather obscure path from Clayhidon, running in an easterly direction to Burnworthy and then south to Churchstanton.

Cleeve Abbey (181) (ST 04-40) The clear waters of the little Washford River run past the very attractive remains of Cleeve Abbey. This is set in a quiet valley, and is surrounded on every side by well mown lawns, a sure sign of the careful guardianship of English Heritage. This Cistercian abbey was founded by the Earl of Lincoln at the end of the 12th century, and although the abbey church has been almost entirely destroyed, the other buildings are remarkably well preserved. The refectory was rebuilt in the 15th century and an inspection of its massive wagon-roof with angel supports more than justifies a visit here. See also the gatehouse built by the last abbot, the well preserved dormitory with garderobes within the thickness of its walls, and the lovely tracery of the rose window in the sacristy.

Clovelly (190) (SS 31-24) This is one of North Devon's, indeed one of Britain's, great tourist favourites; a place of pilgrimage for many generations. Despite this fame, Clovelly has withstood the consequent pressures remarkably well. It should, if at all possible, be approached via the **Hobby Drive**, a one-way, private toll road starting from Hobby Lodge (SS 33-23), which is about eight

Clovelly Harbour.

miles west of Bideford, on the A39 beyond Buck's Cross (see **Tour 10**, page 106). This is a three-mile-long coastal drive, built in the 19th century by Sir James Hamlyn, the Lord of the Manor of Clovelly. The slow driving necessitated by the possibly uneven surface and the modest toll charge are more than justified by the glorious views out over Bideford Bay.

Before walking down to the village, park at the end of the Hobby Drive and call at the excellent Visitor Centre, which is complete with cafeteria and audio-visual show. The steep pull back up to the car park may be avoided by making use of a Landrover service up a road to the west of the village, but this should only be used by those who just cannot

manage the climb. The long cobbled street is so steep in places that it has had to be stepped. It is overlooked by a series of pretty cottages and shops, built almost on top of each other, and bedecked throughout the season with shrubs and flowering plants. Goods are still delivered by donkey or sled, for mercifully the motor car is simply unable to intrude here. The street eventually drops down to an attractive little harbour, above which are towering and splendidly wooded cliffs.

There is an old inn, situated at the very edge of the water, and there are 'trips around the bay' for those who wish to rest before their tiring but well worthwhile climb back up Clovelly's unique street. There is always the Landrover, but think of that sense of achievement, if you toil up unaided!

Clovelly Church is situated on an 'upper level' well to the west of the village, a quiet place, the path to its south door being overhung by a pleasant avenue of yew trees. It is a largely Perpendicular building, although it was heavily restored in the 19th century, with glossy tiles much in evidence. Its long narrow interior is dominated by an exceptional number of wall monuments, mostly to members of the Cary family, who held the manor here until the 18th century, and of the Hamlyns, who purchased it from them. Charles Kingsley's father was rector here from 1830 to 1836, and both Clovelly and the Cary family figure in his famous story, *Westward Ho!* It is possible to walk north-westwards from the church, through Brownsham Wood, to Brownsham (SS 28-26), and then down to rock-strewn Mouth Mill beach (see page 63), with its small stream crossing the shingle.

Clovelly Dykes (190) (SS 31-23), to the right of the A39, well to the south of the village, are earthworks that formed an Iron Age settlement, the complexity of which is probably explained by the requirement of its builders for the protection, not only of themselves, but also of their herds of cattle. The earthworks have not been systematically excavated, but probably date from the first century BC.

Cobbaton Combat Vehicles Museum (180) (SS 61-26) Situated in remote country to the west of the Taw valley, but only about four miles south-east of Barnstaple, this museum contains over twenty World War II British and Canadian fighting vehicles, and many other items of smaller equipment. This is all accounted for as 'a hobby which got out of hand'. *(Tel: Chittlehamholt 414)*

Combe Florey (181) (ST 15-31) 'I am extremely pleased with Combe Florey and pronounce it to be a very pretty place in a very beautiful country'. So wrote the great 19th century reformer and wit, Sydney Smith, in a letter to a friend, a few months after his appointment to the living here. He had always considered life out of London 'to be a mistake', but nevertheless he appears to have taken very easily to Combe Florey. It remains a most attractive village, with colour-washed cottages, a cosy thatched inn — the Farmers Arms, a mill stream, a handsomely fronted manor house and an early 14th century church; all situated in a quiet valley at the eastern end of the Brendon Hills, and not far to the west of the Quantocks.

The manor house was built in about 1675, and was re-fronted in 1730. The gatehouse however is much older, dating from about 1590. The nearby church has a Perpendicular tower, but the chancel was rebuilt in about 1850. The carved pulpit must be contemporary with the tower, also being Perpendicular in style, and there is a good set of bench-ends of about the same period. See also the two medieval brasses to members of the Francis family, and the fine early-14th century effigy of a knight and two ladies, probably Sir John de Merriet of Hestercombe and Combe Florey. The inscription above Sir John's tomb refers to an earlier member of the family, Maude de Merriet, who became a nun at Cannington, near Bridgwater, and whose heart was eventually returned here for burial.

Combe Martin (180) (SS 58-46) A large, exceptionally long village situated in a long narrow combe, which ends in a small bay, with an extensive sandy beach at low tide. There are many rock pools here and the bathing is safe. Combe Martin is renowned for its splendid coastal scenery, and it is possible to walk north-eastwards from here up to the Little Hangman Hill, and on to the Great Hangman and Holdstone Down (SS 61-47) (see page 52). There are fine views from these hills, back down to Combe Martin itself, southwards to Exmoor, and on a clear

Combe Martin, above its sandy beach.

day, out across the Bristol Channel to the Welsh coast. Above the low cliffs leading to the Little Hangman, is a grassy slope called Cobblers Park, and beyond Lester Point there is a small cove – Wild Pear Beach.

In the village, see the interesting Combe Martin Motorcycle Collection, which is close to the main beach car park in Cross Street; and the Pack of Cards Inn, a folly built in the shape of a 'card house'. The largely 15th century red sandstone church is also well worth visiting, with its fine 99 foot high Perpendicular tower, and its beautifully painted rood screen. It also has some well carved 15th century bench-ends, and a medieval chest said to have been used for the collection of *'Peter's Pence'*, a universally unpopular Papal levy imposed from as early as the 8th century, and only discontinued in the reign of Henry VIII.

Combe Martin grew up as a mining town, and in medieval times was well known as a lead and silver producing centre. Iron ore was also mined here, and much of this was shipped to South Wales from Wild Pear Beach (see above). Mining only ceased at Combe Martin in the 1870s, and there are still some remains to be seen from the small road leading up eastwards, over Knap Down. Many shafts and tunnels still exist, some of which once passed under the main street. It should be stressed that all are on

private land, and no attempt should be made to explore.

This combe is so sheltered that its slopes have always been noted for their abundant little market gardens, and on the hillside above these gardens can still be seen the remains of older agricultural strip systems.

Do not miss a visit to the attractive and interesting Bodstone Barton Working Farm and Country Park (180) (SS 57-44), less than two miles to the southwest of the village. *(Tel: 027188 3654.)*

Combe Sydenham (181) (ST 07-36) Here in a quiet valley below the eastern end of the Brendon Hills, is a fine Elizabethan manor house, which was once the home of Elizabeth Sydenham, the second wife of Sir Francis Drake. Now a family home it is being gradually restored, and its attractive features include a fine gatehouse, old walled gardens and ornamental tree nurseries. Here is also a 'Country Park Trout Farm', with lakes and a shop; and there are also ten miles of way-marked, wooded walks, which take in a deserted hamlet, and one of which follows the little woodland stream known as Drake's Leat. Lunches and teas available. *(Tel: (0984) 56284 for further details.)*

Cothay Manor (181) (ST 08-21) Sir Nikolaus Pevsner in his *Buildings of England* series, guide to *South and West Somerset*, refers to Cothay as 'one of the most perfect small English manor houses of the late 15th century', but it is **not open to the public**. It should however be possible to obtain distant glimpses of this delightful house from a small path leading across the River Tone to Appley, but please respect the privacy of the owners.

Cothelstone (181) (ST 18-31) Delightful group of buildings beneath the south-western slopes of the Quantocks, consisting of a church, a farm, a few cottages and an exquisite Elizabethan manor house, like the church in red sandstone. It was from the manor's gatehouse that Colonel Richard Bovet and Thomas Blackmore, two of the Duke of Monmouth's supporters, were hanged after the defeat of his rebel army at the Battle of Sedgemoor in 1685. *Cothelstone Manor is only open by written appointment*.

The largely Perpendicular church has some fragments of 15th century glass in the tops of its north chapel windows, a Jacobean pulpit and, like so many churches in this area, a good set of 16th century bench-ends. There are several monuments to members of the Stawell family, the owners of the manor until the end of the 18th century, notably the 14th century effigy of Sir Matthew de Stawell, and that of Sir John Stawell who was brought home from his Wiltshire estate to *lie amongst his ancestors and by the side of his wife*.

Cothelstone is not a good base for walkers, but there is a pleasant drive from here, up through woodlands, to Park End, and then eastwards for a short distance, leading to **Cothelstone Hill** (181 and 182) (ST 19-32 and 20-32), a large area of open heath, bracken and mixed woodland, which is ideal for a short walk (way-marked walk from car park). There are fine views from the hill-top, which is two thirds of a mile east of the car park.

Countisbury and Countisbury Common (180) (SS 74-49) Small village with a church which, apart from its early 18th century screen, is not of great interest to visitors. The Exmoor Sandpiper Inn was,

COUNTY GATE

Countisbury SCALE 1:25 000 or 2½ INCHES to 1 MILE

County Gate (180) (SS 79-48) Here in wooded, moorland country is the point on the A39 where the counties of Somerset and Devon meet. There are car parks, toilets, and an Information Centre (open between Easter and September). The Glenthorne Nature Trail leading down through woods north towards the coast, starts here, and it is also a good base for other coastal walks. To the north-west of County Gate, there are the earthworks of a Roman fortlet or signal station on Old Barrow Hill (180) (SS 78-49). This circular enclosure with a large mound at its centre, was almost certainly built in the early period of the Roman occupation, to command views of the Bristol Channel and the south coast of Wales, where the Silures, the native tribes inhabiting South Wales, were at that time still unsubdued. There is a similar fortlet near Martinhoe (see page 60), and there probably others. There is also a path leading southwards from County Gate, down to Malmsmead in the Oare valley, where a link could be made to our **Walk 5**, page 116.

Crowcombe (181) (ST 13-36) This delightful village was a well populated borough town in the Middle Ages (note the attractive little market cross), but it now rests quietly below the wooded slopes of the Quantocks, with a few houses and an inn keeping company with handsome Crowcombe Court at the foot of its beautifully wooded park, together with a medieval church house (now the village hall), and a largely Perpendicular church. This fine building has a 14th century red sandstone tower and a beautiful fan-vaulted porch, near which is another medieval cross. Inside will be found a splendid collection of bench-ends with a variety of delightful carved detail, including a mermaid, a 'Green Man' (see Halse, page 49), and small naked men engaged in combat with dragons. See also the handsome 18th century pulpit and rood screen, the exceptionally well carved 15th century font, and the elegantly sculpted classical wall monument to James Bernard by Sir Richard Westmacott, the most distinguished member of a whole family of 18th and 19th century sculptors.

There is a path leading up to the hills from the western end of the village, but for the best walking base near here, drive north-east on the Nether Stowey road, up the steep, wooded hill to Crowcombe Park Gate, and beyond to **Dead Woman's Ditch** (181) (16-38), where there is a large car park (see page 42). To link on to our **Walk 1**, walk back along the road to Crowcombe Park Gate.

Crowcombe Court, beneath the wooded Quantock slopes.

until 1913, a stopping point for the horse-drawn coach that ran between Lynmouth and Porlock. It was also passed by the heroic people of Lynmouth, who on a stormy night in January 1899 dragged their lifeboat on a trolley, up over Countisbury Hill, and down into Porlock, being unable to launch it from Lynmouth, in an endeavour to rescue a threatened ship's crew. After eleven nightmare hours they reached Porlock Weir and were able to launch their boat. They then stood by the rudderless vessel until a tug arrived, and the crew were saved. Read the details of this fine story in *The Ships and Harbours of Exmoor*, by Grahame Farr, or in several other local publications.

Almost all the country around Countisbury is owned by the National Trust, and their excellent leaflet *'Countisbury'* is well worth purchasing. There are car parks at Countisbury village and further east on the A39 (SS 75-49), and from here it is possible to take a variety of walks out over Countisbury Common as far north as Foreland Point, which with its lighthouse, is the most northerly part of mainland Devon. The eastern path to Foreland Point passes through the steep-sided ravine of Coddow Combe, with its dramatic scree-covered slopes overlooked by the jagged rocks of a hill known as Warmersturt, while the western path passes over high Butter Hill. Further to the west it is possible to take a very steep zig-zag path down to Sillery Sands, but this is only for the hardier explorer. Inland from the top of this path, and clearly visible from the A39, which intersects them, are the dramatic earthworks of an extensive Iron Age promontory fort, which are well worth exploring on foot. **Wherever you walk in this Countisbury area, keep well away from cliff edges.**

Crowcombe SCALE 1:25 000 or 2½ INCHES to 1 MILE

Croyde and Croyde Bay (180) (SS 44-39) Attractive little village with thatched cottages and a small clear stream. It is inevitably crowded at holiday times, but away from the coast it has withstood the pressures of tourism, and shown remarkable restraint. The Croyde Gem Rock and Shell Museum, with its shop and craft workshop, is worth visiting *(Tel: Croyde 890407)*. There is a good car park on the far northern side of Croyde Bay (SS 43-39), which gives access to some fine walking country along the coast, to the high cliffs of Baggy Point (see page 24), and back round via Putsborough. The sands of Croyde Bay provide reasonable surfing and fine sandcastle-building opportunities.

At Croyde.

Cruwys Morchard (181) (SS 87-12) Here, in remote, pleasantly wooded country between Tiverton and Barnstaple, and well to the west of the Exe valley, stand just a church and a manor house. The former building has 14th century origins, although the top of its tower was rebuilt in brick in 1689 following a calamitous fire. The alterations in the years after this fire provided a most attractive early 18th century interior, which has since been allowed to stay largely unaltered. There are handsome classical screens with Corinthian columns, a modest pulpit, and old box pews, many of which have place names identifying them with various farms in the parish. On leaving here do not miss the revolving 18th century lych gate. The manor house close by, the home of the Cruwys family since the reign of King John, has a Georgian front, but this feature conceals signs of a much earlier building, dating back at least to the 15th century.

Culbone Church (181) (SS 84-48) This is claimed to be the smallest complete parish church in England. It is in a beautiful setting, sheltered by wooded hills on almost every side, and is close to a small stream, which still has four hundred feet to drop before joining the sea less than a quarter of a mile to the north. The church, which has Norman origins, is a mere thirty five feet long and only twelve feet wide. It has an interesting font and a pleasant 14th century screen.

It was in 1797, at a lonely farmhouse near Culbone, probably Ash Farm just to its east, that the poet Coleridge, having taken two grains of opium — apparently to keep his dysentery at bay — had the strange dream that was to inspire the immortal lines:

In Xanadu did Kubla Khan
A stately pleasure-dome decree:
Where Alph, the sacred river, ran
Through caverns measureless to man
Down to a sunless sea.

There is no public road to Culbone, and lack of this facility further enhances the sense of peace to be experienced here. It can be approached on foot by the Somerset and North Devon Coast Path, either westwards from Porlock Weir, or eastwards from Countisbury and County Gate; north from the A39 at Culbone Stables Inn (181) (SS 82-47); or from the Pittcombe Head car park, further east on the A39 (181) (SS 84-46). It may also be possible to park at a point near the road from Culbone Stables down to Porlock Weir, but a slightly longer walk from one of the other parking places will provide a greater sense of achievement.

Culmstock (181) (ST 10-13) Once a market town, and in medieval times an important wool centre, this still-large village is prettily situated in the Culm valley, below the western end of the Black Down Hills. It is overlooked from the south by Hackpen Hill, while to the north, the western bastion of the Black Downs — Culmstock Beacon — is topped by a beehive shaped 'beacon hut', the only one of its type in Devon. The little River Culm flows beside a road in the centre of the village for several hundred yards, and then passes beneath a bridge believed to date back to the 14th century. The church, a largely 15th century building which is pleasantly sited above the river, is built of flint, a material not often used in Devon. Its interior has been much restored, but it is interesting to note that the present reredos was once part of a handsome rood screen. This screen had been removed by the time that R. D. Blackmore's father became rector here, but it was he that rescued and re-used part of it. See also the splendid 15th century embroidered cope, which has in recent years been restored by the Textile Restoration Centre at Hampton Court; and the stained-glass window by the Pre-Raphaelite artist Burne-Jones.

CUTCOMBE

At Spiceland (181) (ST 08-14), about a mile to the west, there is an elegantly simple Quaker Meeting House, rebuilt in 1815, complete with small burial ground and a store for hay for the use of Friends who had to come long distances by horse to attend their meetings.

R. D. Blackmore grew up in Culmstock and went to school at Blundell's, Tiverton, with another local boy, Frederick Temple, from Axon Farm (ST 08-15) well to the north-west of the village. Temple was later to become Archbishop of Canterbury, while Blackmore gained fame from his writing, especially from *Lorna Doone*, a book that he regarded as far from his best work.

Walk from Culmstock, north and north-east, to Culmstock Beacon (see above), and on beyond to The Wellington Monument (181) (ST 13-17), on the northern side of the Black Down Hills. Return southwards via Pen Cross and Millhayes, and take the quiet road westwards along the Culm valley, to return to Culmstock. It is also possible to walk westwards, from Culmstock, beside the River Culm to Five Fords and Spiceland (see above), and on beside the river to Uffculme.

Cutcombe (181) (SS 92-39) Small village on the southern fringes of Exmoor, just to the north-east of Wheddon Cross, with fine views out over the Brendon Hills, the spine of which runs east from here. Apart from its 13th century tower, the church here was rebuilt in 1862, and is not of great interest to visitors. There is a pleasant walk, heading east from a point opposite the church, over open country, and then north down a deep, wooded valley to join the A396 near Sully.

Dead Woman's Ditch (181) (ST 16-38) (Not shown on Landranger Map.) There is a good parking area here, which provides an excellent base for walks along the top of the lovely Quantock plateau. It lies on the minor road running up over the Quantocks between Nether Stowey and Crowcombe, and is less than a mile to the east of that meeting point of so many Quantock tracks, Crowcombe Park Gate. The 'dead woman' was the wife of a charcoal-burner named Walford, who murdered her in a drunken rage one night in about 1780, while they were returning from the Castle of Comfort Inn near Nether Stowey. He is said to have hidden the body in the ditch, but his crime was soon discovered, and he was subsequently hanged from a gibbet only about a mile to the north-east, at a spot still shown on the map as Walford's Gibbet (181) (ST 17-39). Read the full and pathetic story in Vincent Waite's *'Portrait of the Quantocks'*.

It should be stressed that Walford was certainly not energetic enough to have dug the large earth bank stretching south from the road at Dead Woman's Ditch, and it is believed that this was probably a boundary built to contain cattle, by the Iron Age occupiers of nearby Dowsborough settlement (181) (ST 16-39) (see page 43). Walk from here to join the main spinal trackway along the Quantocks, at Crowcombe Park Gate, or at Halsway Post, not shown on the Landranger map, but just to the north of Hurley Beacon (181) (ST 13-38).

Dodington (181) (ST 17-40) In largely flat countryside beyond the wooded north-eastern slopes of the Quantocks, Dodington consists of a small church

Dodington Hall.

and a fine Elizabethan manor house, Dodington Hall, with a two-storeyed porch, a minstrel gallery and many other interesting features. *(Tel: Holford 422, for appointment to visit, but only on Tues & Thurs.)* The small towered church nearby has an attractive stoup shaped like a miniature font, and fragments of 15th century glass in the tops of the little east window. Near the road back to the A39, there are the scanty remains of a copper mine, which was operated here until the end of the last century.

Dolton (180) (SS 57-12) Modest village in remote, hilly country up to the east of the beautifully wooded valley of the Torridge. Apart from its medieval west tower, the church is largely rebuilt in the 19th century, but is well worth visiting for its strange font. This is made up of two blocks from a Saxon cross, the upper tapering one having been turned upside down and hollowed out, and being ornamented with intertwining serpents, all very Scandinavian in feeling. The lower one has more formal strapwork, and it is assumed that both came from a 10th century cross that possibly once stood at Halsdon (a place name meaning *Holy Stone*), well to the west of the village. See also the stone tablet to Barbara Lister (1696) in the north chancel, surrounded by an elegantly carved wooden frame; and in the south chancel, the three charming tablets in memory of the sculptor J. H. M. Furse and his two wives. These are the work of Laurence Whistler, whose first wife was a daughter of Furse, and who is remembered in the churchyard on a tombstone carved by Laurence's brother Rex.

'Doone Country' (180) (SS 78-45) Had it not been for R. D. Blackmore's classic tale *Lorna Doone*, this name would almost certainly not be marked on our map (see **Walk 5**, page 116). However it would be wrong to dismiss the Doones as a mere figment of his romantic imagination. Legends relating to this savage gang of robbers had long been circulating in the area in the 18th and 19th centuries, many years before the publication of *Lorna Doone* in 1869. It is possible that the Doones were a gang of Scottish freebooters, who settled in this bleak area in about 1620. Blackmore's father was Rector of Oare from 1809 to 1842, and no doubt having heard tales of the Doones when a boy, the author followed these up when staying at Oare, Charles and Withypool in the 1860s. In using this background for the writing of his romantic novel he did no more than many other writers of romantic fiction, but his confident portrayal of the 17th century Exmoor scene has resulted in an unusually strong desire amongst visitors to the area, to identify fiction with fact, and to search for every detail of *Lorna Doone* in the landscape through which they pass. All visitors to the area are advised to read this compelling tale, which captures the spirit of Exmoor so well, and reference to the places involved with the book and with its author will be found in these pages (see Charles, page 34, Culmstock, page 42, Dulverton, below, Oare, page 64, Tiverton, page 74, Withypool, page 86, **Walk 5**, page 116). Let us allow Blackmore to have the last word on *Lorna Doone*, a novel that he certainly did not regard as his best:

> *'If I had dreamed that it ever would be more than a book of the moment, the descriptions of scenery, which I know as well as I know my garden, would have been kept nearer to their fact. I romanced therein, not to mislead any other, but solely for uses of my story.'*

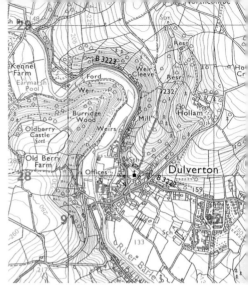

SCALE 1:25 000 or 2½ INCHES to 1 MILE

Dowsborough (181) (ST 15-39) This large Iron Age settlement is situated in high Quantock country, and although much of it is covered by scrub oak, there are fine views northwards from its ramparts, especially north out over Bridgwater Bay. Our **Walk 1**, page 108, comes up a small wooded combe below it to the west. Dead Woman's Ditch (180) (ST 16-38) (see page 42), less than a mile to its south, was probably part of a system of ditches and banks erected by the occupiers of the settlement for the protection of their farm stock. The settlement itself was once called Danesborough, after a skirmish in which a band of Danes was slaughtered here, and there is a local legend of a young Danish minstrel, who ran away from the battle, and who was afterwards put to death despite the entreaties of a young Saxon girl who had fallen in love with him after giving him shelter. His ghost is said to haunt the earthworks of Dowsborough still, gently singing and playing his harp. For details of this story and other local legends, read Sally Jones' *Legends of Somerset*.

Dulverton (181) (SS 91-28) This small, sleepy town is the undisputed focal point for activity in the south-eastern quarter of Exmoor, but it appears to be remarkably unconcerned by its significance. Its

Dulverton . . . in the richly wooded valley of the Barle.

hotels, shops and inns are friendly and relaxed, with real local flavour, and few concessions have been made to the less pleasant pressures of tourism. It is situated in the beautifully wooded valley of the River Barle, only two miles above its confluence with the Exe, and is a natural centre for fly-fishing, and for those who wish to walk north-westwards up the Barle valley; the finest introduction to Exmoor that could be wished for (see **Walk 4**, page 114).

Entering Dulverton from the south, the motorist will first cross the sparkling River Barle by a fine old five-arch bridge, and will soon see the Exmoor National Park Headquarters building, Exmoor House, where there is a most helpful Information Centre. (All those who wish to learn more about this fascinating area are strongly advised to pay a call here.) The church is well beyond, looking down the main street from its neatly mown churchyard. It has a pleasant 13th century tower, but the rest was rebuilt in the mid-19th century and is not of outstanding interest to visitors. Down a lane by the lych gate, just off Bank Square, will be found the Dulverton Weavers studio and shop, where the interesting craft of weaving is carried out on the premises. There is also a wealth of late-Georgian and early-Victorian houses lining the little streets and squares of Dulverton, and a walk around them is well worthwhile. It was at Dulverton that the young John Ridd first set eyes on Lorna Doone, although some years were to pass before they met near the famous waterslide.

The meeting point of the two valleys must have been of great strategic importance in Iron Age times, and there are several settlements above the two rivers: Bury Castle to the east, above the Exe (SS 93-26), Oldbury Castle, above the town to the immediate west (SS 90-28), and Mounsey Castle and Brewers Castle, facing each other across the thickly wooded Barle valley two miles to the north-west (SS 88-29). There are also the fragmentary ruins of an Augustinian Priory at Barlynch Farm, about a mile to the north-west on the west side of the A396 (SS 92-29), but although partly visible from this road, they are not open to the public.

The best walk from Dulverton is north-west, up beside the Barle, to link up with our **Walk 4** at Tarr Steps, about five miles away (see page 114).

DUNKERY BEACON

Dunkery Beacon (181) (SS 89-41) At 519 metres above sea level, Dunkery Beacon is the highest point on Exmoor, and from its bracken and heather-covered slopes there are splendid views northwards to the wooded combes of Holnicote and to the sea at Porlock Bay; south to the gentle valleys of the Barle and Exe; east to the Brendons and the Quantocks, and west towards the central massif of Exmoor itself, where the Badgworthy, Barle, Lyn and Exe all have their source. On a clear day the heights of Dartmoor and Bodmin, the Mendips and Brecon Beacons, may all be seen on the distant skyline, and the reasons for Dunkery's use as a beacon point over the centuries are then abundantly clear. Beacon fires have been lit here on various occasions of national importance or danger, and a supply of faggots was kept here in readiness; but latterly these beacon fires have been used not for the passing of messages, but for the celebration of special events, such as Coronations, Jubilees, Royal Weddings, or in 1969, to mark the centenary of R. D. Blackmore's Lorna Doone.

There are roadside lay-bys on the minor road between Wheddon Cross and Luccombe, leaving about a three quarters of a mile walk to the gentle summit, where there is a viewpoint direction indicator. Dunkery Beacon is within the National Trust's Holnicote estate, and the very best way to visit it is to walk southwards from Horner (181) (SS 89-45) (car park with toilets here), or from Clout-sham (181) (SS 90-43) (car park). There are a variety of delightful woodland walks, many of which have strange names, such as Granny's Ride, Cat's Scramble, and Dicky's Path, bestowed on them by the Acland family, who so generously gave their estate to the Trust. For details of these walks see the specially prepared National Trust leaflet, which is available at National Trust shops and Tourist Information Centres in the area.

Dunster (181) (SS 99-43) Exceptionally picturesque little town, beautifully situated in the Avill valley, between Grabbist Hill, Castle Hill, and the smaller, wooded Conygar Hill to its north, which is topped by an 18th century folly tower rising from amongst the trees. This tower looks down Dunster's broad High Street, out over the charming 17th century Yarn Market, and the Luttrell Arms, a pleasant hotel with several medieval features and once the Duns-ter residence of the abbots of Cleeve. Dominating the far end of the High Street is the splendidly towered and castellated Dunster Castle (see below); while beyond the bend at the end of the street, there is the church (see below); the partly 14th century timber-framed and slate-hung 'Nunnery'; a 17th century water mill with unique twin overshot wheels, now producing stoneground flour again, and open to the public; and finally Gallox Bridge, a medieval packhorse bridge, which is the start of our Walk 2 (see page 110). The hill beyond the bridge was formerly called Gallows Hill, as two of the Duke of Monmouth's luckless supporters were hanged here, soon after his defeat at the Battle of Sedgemoor.

The church was originally part of a Benedictine priory, having been given to the priors of Bath by William de Mohun at the end of the 11th century, and there is still some limited evidence of its Norman origins. However the church is now a fine, largely Perpendicular building, having been built between the mid-15th and the mid-16th centuries.

See especially the handsome tower, with its bells which peal out hymn-tunes, the splendid late-15th century rood screen, and the series of monuments to various members of the Luttrell family of Dunster Castle.

Dunster Castle was built on the site of an earlier Saxon tower, by the de Mohuns soon after the Conquest, and it was sold by them to Elizabeth Luttrell in 1376 for the sum of 5000 marks. It remained in the hands of the Luttrells from that time until 1975, when it was very generously given by them to the National Trust. The earliest surviving structure is the 13th century gatehouse, the ruined Norman central keep having been demolished in the 18th century. In the early 17th century a conventio-nal Jacobean style house was built within the castle walls, and only a few years later the castle was deeply involved in the bitter Civil War struggles for control of the West Country. Thomas Luttrell held it for Parliament until 1643, but it was then surren-dered to the Royalists, who in their turn, only surrendered after a long siege, as late as April 1646. Following this surrender, it was demolished like so many other former Royalist strongholds, leaving only the house and gatehouse.

For the next two hundred years, the Luttrell family fortune ebbed and flowed, the house was improved, and a fine deer park was created. But in 1867 George Luttrell inherited Dunster from his uncle, and he set about a major rebuilding plan, with the help of Anthony Salvin, the great 'neo-medievalist', who is best known for his massive rebuilding of Windsor Castle. The castle we see today is the result of Salvin's genius, for he created a romantic medieval building, making the fullest possible use of the surviving 17th and 18th century features and their outstanding setting. Its interior is full of interest, including plaster ceilings, 17th century staircase and a magnificent set of Spanish leather hangings of the same period. There are magnolias and mimosas, a tropical garden, and a series of splendid views out over Dunster village to the Bristol Channel and the Welsh coast, and inland, above the trees, to the summit of Dunkery Beacon. (Tel: 0643 821314.)

Dunster is deservedly popular, and is still prob-ably the most visited place in the Exmoor National Park. At times it is inevitably very crowded, and it is preferable to come here on a weekday towards the beginning or end of the visitor season. If you wish to explore the village in detail, purchase the excellent leaflet A Walk Round Dunster, published by the Dunster Village Society.

Apart from our Walk 2 (page 110), there are several other walks to be taken from Dunster, the best possibly being the one westwards, along the partly wooded crest that takes in Grabbist Hill and Knowle Hill, to Wootton Courtenay (181) (SS 93-43). It is possible to walk on from here to Dunkery Beacon (SS 89-41), and to return via Luccombe and Tivington, but many will wish to only take part of this very long, but most attractive walk.

There is a car park at the northern end of the town, and if you wish to visit the coast there is another one at Dunster Beach, a mile to the north-east.

Eastacott Cross (180) (SS 62-23) One of only two surviving medieval wayside crosses in Devon, this is roughly carved out of a single piece of granite, and was probably one of a series guiding pilgrims to St

Urith's shrine at Chittlehampton (see page 36). It stands beneath a beech tree, at a Y-junction to the south of Eastacott cross-roads, and there are satisfying views northwards over quiet undulating country towards Chittlehampton. There is a pleasant path westward from near here, down through Pitt Wood, to South Nethercleave, in the Taw valley opposite Umberleigh.

East Buckland (180) (SS 67-31) Minute village in high country to the west of the wooded Bray valley. The church was rebuilt in 1860, utilising the tower of the previous building, in the west side of which is a bricked-up Norman doorway. No other special features of interest.

East Down (180) (SS 60-41) This consists only of a church, a manor house and a few other dwellings, and is situated above the wooded valley of the little River Yeo, not far from its source on Berry Down, to the north-west. The handsome early 18th century manor house was the home of the Pine family for many generations (latterly the Pine-Coffins), and there are several Pine monuments, notably that to Edward Pine, who died in 1663, *'lieutenant-colonel to Sir Hugh Pollard in the late unhappy wars'*. Apart from its 15th century tower, the church was largely rebuilt in the 19th century, but its fittings make a visit here still worthwhile. See especially the marble font with its wooden shaft incorporating early Renaissance panels, the restored 15th century rood screen, the unusual 16th century Spanish lectern, the Elizabethan pews in the Pine chapel, and the quaintly carved figures on the south arcade capitals.

East Quantoxhead (181) (ST 13-43) A delightfully quiet village with a duck pond, and a small church sheltering on the landward side of the Jacobean Court House. This fine old stone house (which is not open to the public) has been in the possession of the Luttrell family for over seven centuries. Built like the Court House, of an austere grey stone, the church dates back to the early-14th century, and although its interior has been over-restored, it contains several items of interest. These include an early-15th century rood screen, an Elizabethan

pulpit, and the canopied tomb of Sir Hugh Luttrell *whe departed. 1522 the fyrst day of february*. See also the east window in memory of one of Sir Hugh's 19th century descendants, A. F. Luttrell, who was rector here for no fewer than seventy years.

As its name implies, this village is situated at the very 'head' of the Quantocks, and it is possible to walk south from here, crossing the A39 at Higher Street, and up to West Hill and Bicknoller Post (181) (ST12-40). It is also possible to walk north to the coast at Quantock's Head, and then eastwards along low cliffs to Kilve, and on to Lilstock.

East Worlington (180) (SS 77-13) Minute village with thatched cottages and church overlooking the steep sided and often wooded valley of the Little Dart River, and very remote from the busy world beyond. The church was almost entirely rebuilt in 1879, but has retained its Norman south doorway with bands of zig-zags and crosses. There is a pleasant path southwards from its bridge (Edglake Bridge) over the Little Dart, and up beside a small stream through Pedley Wood, towards Pedley Barton.

Elworthy (181) (ST 08-35) A quiet hamlet on the eastern end of the Brendon Hills, with fine views east to the Quantocks, and south-eastwards out over the Vale of Taunton Deane. The simple, but rather pleasing church overlooks a small valley. Trees overhang the churchyard gate, and inside there is a Jacobean pulpit reached by what were once the rood loft stairs, and a rood screen, which although dated 1632, incorporates Perpendicular style tracery that must be considerably older. Elworthy Barrows (181) (ST 07-33), on a hill summit about a mile to the south-west, are in fact not barrows at all, but the remains of a large circular Iron Age settlement, now partly destroyed by quarrying. Experts believe that it was never fully completed, but the reasons for this are not clear.

Enmore (182) (ST 24-35) Small scattered village below the wooded Quantock slopes, with a splendidly towered church, which overlooks a mellow brick house with curved baroque gable-ends in the

SCALE 1:25 000 or 2½ INCHES to 1 MILE

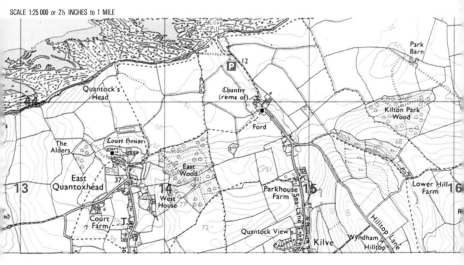

Dutch style. The church has a Norman south doorway and a much restored interior including fine star-vaulting beneath the tower, two 15th century helmets on either side of the chancel arch, a Jacobean pulpit and some 18th century wall monuments. Enmore Castle (not open to the public) is a moated house; all that remains of an 18th century Gothick 'castle', standing in wooded parkland just beyond the churchyard (from whence there are distant views out over Bridgwater Bay).

Walk south from Enmore, and then west, up into the Quantocks, to visit Broomfield (182)(ST 22-32) and Fyne Court, where there is a Visitor Centre for the Quantocks (see page 32). It is also possible to walk north to Barford Park, and on to Spaxton.

Barford Park (ST 23-35), accessible from Enmore by road, is a delightful, small 18th century mansion in mellow brick, with flanking pavilions. There is a pool beside a lawn shaded by a cedar of Lebanon, and pleasant views across to the wooded Quantock slopes. The interior, with its well proportioned rooms, and furniture contemporary with the house, has a warm, lived-in feeling, and visitors are made to feel most welcome. *(Tel: Spaxton 269.)*

Exebridge (181) (SS 93-24) Minute hamlet below steep Hulverton Hill, on the Devon bank of the Exe just to the south of its confluence with the Barle. There has been a large trout farm here since the 19th century, the Exe Valley Fishery, which is now producing over a hundred tons of trout annually. Fishing is available on two small lakes, and the public may visit the farm on payment of a small donation to local activities. Table fish may be purchased on week days. *(Tel: Dulverton 23328.)*

Exford (181) (SS 85-38) Bright, cheerful village astride the little River Exe, and overlooked by high moorland on almost every side. There is a green close to the bridge and a hotel and inn which both add colour to the village. Exford is the centre of the moor's stag-hunting activity, and the Devon and Somerset Stag Hounds have been kennelled here for many years.

The church lies on rising ground to the east of the village, and has a rather cold, grey appearance, owing a great deal to 19th century rebuilders. The interior has also been heavily restored, but the south arcade capitals are pleasantly ornamented with vine clusters. The south aisle was added in the

Bridge over the Exe, at Exford.

16th century, due initially to a local blacksmith who left three pounds in his will towards *the makyng of an yled*. The interesting 15th century screen came from the old church of St Audries, at West Quantoxhead (see page 82), which was demolished in 1858. The screen lay in store for over forty years before a home was found for it at Exford. There is the stump of an old cross in the neat, well tended churchyard.

There are the earthworks of an Iron Age settlement in woodland at Staddon Hill (SS 88-37) two miles to the east of Exford, above the deep-set valley road to Winsford, but this is on private ground. There is another, smaller Iron Age settlement, Road Castle (SS 86-37), above Lyncombe Wood and the River Exe.

The best walk from Exford is south-eastwards, following the infant River Exe, down to the attractive village of Winsford. From here it is an easy walk south-westwards, along quiet roads, past the Caratacus Stone (SS 89-33), to Tarr Steps, where it is possible to use our **Walk 4** to follow the Barle up to Withypool, and then back to Exford, via Chibbet Post (SS 84-37), the site of a gibbet where Red Jem Hannaford, a sheep stealer in *Lorna Doone*, was supposedly hanged. It is also possible to walk north and then east over the high moor, to Dunkery Beacon (SS 89-41), and from there, north again, down into Horner.

Exmoor (180) (181) The Exmoor National Park, with only 265 square miles within its boundaries, is one of Britain's smaller National Parks, but it contains such a variety of coast and countryside, that its very compactness becomes one of its greatest assets. William Camden, in his great survey of the British Isles, *Britannia*, published in 1586, described Exmoor as 'a filthy, barren, ground', and Daniel Defoe, writing over a hundred years later, agrees with him, saying, 'Indeed, so it is', but he goes on to say, 'but as soon as the Exe comes off from the moors and the hilly country, and descends into the lower grounds, we found the alteration; for then we saw Devonshire in its other countenance, viz cultivated, populous, and fruitful'.

Tastes have now changed, and wildness is now appreciated rather than feared or despised; but Exmoor does have its gentler touches, and this point appears to have appealed to Defoe, even as early as 1724. The wilder heather moorland, which is itself lighter and more colourful than its neighbour to the south, Dartmoor, is broken by gentle valleys pushing up from the south, and short torrential streams flowing quickly, often in the company of great tracts of woodland, off steep northern slopes into the sea.

The high moorland is interspersed by the farms that followed the pioneering efforts of the Knight family of Simonsbath (see page 69), but this softening process has in a mysterious way added to, rather than detracted from Exmoor's subtle appeal. Everywhere one looks out towards long moorland horizons, with farmland and wooded valleys relieving any possible monotony in the middle distance, and with luck, there are shafts of sunlight striking out of low cloud-scattered skies, illuminating parts of this magic landscape. Ponies, wild red deer and soaring buzzards are to be seen on the moors and in the high combes, while tree-shaded streams and quiet villages are to be found in the sheltered valley below. The legendary Doones, immortalised by R. D. Blackmore in *Lorna Doone*, never seem very far away, and many visitors will find added pleasure in searching for the various places which he brought into his remarkable story.

It is sometimes claimed that Exmoor has some of the worst weather in Southern England, and records certainly reveal that its higher ground receives up to seventy inches of rain a year. However, do not be deterred. We have spent many happy days exploring the area in spring, summer and autumn, and have always found Exmoor kinder than we had once been led to expect.

Exton (181) (SS 92-33) A minute village clinging to a steep hillside above the Exe valley. The church is not sited high enough for the high moorland to be visible from its churchyard, but there are some fine views westwards to the wooded valley slopes beyond the Exe. Everything here is on a slope and the church is no exception, with a pathway curving up to the porch, overlooked by a 700 year old, castellated tower. The interior has been heavily restored, with ugly pews and glossy tiles much in evidence, but there is an interesting octagonal font with shields around its base. Do not overlook the handsomely lettered panel to Rose, wife of Robert Pierce (1712), complete with macabre trappings including a crowned skeleton, Old Father Time, and a skull and crossed bones. There is a pleasant old bridge over the Exe, at Bridgetown, just to the south of Exton.

Walk north from here, to Coppleham, then north-westward over a hill to West Howetown, and the pretty village of Winsford, from where it is possible to walk up beside the infant Exe to Exford.

Filleigh (180) (SS 66-27) Here are a few attractive cottages and farms and a neo-Norman church, but the great feature here is Castle Hill, a fine Palladian

Castle Hill, Filleigh ... in a park landscaped by William Kent.

mansion, built between 1730 and 1740, in a splendid park landscaped by William Kent. Do not miss the triumphal arch at the end of an avenue, on a hill to the south of the A361. Castle Hill has been the home of the Fortescue family since it was built, and the Fortescues have held the manor of Filleigh since it was acquired by the marriage of Martin Fortescue in the 15th century. Much of the central part of the house was burnt down in 1934, but this was rebuilt under the direction of a distinguished architect, the

Duke of Wellington, who was able to restore it to its original 18th century proportions. The contents of the house include fine 18th century furniture, tapestries, porcelain and pictures; and there are ornamental and woodland gardens and an arboretum. The house is only open by appointment *(tel: Filleigh 227)*; the gardens can be seen by telephoning the Estate Office *(tel: Filleigh 336)*.

The church was moved to its present site in about 1732, and was again extensively remodelled in the 1870s, this time in a richly executed and over-confident Norman style. It is very much a Fortescue church, and the most interesting items are two 16th century brasses, both surprisingly in memory of the same person, Richard Fortescue.

The writer Henry Williamson lived for some years at Shallowford, to the north-east of Filleigh (SS 68-28), and it was here on the banks of the River Bray that he spent much time on research for his book *Salar the Salmon*, although most of the writing was done in his huts near Georgeham (see page 48).

Fitzhead (181) (ST 11-28) Small village in low, but rolling country about mid-way between Taunton and the Brendon Hills. The red sandstone church has a Perpendicular tower, but the rest is largely the result of Victorian rebuilding. There are however some plain 15th century bench-ends, fragments of medieval stained glass, and a fan-vaulted rood screen. In the churchyard will be found a 13th century cross with restored figures beneath its canopied top, and close by, a fine tithe barn, now converted.

Fremington (180) (SS 51-32) Due to ribbon development stretching from Barnstaple almost as far as Instow, this 'village' is now almost a Barnstaple suburb. However its church, which was heavily restored by Sir G. G. Scott in 1867, has retained its 15th century pulpit, a handsome Royal coat of arms of Queen Anne, and a Norman stoop (used for holy water) in its south porch.

Frithelstock (180) (SS 46-19) Minute village in high open country, to the west of the Torridge valley, with an attractively painted inn looking across a small green, where there are daffodils in springtime. Opposite this stands the 15th century church, whose handsome, castellated porch is approached by a long path edged with pollarded limes. The interior of the church has a pleasing flavour, with pretty canopied niches in the arcade columns, a

Church and ruined priory at Frithelstock.

Jacobean pulpit, choir stalls with ruggedly carved ends, and more unusually, carved front panels. Also do not miss the beautiful white plaster Royal coat of arms, dated 1677.

To the immediate east of the church lie the interesting and beautiful remains of Frithelstock Priory, an Augustinian foundation, colonised from nearby Hartland Abbey (see page 50), in about 1220, by Robert de Beauchamp. The three lancet windows of the west front are particularly noteworthy.

Fyne Court. The Visitor Centre for the Quantocks (see Broomfield, page 32).

Gaulden Manor (181) (ST 11-31) This small manor house, with origins in the 12th century, is pleasantly situated in a quiet valley between the Brendon Hills and the Quantocks, just to the south-east of Tolland village. It has a great hall with an outstanding plaster ceiling and fireplace, and off this and divided from it by an oak screen, is a small room known as 'The Chapel'. Both these delightful rooms owe much to the 17th century. The gardens surrounding the house have been lovingly created by the present owners, and include a 'Bog Garden' and an 'Elizabethan Herb Garden'. Gaulden was owned for many years by a branch of the Turberville family, which was immortalised by Thomas Hardy in his *Tess of the d'Urbervilles*; but living here before them was a certain Henry Wolcott, who emigrated to America in 1630, one of whose descendants, Oliver Wolcott, was amongst the signatories of the Declaration of Independence. The guided tour of the house lasts about half an hour, and there are tea rooms in the garden. *(For opening details, tel: Lydeard St Lawrence 213.)*

Georgeham (180) (SS 46-39) Sizeable village, but small compared to Braunton not far to its south-east, Georgeham remains relatively unspoilt, being situated about a mile inland from the splendid Putsborough and Woolacombe Sands. It has many thatched cottages, but its church was unfortunately over-restored by the Victorians, suffering a fate similar to that of far too many English parish churches. It has however retained a screen, put there by restorers working in the classical style in 1762. Happily undisturbed during both the 18th and 19th century restorations, is a 13th century sculpture of the Crucifixion in the north chancel wall. See also the cross-legged figure of a 13th century knight, thought to represent crusader, Mauger of St Aubyn, and the series of late 17th century roundels commemorating various members of the Newcourt family.

The writer Henry Williamson settled in Georgeham soon after returning from the First World War, and he wrote the majority of his books here. These included the beautiful story of *Tarka the Otter*, which was set in the Torridge valley and the surrounding North Devon countryside (see also Weare Giffard, page 78, and The Chains, page 34); and also *The Lone Swallows*, which brilliantly captures the atmosphere of North Devon in the early 1920s, and the life led by Williamson at Georgeham. He first lived at Skirr Cottage, but later moved to Upper House, about thirty yards away. *Tarka the Otter* won the Hawthornden Prize in 1928, and Williamson used the money from it to buy a

field near Oxford Cross, about a mile to the north of the village. He built two huts here, and in them he wrote many of his later works. Although he later moved to Norfolk, he was buried at Georgeham, following his death in 1977.

George Nympton (180) (SS 70-23) Small village with southerly views out over the wooded valley of the River Mole, above its confluence with the Bray. Unusually for this part of the world, the mellow brick church tower was rebuilt in the 17th century. Inside the church will be found an octagonal font, with an 18th century cover, and a stylish wall tablet in memory of William Karslake (1769) complete with obelisk and cherub. There are no walks to be had from here, but there is a pleasantly quiet road running south, down into the Mole valley, and up beyond it to King's Nympton.

Goathurst (182) (ST 25-34) A most attractive village, at the gates of Halswell House (not open), a fine late 17th century mansion in a wooded park on the eastern fringes of the Quantocks, complete with a temple and other typical 18th century curiosities. In the village there are 18th century almshouses, with colourful cottage gardens, and below them a pleasant lych-gate leading to the church which has a tower built, like the almshouses, of red sandstone.

In the churchyard there is an unusual 18th century equivalent of a churchyard cross ... an elegant piece of ornamented pillar topped by an urn. The interior contains a fine Jacobean pulpit complete with tester, and a wonderful assortment of Tynte family (of Halswell House) monuments including works by Rysbrack and Nollekens, two of England's most fashionable 18th century sculptors. The family pew has a squint cut through a wall to the altar and a handsomely plastered 18th century ceiling in the Elizabethan style. Do not miss a visit here; it lies some distance to the east of the area covered by our guide, but is well worth the diversion.

Goodleigh (180) (SS 59-34) Situated on the slopes of a small valley just to the east of Barnstaple, this village has a church which, apart from its Perpendicular tower, was rebuilt in the 1880s. Coombe Farm, to the south-west of the village, used to be the home of a branch of the famous Acland family, and there is a modest monument in the church to James Acland, who died in 1655, complete with a miniature portrait.

Grand Western Canal (181) (SS 98-12) — (ST 07-19) It was originally intended to link the Bristol Channel and the English Channel by building a canal from Taunton (which was finally linked in 1827 to the Bristol Channel by the Bridgwater and Taunton Canal), to Topsham just south of Exeter. The route was surveyed by the great civil engineer John Rennie in 1794, although it was not until 1810 that the first turf was cut. The initial stretch to be dug was a branch canal from Burlescombe (181) (ST 07-16) to Tiverton, and this was opened in 1814, by which time the main project of a canal south to Topsham had been abandoned due to lack of capital. The stretch from Burlescombe to Taunton was however thought to be worth retaining, but even this was not completed until 1838, and then to a much smaller gauge than was originally intended.

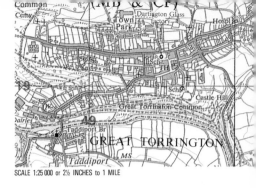

SCALE 1:25 000 or 2½ INCHES to 1 MILE

The canal was never a great success, and the opening of the Bristol and Exeter railway line in the 1840s was followed some years later by the sale of the canal to the railway company. Disused since 1924, it appeared to be doomed by the 1960s, but the efforts of the Tiverton Canal Preservation Society led eventually to its restoration by the Devon County Council, from Tiverton to a point on the Somerset border near Holcombe Rogus (181) (ST 07-19). This delightful stretch of waterway has been designated as a Country Park, and provides facilities for walkers, anglers, boating enthusiasts, and lovers of wildlife. There is a car park at the Tiverton canal basin, with toilets and picnic facilities, and the Grand Western Horseboat Company operates an unusual horse-drawn passenger service from the basin. Licences for the use of private unpowered craft may be obtained from County Hall, Exeter, or from the G.W.Horseboat Company *(tel: Tiverton 253345)*, who will also provide details of their horse-drawn passenger service. Visit Tiverton Museum to see a display relating to the canal's history; and if you wish to explore the towpath, and the footpaths that follow much of the long abandoned sections beyond Holcombe Rogus, read the very interesting account in Ronald Russell's excellent book, *'Lost Canals & Waterways of Britain'*.

Great Torrington (180) (SS 49-19) Attractive little market town situated on a steep hill overlooking the lushly wooded valley of the Torridge, and the rolling countryside beyond. The view southwards from the car park close to the bowling green (the site of Torrington's early 13th century castle) is especially

The handsome Town Hall at Great Torrington.

fine and there are pleasant paths zig-zagging across the slopes stretching below to the river bank. Behind Castle Hill there is a Pannier Market, which now houses the town's library, and beyond this, a passage leading to the church. This was used as a powder magazine during the Civil War, and shortly after the defeat of the town's Royalist garrison, it was blown up by accident, killing a large number of unfortunate Royalist prisoners and their guards. It was rebuilt soon afterwards, but suffered extensive 'restoration' in 1864, and is not now of great interest to visitors, apart from the handsome late 16th century pulpit. However there are pollarded limes and cobbled pathways in the churchyard, and the

handsome Palmer House close by. This was built in 1752 by John Palmer, the husband of Mary Reynolds, who was the sister of Sir Joshua Reynolds. The great painter visited her at Torrington from time to time, and on one such visit in 1762, he brought with him his friend Dr Samuel Johnson.

There are, unfortunately, many Victorian terrace houses built of harshly coloured brick and granite, but in addition to Palmer House there are also many pleasant Georgian buildings. The old cattle market site is now occupied by a large heated indoor swimming pool, and there is a small museum in the Town Hall ... Georgian, but rebuilt in 1861. Do not miss a visit to one of Torrington's inns, amongst which are the largely 17th century Black Horse Inn in the Market Square and the Torridge Inn. But for many visitors, the most interesting feature of Great Torrington, is the Dartington Glass factory in Linden Close, off School Lane *(tel: 0805 22321)*, which offers guided factory tours, and a shop and cafeteria.

Taddiport Bridge, crossing the Torridge to the south-west, dates back to the 17th century; while Rothern Bridge, a little further downstream, was built two centuries earlier. Between here and the town there are gorse- and bracken-covered commons with a picnic site close to the A386, Bideford road; while at Darracott, two miles to the north-east (180) (SS 51-21) there is a reservoir offering excellent coarse fishing. Permits may be obtained at Town Mills, to the south of the town where the A386 Okehampton road crosses the Torridge. For details of the Torrington Canal, see page 75.

Halberton (181) (SS 00-12) A large village within a wide bend in the meandering Grand Western Canal, now designated as a Country Park (see page 48), and access to which can be gained at the red sandstone Greenway Bridge, on the small road heading north from the village towards Uplowman. The large pond between the two parts of the village, Higher Town to the east, and Lower Town to the west, is reputed never to freeze over due to its being fed by a warm spring. The large church, built of red sandstone (a favourite local building material), dates back at least to the 14th century, and its contents include a stout Norman font, a fine 15th century rood screen and a beautiful pulpit of about the same date. Inevitably the best walks from Halberton are along the Grand Western Canal's towpath, either westwards into Tiverton, or east towards Sampford Peverell.

Halse (181) (ST 14-27) Situated in valley country between the Brendon Hills and Taunton, with pleasant views north-westwards to the Quantocks. Several old cottages line the village street, while to the south of the main village will be found a small but most interesting church. This has a Norman south doorway, but the tower and much of the rest date from the 13th and 14th centuries. There is strange carving between the arches of the north aisle arcade, thought to represent a 'Green Man', a popular folk figure in medieval times, who was ritually killed on each May Day, and who was regarded as a bringer of fertility. (There is another example at Crowcombe, see page 40.) Other features of interest include an outstanding 15th century rood screen, two painted panels from Italy, six beautiful 16th century stained glass roundels, which originated in Bruges, and a circular Norman font.

Field Marshal Montgomery, the victor of Alamein, use to stay at Halse as a boy, when his uncle was the rector here.

Hartland (190) (SS 25-24) This little town lost its market status as long ago as 1780, and was never nearer than thirteen miles to a railway station. It is probably for this reason that it has retained its delightful early-19th century flavour, with simple houses and shop fronts and a 'chapel of ease' to the parish church (see Stoke, page 71), built in 1837, on the site of its old Town Hall. This has an unspoilt interior with old box pews and a 17th century clock, that used to hang in the Town Hall. Bringing further character to the town are a group of craftsmen operating as 'Hartland Workshops', including two potteries, two furniture workshops and one of the oldest established forges in Devon.

Hartland Abbey is an 18th and 19th century mansion incorporating the cloisters of an Augustinian abbey, founded here in 1189. It is delightfully situated in a wooded valley just over a mile to the west of the town, but it is not open to the public.

Hartland Forest Information Centre (190) (SS 27-20) This is situated on the A39, fifteen miles from Bideford and eleven miles from Bude, and provides information on walks, trails and picnic places in both Devon and Cornwall. There are displays on the birdlife of forest and moorland, and on forestry and timber production. The Welsford Forest Trail starts from here, and a second trail, the Summerwell, starts from a point three quarters of a mile to the south, off the A39 at Summerwell (190) (SS 27- 19).

Hartland Point (190) (SS 22-27) The remarkable traveller Celia Fiennes, writing in her diary in 1698, describes her journey to this wild headland thus, *'Here I rode over a Common or Down 4 miles long in sight of the north sea and saw Hartly Point, which is the Earle of Baths just by his fine house called Stow* (now Hartland Abbey), *his fine stables and horses and gardens; there I discern'd the Poynt very plaine and just by I saw the Isle of Lundy'.* Today it is possible to drive almost the whole way from the A39, at Clovelly Dykes (190) (SS 31-23) to this three hundred and twenty five foot high headland, which forms the north-west extremity of Devon. It is topped by a Coastguard Station and is accompanied by a lighthouse, on a small plateau two hundred feet lower down. There are fine views on a clear day, out to Lundy and the Welsh coast.

To explore the coast eastwards from here as far as Mouth Mill (see page 63), use the excellent National Trust leaflet, *Clovelly to Hartland Point.*

Hartland Quay (190) (SS 22-24) This was built in the 15th century to deal with local coasting trade in grain and building materials. It was breached by storms in the 19th century and as coastal trade had by then declined, it was never repaired. Here will be found a pleasant hotel, and a small museum devoted to the Hartland coastline and its shipping and shipwrecks. Car parking is ample at Hartland Quay and **Walk 11**, page 128, starts from here. Coastal scenery is highly dramatic both to north and south, and the North Devon Coastal Path is well worth following, but be prepared for some steep sections from time to time. Half a mile to the north the long vanished Blackpool Mill once stood on the little Abbey River just above the point where it ran into the sea, over a rocky, but still unspoilt beach.

Hawkridge (181) (SS 86-30) Small village on a ridge, as its name indicates, above the wooded Barle valley, with a small road leading northwards, down to Tarr Steps (do not try to drive across the ford near the Steps). Hawkridge church has a Norman doorway and font, and is a simple building admirably suiting its elemental moorland setting. Walk from here to link on to **Walk 4**, page 114, at Tarr Steps. There is also a good walk westwards across the valley of the little Dane's Brook to Anstey Common, and then south-west to Molland, with its most attractive church (see page 62).

Hawkridge Reservoir (182) (ST 20-36) This is attractively set in the eastern foothills of the Quantocks, to the north of Aisholt. There is roadside parking provided on the southern side of the reservoir, and colourful sailing dinghies can usually be observed in summertime. Anglers will be interested to learn that there are brown and rainbow trout here, and that self-issue tickets are available at a shelter near the car park, which is situated close to the public road, to the south of the dam.

Heanton Punchardon (180) (SS 50-35) Compact village situated at the western end of a two hundred foot high ridge overlooking the Taw estuary. There are wide views out over Braunton Burrows towards the dark cliffs above Clovelly, and in the churchyard are buried many young Dominion airmen who were stationed at nearby Chivenor airfield during the 1939-45 War. The Perpendicular church has a tall west tower and a beautiful white plastered interior, enriched by several interesting monuments. Do not miss the 16th century canopied tomb of Richard Coffin, which probably served as an Easter sepulchre, in a similar manner to the tomb at Bishop's Nympton (see page 29). See also the grave of Edward Capern (1819-94), known as 'The Postman Poet', which is complete with his postman's handbell. His book of poems, now seldom read, earned him the praise of Walter Savage Landor, who dedicated one of his own poems to him, and who referred to him as 'The Burns of Devon'. For further details of Capern's life and work, visit the little museum at nearby Braunton (see page 30).

Heasley Mill (180) (SS 73-32) Pretty hamlet in the wooded valley of the Mole, with a pleasant hotel looking out over a small green. Mining in this area certainly dates back to the Norman period, as the Domesday Book refers to iron-workers being in the parish at that time. There are also records of 17th century mining and revivals on a considerable scale in the 19th century, with a tramway running down the Mole valley, through North Molton and connecting to the railway at South Molton. There are distant memories in North Molton of wild times in the many inns there, before the miners set off late at night, back to Heasley Mill (there is still a 'Miners Arms' at North Molton). Iron and copper were the main source of wealth, but lead, silver and gold have also been found in the area in smaller quantities. Very little trace of the workings remains, although there are several disused mine shafts in the woods to the north of Heasley Mill which are marked on Pathfinder Map SS 63/73. However these are liable to be dangerous and are on private ground.

Heddon's Mouth (180) (SS 65-49) This is where the beautiful Heddon Valley meets the sea. It is an easy one mile walk from a good car park at Hunter's Inn (SS 65-48), and is also on our **Walk 8**. For further details see page 122, and also refer to the excellent National Trust leaflet, *'Heddon Valley and Woody Bay'*.

Heddon Oak (181) (ST 12-37) Until recently an ancient oak stood at these cross-roads not far to the west of the Quantock slopes. It is believed that shortly after the Battle of Sedgemoor in 1685, the mutilated bodies of six of the Duke of Monmouth's followers, three from Stogumber and three from Crowcombe, were hung from this tree. For years afterwards groans and the rattle of chains were said to be heard here on dark nights, and Judge Jeffreys' dreadful series of trials and executions are still recalled in these parts with understandable horror. For further details of ghostly 'goings-on' read Sally Jones' book, *Legends of Somerset*.

Hele Mill (180) (SS 53-47) Situated just off the A39, about a mile to the east of Ilfracombe, this small watermill dates back to 1525. After being derelict for many years it has been painstakingly restored to full working order, and is now producing wholemeal flour. There is an eighteen foot overshot waterwheel, and inside there are many interesting items of mill machinery to be seen by visitors.

Hemyock (181) (ST 13-13) Large and rather unexciting village below hill slopes on the southern side of the Culm valley. The church was largely rebuilt in 1847 and apart from its square Norman font, is not of great interest to visitors. Nearby is the gateway of 13th century Hemyock Castle, and other fragments incorporated in farm buildings. In the little Square is an extravagantly decorated cast-iron village pump, a real period piece reflecting taste at the very beginning of the 20th century.

Hestercombe Gardens (193) (ST 24-28) Situated about two miles to the north-east of Taunton, Hestercombe House is the Headquarters of the Somerset County Fire Brigade and is a largely 19th

century building. However the gardens, with their lovely orangery, pools and stone terraces looking out over the Vale of Taunton Deane to the long line of the Black Down Hills, were the work of Sir Edwin Lutyens and his close associate Gertrude Jekyll, between the years 1904-9. Happily these have been rescued from decay by the County Council, and are now well worth visiting.

High Bickington (180) (SS 59-20) Set in high rolling hills to the west of the Taw valley, countryside more Cornish than Devonian in character, this is an austere little village, with its cottages and thin towered church. However this church has a Norman south doorway and a Norman font, and an

High Bickington Church . . . a wealth of bench-ends within.

amazing series of bench-ends. There are seventy of these in all, some late medieval, some early Renaissance, with their subjects ranging from Instruments of the Passion, to cheerful bucolic cherubs blowing trumpets.

Hillfarrance (181) (ST 16-24) Small village in valley country just to the north of the Tone. The church has a tower with an attractive 16th century parapet, and the interior, though much restored in 1857, contains some good bench-ends.

Hobby Drive (190) (ST 33-23) Do not miss this. See Clovelly, page 38, for details.

Hockworthy (181) (ST 03-19) Pleasantly sited on a hillside beneath high Chimney Down, this small stone village has a church which, apart from its medieval tower, was rebuilt in 1865. It has a Norman font, but is not otherwise of great interest to visitors. Walk north-east from here over hill and valley, and across the county boundary into Somerset, to visit Ashbrittle.

Holcombe Rogus (181) (ST 05-18) Sloping village looking east, out over the Tone valley, and backed by woodlands. The village street climbs up until, beyond an attractive vicarage and a 'priest's house', it reaches a group of buildings, the beauty of which makes a journey here well worthwhile. Here is a fine Perpendicular church standing close to one of Devon's finest Tudor buildings, Holcombe Court, with its tall gatehouse tower and great hall, and

51

large circular dovecote nearby. The Court (not open to the public) stands in beautifully landscaped grounds with serpentine lake and fishponds, beneath sloping parkland. It was built by the Bluett family in about 1530, and it remained in their hands until gambling debts appear to have forced them to sell it in 1858.

The church has a handsomely vaulted south porch and an unusually pleasant and interesting interior. There is an unceiled 15th century wagon-roof in the north aisle, a 16th century rood screen thought to have been brought here from St Peter's church at Tiverton, and an unusually complete example of a Jacobean family pew ... the Bluett Pew, with a screen, the rich carving of which includes a series of medallions with scenes from Genesis and Exodus. The north chancel chapel contains a series of Bluett family monuments, and provides a wonderful illustration of changing tastes and fashions throughout the 17th and 18th centuries.

Walk east from here to link on to the Grand Western Canal (see page 48), the surviving 'Country Park' section of which terminates near Burnhill Farm (181) (ST 07-19).

Holdstone Down and Trentishoe Down (180) (SS 61-47 and SS 63-47) Here on high country just inland from the coastal cliffs between Combe Martin and Hunter's Inn, are two good car parks from which there is access to the two hill-tops, both of which are accompanied by Bronze Age round barrows. There are fine views in every direction, especially out over the Bristol Channel to the Welsh coast. In the closing years of the last century the landowner endeavoured to develop this area and laid out tracks (one of which was called 'Seaview Road') and even sold some plots of land for bungalows. Due largely to the lack of available water, the development never took hold, and as a result we are fortunately left with some grand countryside. Walk a short distance east from Trentishoe Down to link with our **Walk 8**, page 122.

Holford (181) (ST 15-41) Delightful little village below the deeply indented eastern slopes of the Quantocks, with a multitude of paths leading up through several wooded combes, to Wordsworth's *smooth Quantock's airy ridge*, including our own **Walk 1** (see page 108). Handsome Alfoxton Park, which Wordsworth and his sister Dorothy rented in July 1797 for the modest sum of twenty three pounds for the year taxes paid, is now a hotel. During the year they stayed here, they saw much of the friend that had recommended it to them, the poet Samuel Taylor Coleridge, who was living at nearby Nether Stowey. Together they roamed the area, and Dorothy records much of these happy times in her *Alfoxden Journal*, which she kept between January and May 1798. For further details read Berta Lawrence's fascinating book, *Coleridge and Wordsworth in Somerset*.

Holford church, with its minute saddle-back tower, was rebuilt in about 1850, and apart from the unusual dog pound close by, is not of outstanding interest to visitors. The village itself is very pleasant, with thatched cottages, and a small stream coming off the hills.

Holnicote (181) (SS 91-46) The manor house of the Aclands is now gone, and only a gateway remains.

But Holnicote is the centre of the great estate given to the National Trust by Sir Richard Acland, Bt. in 1944, and all those who love Exmoor and its surroundings remain very much in his debt.

Horner (181) (SS 89-45) This delicious little hamlet should be seen early in the morning, or in spring or late autumn, when the number of other visitors is at its lowest. Here are thatched cottages, one of which has a tea garden and gift shop, and a little stream, the Horner Water, crossed here by a small packhorse bridge. There is also a car park which

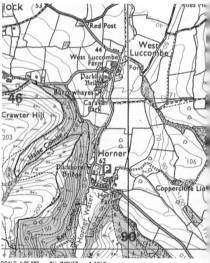

SCALE 1:25 000 or 2½ INCHES to 1 MILE

makes an excellent base for the splendid walks through the Horner Woods, partly beside the Horner Water, up to Cloutsham, Dunkery Beacon and Stoke Pero.(See the specially prepared National Trust leaflet, or simply follow the signs through the woods.) Day tickets are available for trout fishing on the Horner Water, from John Lynn and Co, Porlock.

Horns Cross (190) (SS 38-23) Hamlet on the A39, to the west of Bideford, with a character pub, the long, low and thatched Hoops Inn, at its western end. This is not far from the route of our **Walk 10**, page 126.

Horwood (180) (SS 50-27) There are fine views of the Taw and Torridge estuary from this pleasant village, situated at the western end of a long ridge. It has a small church, inside which is a delightful alabaster effigy of a 15th century lady, with horned headdress, and small figures of children beneath her cloak. This is in the north aisle, which was built by John Pollard, and the effigy is thought to be that of his wife, Emma. There are also some interesting bench-ends, a Jacobean pulpit and altar rail, and some medieval Barnstaple tiles.

Huish Champflower (181) (ST 04-29) Small village set in lovely wooded countryside between the

Brendon and Heydon hills, and like neighbouring Clatworthy, overlooking the headwaters of the River Tone. It has the edge over Clatworthy however, as it has an inn, The Castle, serving bar snacks and beer from the wood, and it also has a more interesting church. This has a fine 14th century tower and a light airy interior created by much plain glass, and a floor re-flagged with plain grey stone. The east window of the north aisle contains some medieval stained glass, with its splendid reds and blues reminiscent of Chartres. This glass is thought to have come from the ruined priory of Barlynch, about a mile to the north-east of Dulverton (see page 43). See also the simple tub font, and the finely carved medieval eagle lectern.

There is a pleasant walk southwards from here, first down the road to Washbattle Bridge (the reason for its name, we do not know), and then largely through woodlands beside the Tone down to Waterrow. From here it is possible to go even further beside the Tone, to Stawley (181) (ST 06-22).

Hunter's Inn (180) (SS 65-48) This hotel is situated in the thickly wooded valley of the little River Heddon, about a mile to the south of Heddon's Mouth (see page 51). **Walk 8**, page 122, starts from the large public car park, and the excellent National Trust leaflet, *Heddon Valley and Woody Bay* may be purchased here. It is also possible to walk eastwards from here to Martinhoe to start our **Walk 7**, page 120, exploring further east to Woody Bay. There is a shop and refreshment facilities at Hunter's Inn, in addition to the hotel itself.

At Mannacott Farm (SS 66-48), just above Hunter's Inn on the minor road eastwards to Martinhoe, will be found the Exmoor Farm Animal Centre. This is a working farm producing mainly beef, wool and sheep, where visitors are allowed to wander around a selection of about fifty breeds of cattle and sheep. There is a Pets' Corner, a display of horse-drawn implements, and on certain days, working demonstrations, including spinning. *Tel: Parracombe 227.*

Huntsham (181) (ST 00-20) Small village tucked away in the hills to the south of Bampton Down, with an over-restored church of little interest to visitors. Huntsham Castle (181) (SS 99-17) about two miles to the south is an Iron Age settlement on an impressive hill-top site.

Huntshaw (180) (SS 50-22) Quiet hamlet in wooded country to the north of Great Torrington. Funds must have been short around here in the 1430s, as an indulgence was granted in 1439 to all those who contributed to the rebuilding of the church. This move appears to have had excellent results, for most of the church, apart from the chancel, which is 12th century work, dates from this time. Do not miss the figures among the leaves on the north aisle arcade capitals. Pevsner, writing his invaluable Penguin *Buildings of England* North Devon volume in 1952, refers to a 'tumbler in an unseemly posture', and this figure no doubt typifies the robust medieval carvings so often found in English parish churches; carvings which so charmingly reflect the life and times of medieval England.

One of the rectors here, a native of Barnstaple, Cuthbert Mayne, was brought up a Protestant and converted to Roman Catholicism while an undergraduate at Oxford. He was however instituted as rector of Huntshaw in 1561, some years before leaving for the Continent, where he was ordained at the famous seminary at Douai. In 1576 he was sent secretly to England, being based in the neighbouring county of Cornwall, but within a year he was betrayed and arrested for saying Mass, and in 1577 he was executed at Launceston. The first of the martyred seminary priests, he was beatified as recently as 1886, and is now known as St Cuthbert Mayne.

Ilfracombe (180) (SS 51-47) Lively holiday resort town with something to offer every member of the family. Its harbour was developed by the Bourchiers (Earls of Bath) of Tawstock, but as a seaport it never achieved the importance of Bideford or Barnstaple. However with its splendidly romantic setting, it soon attracted the attention of the early 'holidaymakers', and developed rapidly throughout the last half of the 19th century. This is all too evident in the largely Victorian character of the town, but the bright little harbour, the series of small shale-sand beaches and the dramatic cliff walks, make Ilfracombe an ideal family destination.

There is a **Tourist Information Centre** on the Promenade, and **Ilfracombe Museum** in Wilder Road has collections relating to local history, dolls, model ships, mammals and butterflies; and there are many exhibits brought back from South America, by its founder the late Mervyn Palmer. There is

SCALE 1:25 000 or 2½ INCHES to 1 MILE

Ilfracombe

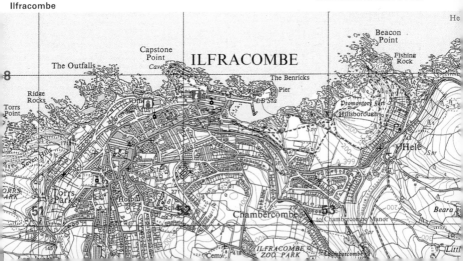

an Art Society Exhibition in the **Pavilion** on the Promenade throughout the summer season, and a pottery in the High Street.

Bicclescombe Park comprises attractive Municipal Gardens, which have a wide range of sporting facilities for young and old, and more unusually, a restored 18th century Corn Mill, complete with working waterwheel and internal machinery.

The Parish Church dates back to Norman times and has splendid 15th century ceiled wagon-roofs, a beautiful structure above the former rood screen, and a fine Elizabethan pulpit. **St Nicholas Chapel**, a lighthouse since the 18th century, stands above the entrance to the harbour. It has now been restored and contains a number of old prints of Ilfracombe. **Hillsborough Pleasure Grounds**, above and to the east of the town have a series of attractions including 'karting' for children. It is also possible to walk to Capstone Hill, and to Torrs Walk to the west of the town, from whence it is possible to walk to Lee Bay (see page 57, and **Walk 9**, page 124). See page 34 for neighbouring Chambercombe Manor, and page 51 for Hele Mill, both places that are well worth visiting.

Instow (180) (SS 47-30) Popular holiday village with a minute quay, from which there is a ferry service to Appledore, and a fine sandy beach (best access from car park at north end of village), which looks across the Torridge estuary to the steep streets and terraces of Appledore. There are also splendidly open views across the union of the Taw and Torridge, to the sandy wastes of Braunton Burrows. In the old part of the village, which stands well above the shore, there is a church with 14th century origins. There is an inscription on one of the

Instow ... a view from Appledore.

north aisle arcade capitals stating that Richard and Emma Waterman built this aisle in 1547, while the south transept contains a pleasant wall monument in memory of the son of a rector here, John Downe, who died while an undergraduate at Oxford in 1640. Humphrey Sibthorp, a renowned 18th century botanist, was buried at Bath, but he is also remembered by a handsome oval wall monument in the church here.

There is a path north from here, just above the shoreline, extending as far as Lower Yelland, with good bird watching opportunities especially in winter. However there is no right of way leading back to the road at Lower Yelland, and a return will almost certainly have to be made to Instow.

Kentisbury (180) (SS 62-43) Scattered parish, with no more than a 17th century farmhouse and a church at its centre, from which there are views westwards out over a quiet valley. The church has a Perpendicular tower of dark slate, and a south porch of the same period, which retains some of its original roof bosses. However the rest was ruthlessly 'restored' in 1875, and medieval flavour has been replaced by Victorian tidiness, with a pulpit of coloured plaster and a coloured roof. However do not miss the attractive 18th century sundial.

Use Pathfinder Map SS 64/74 for a pleasant walk north-eastwards, up over Silkenworthy Knap, and then largely beside a small stream, which leads to Trentishoe and Hunter's Inn, linking on to **Walk 8**, page 122.

Kilton (181) (ST 16-43) Secluded hamlet on rising ground between the Quantocks and the sea, with a small church at its northern end, rebuilt in 1862, by John Norton, the architect who was also responsible for the church at West Quantoxhead. However it has retained its handsome Perpendicular font and a 16th century brass with a long verse in memory of Charles Stenninge, which concludes thus:

His bodie here entombed is;
His sowle in heaven withe God dothe and
well;
God grant all men perusing this
Maie live with him and so fare well.

Walk north from here to link on to the coastal path.

Kilve (181) (ST 14-43) The major part of this small village lies astride the A39, where there is a lively inn, the Hood Arms, where stories of *'glatting'* are still told. This was a local sport, the hunting with an assortment of dogs for conger-eels, which are still sometimes to be found under stones on the muddy Kilve foreshore. Near the end of the road down to the shore, there is a small church, a stout grey stone building, with a squat tower and a white plastered interior containing early 19th century commandment boards and partly Jacobean choir stalls. Past the church are the ivy-covered remains of a medieval chantry chapel, the ruination of which in 1848 may have been caused by smugglers using it as a store for spirits, for there had been a long tradition of smuggling along this low and remote shoreline.

Well beyond the chapel, there is a good park, from whence it is only a short walk down to a rocky shore, backed by low cliffs. Walk west and south from here, to East Quantoxhead, or eastwards along the coastal path to Lilstock. The range here is used for dive-bombing practice at sea, and if a red flag is flying, please take heed of any warning notices that may be displayed. The poet Wordsworth would no doubt not have approved of all this, for in later life he and his sister Dorothy had fond memories of times spent here with their friend Coleridge, beside *Kilve's delightful shore*.

King's Nympton (180) (SS 68-19) Large village to the east of the Taw valley, not far from the confluence of that river with its tributary the Mole. Its small streets are full of character, with shops, inn and church all adding flavour to that of white painted cottages and modest houses. The thatched Grove Inn serves good bar meals in unspoilt

Copper-spired King's Nympton Church.

surroundings. The largely 15th century church has a stout tower topped by a copper spire. Its interior was spared the far too usual excesses of Victorian 'improvement', and is a delightful blend of late medieval and 18th century work. See especially the fine unceiled wagon-roofs to the nave; the richly carved bosses to all the roofs, even that of the south porch; the 15th century rood screen; the Jacobean panelling in the south chancel; the simple 18th century box pews; the reredos, also from the 18th century, but this more elegant; and the early 19th century painted ceiling to the chancel.

Kingsnympton Park is a handsome early Georgian mansion, in a well-wooded park above the Mole, well to the west of the village. It is not open to the public.

Head Mill Trout Farm is situated near the point where the B3226 crosses the River Mole, about a mile to the south-west of the village (180) (SS 66-18). Here visitors may stroll around the farm and see trout in various stages of production. *Tel: (0769) 80862.*

Kingston St Mary (193) (ST 22-29) This attractive village below the southern end of the Quantocks is dominated by the splendid 15th century tower of its church. The nave is two centuries older than the tower, but the finely vaulted porch and the chancel are contemporary with it. Inside, amongst many items of interest will be found a great 14th century tomb chest and a wonderful collection of medieval bench-ends. One of these depicts a weaver's shuttle, which should remind visitors to visit Church Farm Weavers, who have an attractively laid out hand-loom weaving workshop and gallery in a restored barn below the church. *Tel: Kingston St Mary 267.*

Kinsford Gate (180) (SS 73-36) These cross-roads are situated high up on the south-western confines of Exmoor, on the border between Somerset and Devon. At this point the border appears to follow a prehistoric trackway, north-westwards and then north from here, and in its vicinity are the remains of many Bronze Age round barrows and tumuli: Five Barrows, Setta Barrow, Wood Barrow, Longstone Barrow, and not far away, Chapman Barrows. If Bronze Age barrows are not your thing, do not be deterred, for this is splendid country, with ponies often to be seen on the skyline, and much wildlife to be spotted.

Kittisford (181) (ST 07-22) Small village in the valley of the Tone, with a path across the fields to Cothay Manor, beyond the river to the south. The pink-washed church tower has high stone buttresses, while inside there is a rare feature in the shape of arcading in wood, rather than in stone. There is also a 17th century north chapel, a slightly earlier pulpit from the same century, and a brass of Richard Bluett and his wife (1524), the Bluetts being the owners of Cothay (see page 39).

Knightshayes Court (181) (SS 96-15) Now owned by the National Trust, Knightshayes was begun in 1869, and is a rare domestic example of the work of one of the most talented 19th century architects, William Burges, best known perhaps for his work on Cardiff Castle and Castle Coch, two supreme examples of High Victorian Gothic. The house has a richly decorated Victorian interior, and stands in one of the finest gardens in Devon, looking out westwards over the Exe valley. This garden was developed by the late Sir John Heathcoat-Amory and his wife in the 1950s, 60s and 70s, and is noted for its fine specimen trees, formal terraces, and rare shrubs. There is a Garden Shop and a Licensed Restaurant. *Tel: Tiverton 254665.*

Sir John Heathcoat-Amory, one of the developers of the garden, was the grandson of the man who built Knightshayes, who himself was the grandson of the remarkable John Heathcoat, the inventor and mill owner, who, in the true spirit of the Industrial Revolution, built himself a mill at Tiverton, after his original lace mill had been wrecked by Luddites in 1816. It is good to report that John Heathcoat and Company still operates at Tiverton *(see page 75).*

Knowstone (181) (SS 82-23) Small village in bleak countryside above two wooded valleys through which flow the Crooked Oak Stream and a smaller tributary. There is a hospitable little inn here, the thatched Masons Arms, serving beer from the wood and a good selection of bar and restaurant meals, which are understandably popular with walkers coming through on the Two Moors Way (see page 76). The small church has a modest Norman south doorway and an interior which includes some unspoilt 18th and early 19th century pews, and a pleasant series of 17th century wall monuments. Sir Nicholas Wadham, the founder of Wadham College, Oxford, was born at Wadham, a

Thatched roofs and diamond-paned windows, at Knowstone.

LANDACRE BRIDGE

farm about a mile to the north-west of the village. Sir John Berry, later to be knighted by Charles II for his part in the naval battle of Sole Bay in 1665, was born at the vicarage here; but a 19th century vicar, 'Parson Froude', brought less welcome attention to the village. He eventually died from a heart attack, due to his loss of temper with a parishioner, but not before earning himself, over many years, a reputation for lawlessness and heathen-like behaviour in the two livings in his care.

Walk north from here, then west along the valley of the Crooked Oak, to Wadham Bridge, and back up to the village. The Two Moors Way has to use a public road to the south-east of the village, but walkers going north from here move up a quiet roadway to Owlaborough, and then on a path up to the B3227, along which they head east for a short distance to the Jubilee Inn, which offers accommodation and buffet meals.

Landacre Bridge (181) (SS 81-36) Attractive old bridge spanning the River Barle, about two miles above Withypool, with stout sandstone piers and five arches. The area near the bridge can become crowded at peak holiday times, but at others, it is well worth visiting. Jeremy Stickles, King's Messenger and friend of John Ridd, escaped here from an ambush by the Doones in Blackmore's story *Lorna Doone*.

There is a path eastwards from here, parallel with the Barle, to Withypool, and the Two Moors Way runs in an east-west direction, not far to the north.

Landcross (180) (SS 46-23) The smallest parish in Devon sits astride the busy A386, about two miles south of Bideford, on a narrow spit of land between the Torridge and the Yeo. The small 15th century church has, beneath its charming barrel-shaped ceiling, a Norman font, a pulpit made up of old bench-ends, and despite this, a series of other bench-ends still in their original use. Christened here on 11th December 1608, was the infant George Monk, who was to become one of Cromwell's great Generals, and who was largely responsible for the recall of Charles II in 1660, when the Commonwealth was in disarray following the death of Oliver Cromwell in 1658.

It was near this village that Henry Williamson's 'Tarka the Otter' finally met his death at the end of the epic fight with the otterhound Deadlock, only about a mile downstream from the place of his birth, below the Canal Bridge between here and Weare Giffard.

Landkey (180) (SS 59-31) A scattered village to the immediate east of Barnstaple. It does however have a handsome 15th century church, with a well proportioned tower and a porch containing a curious roof boss depicting four stags devouring a man's head. The chancel was rebuilt in 1870, but the nave and aisles have fine roofs, supported on interesting corbel heads, and many charming roof bosses. See also the three medieval stone effigies in the north aisle and the beautifully coloured monument to Sir Arthur Acland (1610) in the south transept.

Landacre Bridge ... open spaces and memories of Lorna Doone.

Do not miss a visit to the interesting North Devon Farm Park, at Marsh Farm well to the east of the village. Features here include rare breeds of sheep, cattle, goats and pigs; farm machinery, ponds and woodland walks; refreshments and shop. *(Tel: 0271 830255.)*

Langford Budville (181) (ST 11-22) Small village on a hillside, with views out across the Tone valley to the Wellington Monument on the Black Down Hills above Wellington town. The red sandstone church is largely 15th century, but early in the following century a certain John Peryn of Wellington bequeathed money for the building of a new tower, and the fine Perpendicular specimen built with John's money survives to this day. The interior, beneath its ceiled wagon-roof, contains a handsome 15th century font, and on one of the south arcade capitals, the delicate and possibly unique carving of a needle and thread.

There are attractive unfenced roads leading through woodland to the west and north-west of this village, 180 acres of which is now a Nature Reserve.

Langtree (180) (SS 45-15) Sitting comfortably astride the B3227, this small village of cob and thatch is in high country well to the west of the Torridge valley, and there are fine views out over the surrounding fields and woodlands. The 15th century church has a richly ornamented late 17th century pulpit, two Victorian chairs, which both incorporate interesting 16th century Flemish panels, and an ambitious Royal Arms of George II in plaster. At Withacott Farm, on the B3227 to the west of the village, flowers are specially grown and dried for display purposes, and its showroom is open from Monday to Friday *(tel: Langtree 246)*.

Lee (180) (SS 48-46) Pretty village at the end of a combe, on the rocky shore of little Lee Bay (good bathing at low tide). There are tea gardens, the well known 'Old Maids Cottage' and a 'smuggler's cottage'. The church was only built in 1837, but has a wealth of 17th century oak furnishings. Walk westwards from here above Damage Cliffs (bright with primroses in springtime), to Bull Point, or eastwards to Ilfracombe via Torrs Walk. Lee is on our **Walk 9**, page 124, and there is a car park here.

Lilstock (181) (ST 16-44) Here are a few houses and a small church, which consists only of the chancel — all that remains of a medieval church otherwise demolished in 1881. There is a car park close to the shingly shoreline, and the possibility of a pleasant walk westwards along the coastal path to Kilve and East Quantoxhead, but take note of any warning signs (see Kilve, page 54).

Littleham (180) (SS 43-23) Small village in hilly country above the valley of little River Yeo, with a church and rectory situated well to its east. Inside the church will be found a series of mid-16th century bench-ends with a Renaissance rather than a medieval flavour, and an impressive tomb chest, upon which lies the alabaster figure of a bearded military man, General Hope Crealock, who died in 1891. There is a path leading southwards off the lane to the church, down to the Yeo valley near Edge Mill.

Little Torrington (180) (SS 49-16) This compact village is poised high above the wooded western slopes of the winding Torridge valley, with views over to Great Torrington, less than two miles to the north. The church was largely rebuilt in the 19th century, but there is a small brass to be found on a window ledge on the south side of the chancel. This is to Jone Phesant, who died in 1635, *'esteemed for her grave and matronlike conversation'*.

The Long Stone (180) (SS 70-43) An impressive Bronze Age standing stone, no less than nine feet high. This stands on windswept moorland 1525 feet above sea level, between Chapman Barrows (to the west) and Longstone Barrow (to the south-east). It was probably put here, between 1500 and 1000 BC, as a memorial to a local chieftain. It is best approached south-eastwards from Parracombe, or northwards from the vicinity of Challacombe. If you wish to avoid summer crowds, this should provide a splendid opportunity, but at all times of the year, go properly equipped.

Loxbeare (181) (SS 91-16) Scattered parish much disturbed by the busy North Devon Link Road, with a few houses and a small church dating back to the 12th century. This has a Norman south doorway and in its partly Norman tower there is a set of bells cast in Exeter as long ago as the 15th century. Despite being 'gone-over' in the early 19th century, much of interest has been spared, including a Jacobean pulpit, altar rail and little west gallery. Although sited above the valley of a small tributary of the Exe, Loxbeare stands only a mile from the source of what many would regard as Devon's loveliest river, the Dart, which rises in a field about 1½ miles west of the village (SS 89-16).

Loxhore (180) (SS 61-38) Here is yet another scattered parish, this one above the wooded valley of the Yeo. This river, which joins the Taw at Barnstaple, is not to be confused with the Yeo that flows into the Torridge near Bideford. The largely 15th century church stands on a hillside to the north of the parish, and has a north arcade supported on wooden pillars, and a painted 16th century font cover.

Luccombe (181) (SS 91-44) Out of season this is a beautifully quiet village, with several thatched cottages overlooking a well tended churchyard. The largely Perpendicular church has a fine, well proportioned tower with shields carved upon its castellations, accompanied by some nicely aggressive gargoyles. Do not overlook the tomb of Henry Byam, rector here during the Civil War. A staunch Royalist, his four sons fought for the King in a troop that their father helped to raise. Although he lived to see the restoration of the monarchy, his wife and daughter were sadly both drowned while trying to escape from the Parliamentary forces.

With the woods of Horner and Cloutsham, and the moorlands of Dunkery all not far away, this is splendid walking country, but motorists are advised to head for the car park at Webber's Post, about a mile to the south-west (SS 90-43). It is however possible to walk eastwards, via Blackford and Tivington, and through extensive woodlands beyond, to Dunster.

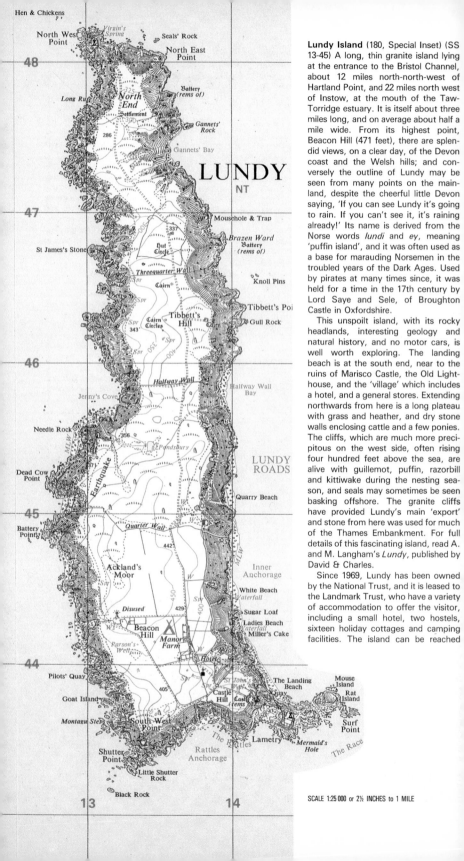

Lundy Island (180, Special Inset) (SS 13-45) A long, thin granite island lying at the entrance to the Bristol Channel, about 12 miles north-north-west of Hartland Point, and 22 miles north west of Instow, at the mouth of the Taw-Torridge estuary. It is itself about three miles long, and on average about half a mile wide. From its highest point, Beacon Hill (471 feet), there are splendid views, on a clear day, of the Devon coast and the Welsh hills; and conversely the outline of Lundy may be seen from many points on the mainland, despite the cheerful little Devon saying, 'If you can see Lundy it's going to rain. If you can't see it, it's raining already!' Its name is derived from the Norse words *lundi* and *ey*, meaning 'puffin island', and it was often used as a base for marauding Norsemen in the troubled years of the Dark Ages. Used by pirates at many times since, it was held for a time in the 17th century by Lord Saye and Sele, of Broughton Castle in Oxfordshire.

This unspoilt island, with its rocky headlands, interesting geology and natural history, and no motor cars, is well worth exploring. The landing beach is at the south end, near to the ruins of Marisco Castle, the Old Lighthouse, and the 'village' which includes a hotel, and a general stores. Extending northwards from here is a long plateau with grass and heather, and dry stone walls enclosing cattle and a few ponies. The cliffs, which are much more precipitous on the west side, often rising four hundred feet above the sea, are alive with guillemot, puffin, razorbill and kittiwake during the nesting season, and seals may sometimes be seen basking offshore. The granite cliffs have provided Lundy's main 'export' and stone from here was used for much of the Thames Embankment. For full details of this fascinating island, read A. and M. Langham's *Lundy*, published by David & Charles.

Since 1969, Lundy has been owned by the National Trust, and it is leased to the Landmark Trust, who have a variety of accommodation to offer the visitor, including a small hotel, two hostels, sixteen holiday cottages and camping facilities. The island can be reached

SCALE 1:25 000 or 2½ INCHES to 1 MILE

on the supply ship *Oldenburg* from Bideford or Ilfracombe (two and a half hours), but bookings must be made in advance. (*For Day Visit sailings, tel: 02372 70422.*) All other details relating to accommodation and the booking of transport may be obtained from: *The Landmark Trust, Shottesbrooke, Maidenhead, Berks. Tel: (0628-82) 5925.*

Luxborough (181) (SS 97 38) A minute village on the northern side of the Brendon Hills, with a small church looking eastwards down a valley towards Druid's Combe. This has a saddleback tower which only dates from the 19th century, when extensive restoration of the whole building took place. There is an octagonal font, and in the churchyard, the base of a medieval cross, with a stump in red sandstone.

There are fine walks northwards, through extensive Forestry Commission woodlands to Timberscombe and Dunster, and for those who do not wish to walk, there is an attractive road through part of these woods, with a Picnic Place at Croydon Hill (SS 97-41). (Link here with our **Walk 2**, page 110.) It is also possible to walk south, up through Chargot Wood to the Chargot Wood Picnic Place, on the Brendon Hills east-west spine road (SS 97-35), or up to the Kennisham Picnic Place, which is on the same road, about a mile to the west (SS 96-35).

Lydeard Hill (181) (ST 18-33) There is a good car park on the Quantocks, above West Bagborough. This makes an excellent starting point for a long and exhilarating walk north-westwards along the spine of these glorious hills, passing the Triscombe Stone, Crowcombe Park Gate, and Bicknoller Post, before descending to the car park at Staple Plain

(ST 11-41), near West Quantoxhead. If you cannot find friends to collect you from Staple Plain, make a circular walk taking in the Triscombe Stone, Cockercombe and Aisholt. Come up here soon after dawn and you may be rewarded by the sight of deer not far away.

Lydeard St Lawrence (181) (ST 12-32) Small village in wooded countryside with low hills between the Quantocks and the Brendons, with fine views eastwards to the former. The red sandstone church has a 14th century chancel in the Decorated style, but is otherwise Perpendicular. See especially the carvings on the north aisle arcade capitals, including one showing a fox with a goose in its mouth; the handsome Jacobean pulpit, and the font, which appears to incorporate the remains of two Norman fonts, one of which is inverted. The churchyard no longer contains the quaint epitaph to William Rich, but luckily its content has been recorded:

> Beneath this stone in sound repose,
> Lies William Rich of Lydeard Close:
> Eight wives he had yet none survive,
> And likewise children eight times five;
> From whom an issue vast did pour
> Of great grand-children five times four.
> Rich born, Rich bred, but fate adverse
> His health and fortune did reverse.
> He lived and died immensely poor.
> July the 10th aged ninety-four.

There is a station on the West Somerset Railway, and a Youth Hostel, both about a mile to the north-east of the village.

Lynmouth (180) (SS 72-49) An exceptionally

Lynton and Lynmouth   1 Tourist Information Centre   SCALE 1:10 000 or 6 INCHES to 1 MILE

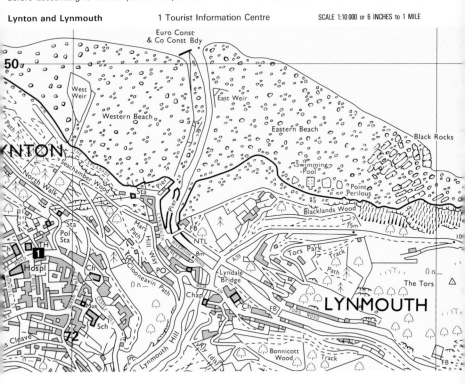

beautiful 'fishing village' sheltering at the mouth of the East and West Lyn Rivers, with cliffs nearly a thousand feet high on either side. The first visitors came here in the early years of the 19th century, when the wars with Napoleon prevented them from travelling to the Continent. The poet Southey stayed here with his young wife in the summer months of 1812, and in letters to friends, made references to Lynmouth's *'indescribable fertility and grandeur'*, and to the mildness of its climate. Several of the houses date from this early period, and others from the later years of the 19th century, although the thatched 'Rising Sun' hotel is certainly much older. This overlooks the little harbour, whose focal point is the 'Rhenish Tower', an attractive structure built by a retired general in about 1860, to store sea water for indoor bathing. Beyond the harbour, just to its west, is the lower 'station' of a dramatic cliff railway up to Lynton, built in 1890 by a local builder, and largely financed by the publisher, George Newnes. This consists of two cars linked by steel cables. Both cars have large water tanks beneath them, and the descending car has its tank filled with water, thereby pulling up the ascending car which has an emptied tank. But before ascending to Lynton, do try to do at least a little of our **Walk 6**, (page 118), which starts from the car park to the south-east of Lyndale Bridge. Also visit the gardens of Glen Lyn House and the Exmoor Brass Rubbing Centre close by in Watersmeet Road *(tel: Lynton 52529).*

New pathways have been built here, and the river generally has been greatly tamed by civil engineers since the great flood disaster here on the night of 15th August, 1952, when thirty four people died, and great damage was inflicted upon the village. The passing of the years has healed the scars, but those who survived will never forget that night, when ninety million gallons of water fell in a few hours, when light and power failed, and all was blackness and roaring water, until the morning revealed the extent of the West Country's greatest tragedy. For details of this tragic story, read E. R. Delderfield's *The Lynmouth Flood Disaster*.

For details of the Lynmouth Lifeboat's epic overland journey to Porlock Weir, see Countisbury, page 40.

Lynton (180) (SS 71-49) Lively little hill-top town with splendid views and a cliff railway linking it with its neighbour Lynmouth far below. It grew up in the heyday of 19th century holidaymaking, and its architecture is largely Victorian and Edwardian. However it has many busy little shops, and a wide variety of accommodation for visitors. Do not miss the Lyn and Exmoor Museum in the attractive St Vincent's Cottage. There is a **Tourist Information Centre (1)** at the Town Hall in Lee Road *(tel: Lynton 52225).* Walk or drive, along a minor road westwards, to visit The Valley of Rocks (see page 77), and the car park at Lee Abbey (to link on to our **Walk 7**, page 120).

Lynton and Barnstaple Railway (180) (SS 67-46 etc) This two foot gauge miniature railway was opened in 1898, and although it never paid its way, it must have provided visitors with a delightful scenic run. Signs of its embankments and cutting may be seen at several points between Lynton and Barnstaple, especially near Parracombe and Bratton Fleming. It was only closed in 1936, and it was a great tragedy that it did not just endure long enough to enter the age of the pleasure railway revival.

Malmsmead (180) (SS 79-47) Here, a short distance above the confluence of the sparkling Badgworthy Water and Oare Water, is a ford with a pleasant old bridge beside it. This is in the very heart of R. D. Blackmore's *Doone Country*, and our **Walk 5**, page 116, starts from here, following up beside the Badgworthy Water. There are car park, picnic site, souvenir shop and refreshment facilities at Lorna Doone Farm, which overlooks the bridge, while opposite the turn to Cloud Farm there is an interesting Natural History Centre *(tel: 0643 2075)*, with displays relating to Exmoor wildlife. Cloud Farm also provides a wide range of refreshments.

Marsland Mouth (190) (SS 20-17) Small beach overlooked by dark cliffs, at the border between Devon and Cornwall, here marked by a small stream flowing over the rock strewn, shingly shore. This is best approached by our **Walk 12**, page 130.

Martinhoe (180) (SS 66-48) Scattered parish bordered on the north by great hog-backed cliffs, inland from which are the small earthworks of a Roman fortlet or signal station (SS 66-49) similar to that on Old Barrow Hill (see also County Gate, page 40). Archaeologists believe that it was in use only for about twenty years, from about AD 58 until the time when the Roman army had gained effective control over the tribes of South Wales. The small church, with only a few houses for company, was heavily restored in 1866, and contains little of interest to visitors. However it is situated about eight hundred feet above sea level, and there are splendid views north-eastwards out over Woody Bay. Our **Walk 7** starts from the car park to the east of the hamlet.

Marwood (180) (SS 54-37) Pleasant village in rolling countryside, less than four miles north of Barnstaple. The church dates largely from the 14th century, and looks westward over a quiet, wooded valley. Its interior is well worth visiting, and includes a fine series of bench-ends, a lovely 16th century screen with carved Renaissance figures, and several other features of interest. Do not miss the 18th century sundial on the south porch, which indicates the approximate time in Jerusalem and various European capitals; Rome however being excluded, no doubt on account of local anti-Papist prejudice. Read Sally Jones' *'Legends of Devon'*, for the full story of *The Candle of Marwood*, in which the devil is thwarted by a resourceful mother protecting a wayward daughter who had courted disaster by paring her nails on the Sabbath. All good stuff!

Marwood Hill, opposite the church, has a delightful garden with an extensive collection of camellias, rhododendrons and flowering shrubs in a sheltered valley with pools. There is also a rock and alpine garden.

Melbury Woods (190) (SS 37-18) There is a Forestry Commission Picnic Place beside an avenue of beech, near Powler's Piece cross-roads (on a minor road between Parkham and West Putford).

Leading off from this picnic place are two short forest trails through plantations of young spruce and pine (one a mile in length, and one about half a mile). For further information, visit Hartland Forest Information Centre (see page 50).

Merton (180) (SS 52-12) A rather featureless village astride the A386, in hill country above the densely wooded valley of the little Mere River. There are views southwards to the dark outline of Dartmoor from the vicinity of the sadly over-restored church. Apart from its Norman font with Jacobean cover, there is not a great deal of interest within this building. Walter de Merton, the founder of Merton College, Oxford, was born here early in the 13th century. Great Potheridge (SS 51-14) was the family home of the Monks, but little survives of the great house built by General George Monk, who will always be remembered for his leading role in the restoration of Charles II to the English throne in 1660. *(See also Landcross, page 56.)*

Milky Way (190) (SS 32-22) Situated two miles east of Clovelly, just south of the A39 road towards Bideford, this 205-acre working farm has various attractive visitor facilities. These include a special viewing gallery to see the dairy herd being milked, a fine display of historic farm machinery, a restaurant and shop. *(Tel: 02373 255.)*

Milverton (181) (ST 12-25) Delightful little town on a small rise, and now mercifully relieved from traffic along the busy B3227. The little sloping streets, at least one of which has a raised cobbled pathway, are lined with pleasant Georgian houses, with a few 17th and later 19th century buildings to add further character. Near the church is a fine late-15th century parsonage, and the church itself is a handsome late-14th and early-15th century building in mellow red sandstone. Before looking inside do not miss the pleasant views from the south porch out over the Vale of Taunton Deane, to the Wellington Monument on the Black Down Hills. The interior is full of interest, with a Norman font, 15th and 16th century benches, bench-ends, and choir-stalls, and a 16th century rood screen. The beautifully detailed carving of all this woodwork is well worth inspecting.

It is possible to walk westwards from here, by road to the vicinity of Farthing's Farm, and then across country, via Nunnington Park Farm, to Waterrow.

Minehead (181) (SS 96-46) Bright and busy holiday resort town reinforced by the vigour of a giant holiday camp. Apart from its two mile long sand and pebble beach, it has a great variety of accommodation, many shops and amusements, and colourful gardens just behind its Esplanade. There is also a **Tourist Information Centre (1)**, in the Market House, on the Parade *(tel: 0643 2624)*.

But apart from all this, Minehead has quieter corners to offer. Quay Town has a long row of 'fishermen's cottages', and beyond these is a small harbour, described by Daniel Defoe in the 1720s as

Minehead	1 Tourist Information Centre	SCALE 1:10 000 or 6 INCHES to 1 MILE

MOLLAND

'fairer, and much deeper, than those at Watchet and Porlock'. It is possible to visit the Lifeboat Station here. Above the harbour is Higher Town, with its steep streets bordered by brightly painted cottages, and leading up to a handsomely towered 15th century grey stone church. Inside see especially the late 15th century screen, possibly by the same craftsmen who made the screens at Carhampton and Dunster, the elegant Perpendicular font, the Jacobean pulpit, and the 15th century brass of a lady with a tall hat. Walk or drive beyond to North Hill and Selworthy Beacon (see pages 63 & 68). Also walk far beyond the harbour, through woodlands above the coast, to the ruined Burgundy Chapel (SS 94-48), which lies beyond Greenaleigh Point; or walk to Bratton with its ford and 15th century manor house, by way of the Parks Walk, Woodcombe Walk, and Bratton Walk.

Molland (181) (SS 80-28) Small village on a hillside below the moors, overlooking gentle valleys to the south. Its delightful church was so effectively restored in the mid-18th century that it entirely escaped the attentions of those over-enthusiastic Victorians. Here therefore is a perfect rural Georgian interior with uneven, white plastered walls, high box pews, three-decker pulpit, and a screen with the Royal coat of arms. Do not overlook the

Molland Church ... an unspoilt Georgian interior.

interesting little figure in a niche in one of the north arcade pillars, nor the ornate series of 17th and 18th century Courtenay monuments, which provide so perfect a foil for the plainer walls and furnishings. Do not miss this most satisfying little building.

Molland was the home of Henry and James Quartly, two brothers who, in the late 18th century, established the famous strain of Red Devon cattle by selective breeding.

Walk north-eastwards from here, via Smallacombe, up over West Anstey Common, and on to Hawkridge and Tarr Steps.

Monkleigh (180) (SS 45-20) Attractive village in high country above the Torridge valley, with a long street lined with many thatched cottages, and a most interesting church. This was rebuilt in the early-16th century, with funds provided by the will of Sir William Hankford of Annery, an estate well to the north of the village (SS 45-22). Sir William was Chief Justice of the King's Bench in the reign of

Henry V (see also Bulkworthy, page 33), and his impressive canopied altar tomb stands in the south-east chapel (the Annery Chapel). The other contents of this fine Perpendicular church include a handsome 16th century parclose screen (can you spot the pelican?), a Norman font, some carved bench-ends, a brass to James Coffin, who died in 1566, and a 17th century wall monument to William Gaye and his wife. Gaye's epitaph is well worth reading and from it we learn that:

*'Oxford's Academie soe prized his parts
That it did crowne him Lawreate of Arts.'*

We wonder if this Gaye was an ancestor of John Gay, the composer of *The Beggar's Opera*? We do know that some of his ancestors lived at Goldworthy, near Parkham, a few miles to the west of Monkleigh.

Walter de Stapledon, Bishop of Exeter, and founder of Exeter College, Oxford, was born at Annery (see above) in 1261. No trace of the medieval house remains, but there is a fine Georgian building here.

Walk south from Monkleigh, over the fields to Frithelstock, and on to Watergate Bridge (SS 46-17).

Monksilver (181) (ST 07-37) Pleasant village set in a well wooded valley, with many thatched and colour-washed cottages, and a pleasant inn, the Notley Arms. The church overlooks the village from its sloping churchyard, and rose trees line the path to its 15th century south door. It has a Norman tower, but is otherwise mainly Perpendicular. Inside there is a wealth of good carving — on bench-ends, on the panels of the rood screen, and on the pulpit. Do not miss the gargoyle that appears to depict a painful piece of medieval dentistry.

The best walk from here is south-westwards, up through woodlands below Bird's Hill, and over to Sticklepath (ST 04-36). It is possible to return from here to Monksilver, via Chidgley and Birchanger Farm, or to walk on west and north, to Roadwater, following the course of the long-dismantled railway line that once linked the mines on the Brendon Hills with the port of Watchet. *(See Brendon Hills, page 31.)*

Morebath (181) (SS 95-24) Small village on a hillside above a quiet valley, with a largely Perpendicular church, over-restored in 1875. However it has retained its saddle-backed 13th century tower, and we are indebted to the Victorians for the impressive black marble font.

Mortehoe (180) (SS 45-45) Pleasant coastal village with a small-scale church of Norman origin, situated in an equally minute churchyard. See especially the fine altar tomb of Sir William de Tracey, vicar and probable founder of Mortehoe church, who died in 1322; the carved bench-ends; and the impressive mosaic over the chancel arch. The National Trust owns almost all of the coastal area hereabouts, and there are fine walks along the jagged cliff country of Morte Point and Bull Point (see the excellent National Trust leaflet, *Ilfracombe to Woolacombe*). This coast was always a great hazard to shipping until the Bull Point lighthouse was built in 1879, and in the winter of 1852 no fewer than five ships went down off the treacherous Morte Stone, off Morte Point. Our **Walk 9**, page 124, starts from here.

Mouth Mill (190) (SS 29-26) There is access to the rocky coast at Mouth Mill, down a beautifully wooded combe, starting from a National Trust car park in the vicinity of Brownsham Farm. It is possible to walk eastwards from here, along a section of the North Devon Coastal Path, parallel with the four hundred foot high Gallantry Bower cliffs, to Clovelly. Use the excellent National Trust leaflet, *Clovelly to Hartland Point*, to explore westwards to Hartland Point.

Muddiford (180) (SS 56-38) Small village in the deep, wooded valley of the little Bradiford Water, with a four-acre fly fishing lake, owned by Blakewell Fisheries. Visitors not wishing to fish are encouraged to wander around the trout rearing ponds and to feed the fish. The farm shop is well stocked with fresh and smoked trout. *(Tel: Barnstaple 44533.)*

Nether Stowey (181) (ST 19-39) The little streets of this village are full of character, and a small stream flows beside two of them. Coleridge Cottage in Lime Street (National Trust) was rented by the poet from late 1796, and although he only spent three years at Stowey, some of his best verse was written here, including *The Ancient Mariner, Kubla Khan* and the first part of *Christabel*. Otherwise Coleridge found 'scanty maintenance by writing verses for a London morning paper'. William Wordsworth and his sister Dorothy, who stayed at Alfoxton for a year in 1797/8 (see also Holford, page 52), spent much time with Coleridge, and Charles Lamb also came here. Only one room of the cottage is open, but it is full of interesting Coleridge material, and well worth visiting. For further details read Berta Lawrence's *Coleridge and Wordsworth in Somerset*.

Nether Stowey church is almost marooned on the far side of the busy A39, and has little sense of antiquity within, having been largely rebuilt in 1851.

Nether Stowey Church.

Next door to the church is Stowey Court (not open to the public), hiding behind a high brick wall, which is itself ornamented by an attractive 18th century gazebo. At the southern end of the village there is a grassy mound topped by the ruined foundations of a square keep; all that remains of a stout Norman castle.

Drive south-west from here, up on to the Quantocks, for the car parks at the Triscombe Stone (see page 76), or at Dead Woman's Ditch (see page 42); both of which make excellent bases for exploring this delightful hill country.

Nettlecombe (181) (ST 05-37) Here in a quiet valley running northwards from the Brendon Hills is an interesting red sandstone church and Nettlecombe Court, a fine Elizabethan manor house, with a Georgian west front. The Court, which was the home of the Raleigh family and then the Trevelyans for many hundreds of years, is now a Field Study Centre. Details of courses may be obtained from: *The Warden, Nettlecombe Court, Williton, Taunton, TA4 4HT*.

The church has retained its 15th century tower, but is otherwise a 19th century building. However it contains several interesting monuments, some 16th century bench-ends, a richly carved Perpendicular font, and a fine 18th century pulpit; all of which make a visit here worth while.

Newton St Petrock (180) (SS 41-12) Minute village in undramatic country, on the slopes of a valley through which the infant Torridge flows. The small, mainly Perpendicular church has a pleasant series of 16th century bench-ends, a 19th century pulpit incorporating some medieval panels, and a 17th century altar table.

Newton Tracey (180) (SS 52-26) An undistinguished little village strung out along the B3232, with a small church harshly restored by the Victorians. The Norman font, with its leaf and cable patterns, has survived.

Northam (180) (SS 44-29) There is a bright, busy atmosphere in Northam's little square, which is overlooked by a tall-towered church (used as a shipping mark for centuries). Its large interior was heavily restored in the mid-19th century, and is not of great interest to visitors. However there are fine views northwards out over the green expanse of Northam Burrows, part of which is now designated as a Country Park. Here is an interesting Visitor Centre and 650 acres of common land, where ponies are usually to be seen contentedly grazing, and where the sound of the skylark may be heard in early summer. There is also a golf course, The Royal North Devon. (See also Westward Ho!, page 82.)

North Hill (181) (SS 94-47) A fine stretch of open country lying to the west of Minehead, and just to the south of the coast. There are car parks at North Hill itself, and further west, at Selworthy Beacon (SS 91-47). There is a nature trail and a camp site at North Hill, and a viewpoint indicator at SS 93-47. It is possible to walk down to the shore near the ruined Burgundy Chapel (SS 94-48), to walk east to Minehead, or west to Bossington and Porlock. See also Selworthy, page 68, and Minehead, page 61.

North Molton (180) (SS 73-29) Once a borough, which at various stages of its history grew reasonably prosperous from the woollen trade, and from local mining activities (see Heasley Mill, page 51). It is still possible to trace parts of the mineral railway that ran through North Molton, between the mines at Heasley Mill and the main line at South Molton, but both the woollen trade and the mining have long since died out, leaving a rather gaunt village with a wide square and a handsome church, both too large for present day needs.

This grey stone building has a fine Perpendicular tower, with a tall figure of the Virgin Mary in a niche on its south side. The spacious interior is well lit by clerestory windows which are an unusual feature in North Devon. The 15th century font has figures of saints and bishops around its stem, including the martyr St Urith of Chittlehampton (see page 36), who appears with a head in her hands, and for good measure, one in its expected place as well. There is a dark 15th century rood screen, and beyond it a chancel with heavy 17th century panelling. Do not miss the fine medieval timber pulpit, the clock made in Barnstaple in 1664, nor the beautiful 17th century monument to Sir Amyas Bamfylde, with his wife sitting sadly at his feet, and a bible open on her knees.

Tom Faggus, the highwayman cousin of John Ridd in *Lorna Doone*, had his smithy in the Square at North Molton. The best walk from here is down the valley of the River Mole to South Molton, partly along the course of the old mineral railway.

Summer evening at Nynehead.

the north of the village, was erected here to commemorate the World Ploughing Championships held here in 1971, and incorporates bricks made from materials from the twenty one competing countries.

Walk south from the east side of the village, over the aqueduct that once carried the Grand Western Canal over the Tone, and then follow the course of the canal west and then south towards Holcombe Rogus (for Grand Western Canal, see page 48).

Norton Fitzwarren (181) (ST 19-25) Much enlarged in recent years, Norton Fitzwarren is noted for its Taunton Cider Visitor Centre. In addition to its exhibition illustrating the history of cidermaking, there is a mini-orchard, a shop and 'Morses Place', an atmospheric West Country pub. *(Tel: 0823 283141.)* The church has a medieval tower, but was largely rebuilt in the 19th century. The rood screen has a series of fascinating carvings on its lower frieze telling the story of the *Dragon of Norton Camp*, a mythical beast that is said to have haunted the earthworks of the Iron Age settlement on a small hill to the north of the church. Having made itself thoroughly objectionable for many years by carrying off the screaming children of the villagers, the dragon was eventually slain by local hero, Fulke Fitzwarren. The rood screen that portrays this story was once thrown out of the church, but in 1886 was rescued by the rector from a Taunton junk shop; one of the occasions when a Victorian 'restorer' really earned this description. Read the full story of the Dragon in Sally Jones' *Legends of Somerset.*

Walk south-west from here, beside the River Tone, to Nynehead, and onwards, following much of the line of the Grand Western Canal (see page 48).

Nynehead (181) (ST 13-22) Small village in the Tone valley, not far to the north of Wellington, with the 17th century Nynehead Court standing close to a largely Perpendicular red sandstone church. This building was considerably altered by the Rev. John Sanford, a member of the family who had owned the Court since about 1600, but we can forgive him for this in view of his enlightened provision of various works of art from Italy, including exquisite sculptures by the 15th century Florentine artists Luca della Robbia and his nephew Andrea. There are Sanford monuments, and also a monument to Edward Clarke and his wife, with the two of them kneeling opposite each other at a prayer desk. The Clarkes lived at nearby Chipley Park, where they often used to entertain their friend, the philosopher John Locke.

The 'Cairn of Peace' at Haywood Farm, just to

Oake (181) (ST 15-25) Minute village in flat willow-bordered, meadow country to the north of the Tone, with a small red sandstone church tucked away behind its Manor Farm. This church has a Perpendicular window complete with stained glass, thought to have come from Taunton Priory. Walk south from here, across the meadows to Nynehead, and return northwards via Weekmoor.

Oakford (181) (SS 90-21) Steeply sited on the side of a ridge between the deep, wooded valleys of the Exe and the Iron Mill Stream, this small village is dominated by the medieval tower of its otherwise rather plain 19th century church. To the north-west of the village is Oakfordbridge, a pretty hamlet beneath steep woods, with an old mill on the Exe.

Walk south-west from the village, along a quiet road to Spurway Mill, then north up a wooded valley, and return eastwards along the road from Bowdens.

Oare (181) (SS 80-47) This scattered parish in the steep sided Oare Water valley was the location for the fictitious *Plovers Barrows Farm*, the home of John Ridd of R. D. Blackmore's *Lorna Doone,* and the old manor house that still stands close to the church was the fictional home of Farmer Snow, John Ridd's neighbour. The little church, which stands close by the manor, was the scene of one of the great dramas of *Lorna Doone*, the shooting of Lorna by the villainous Carver Doone on her wedding day, and for this reason alone, the church is over-visited. However it is a charming building in its own right, with early-19th century box pews, a fascinating piscina in the shape of a man's head held by cupped hands, and some attractively lettered monuments to the Spurrys, one of whom painted the weird panel nearby depicting Moses.

There is also a monument in the church to the man who brought such fame to the parish, the author of *Lorna Doone*, R. D. Blackmore himself, whose grandfather was the rector here from 1809 to 1842. Blackmore, who stayed with his grandfather as a boy, later came back here, and is said to have written parts of *Lorna Doone* while staying at nearby Parsonage Farm, which he used, along with Yenworthy Farm (between the A39 and the coast) as settings for raids by the Doones.

Our **Walk 5**, page 116, starts from Malmsmead, a little to the west, but it is also possible to walk due south, up over South Common, and then south-west, past Larkbarrow and Alderman's Barrow, and on to Exford (SS 85-38). It is also possible to walk north, to the car park on the A39 near Yenworthy Common, and then east to Culbone, or west to County Gate and on northwards to Glenthorne.

Old Cleeve (181) (ST 03-41) Compact village on a small hill looking westwards along the coast to Minehead and the outline of North Hill beyond. The handsome limestone church is almost entirely Perpendicular and owes some of its highly refined style to its connections with Cleeve Abbey, although money for the construction of the tower was actually left to the parish in 1533, in the will of a certain John Tucker. See especially the octagonal font, the elegant 18th century brass chandelier, and the effigy of a 15th century civilian in a recess, with a cat at his feet trapping a long tailed mouse beneath its paw. There is a tombstone in the churchyard of blacksmith, George Jones, with a charming epitaph which concludes:

My Coal is burnt, my Iron's gone,
My Nails are drove, my work is done.

At Linton, on the west side of the village, is the interesting factory of John Wood, which has been making a range of sheepskin products for over a hundred years. It is possible to visit the factory, showroom and seconds shop. *(Tel: 0984 40291.)*

Over Stowey (181) (ST 18-38) Quaint little village at the foot of the wooded combes that characterise the eastern slopes of the Quantocks. The over-restored church contains carved bench-ends, and an attractive early-19th century wall monument. At Adscombe, to the south, there are the ivy-clad ruins of a medieval chapel, known as 'Monks' Chapel'. For details of a nearby Forestry Commission car park, camp site, picnic place and forest walk, see Rams Combe, page 67. For an interesting account of life in Over Stowey and the surrounding countryside in the early years of the 19th century read *'Paupers and Pig Killers'*, the diary of William Holland, who was vicar here from 1779, and who kept this record between 1799 and 1818.

Parkham (190) (SS 38-21) Modest village in undulating country between the valley of the little River Yeo and the woodlands of Melbury Forest. The thatched Bell Inn serves beer from the wood and a good selection of food. The largely 15th century church has a fine Norman south doorway, and a font of the same period, standing on a floor of medieval Barnstaple tiles. Some of the ancestors of John Gay, of *The Beggar's Opera* fame, lived at Goldworthy, a hamlet about a mile to the north of the village.

Parracombe (180) (SS 66-44) Steeply sited village tucked away in the valley of the Heddon, only two miles from its source, 1300 feet up on Exmoor. The main A39 road and the course of the old Lynton and Barnstaple Railway (see page 60) curve round the hillside above it, and between the two is situated Parracombe's old church. This was almost demolished in 1878, when the new church was built, but a protest by John Ruskin, among others, led to its rescue. Having never been 'restored' by unsympathetic Victorians, it remains one of those rare churches with an unspoilt 17th and 18th century interior, with box pews, a screen with tympanum, and a pulpit with reader's and clerk's desks attached. Holwell Castle is a medieval motte and bailey castle, the circular earthworks of which are situated to the south of the new church.

Walk south-east from Parracombe to visit Chapman Barrows and the Long Stone (see page 57), and experience some of the remote 'high places' of western Exmoor. Also walk northwards, down the wooded Heddon valley to Hunter's Inn, linking with our **Walk 8**, page 122.

Pilton (180) (SS 55-34) In Saxon times, this was more important than neighbouring Barnstaple, and although it now appears on the map to be no more than a suburb of this large and busy town, it has retained its own highly individual flavour. There are several pleasant old stone houses near the church, which is itself approached beneath an archway in the convincingly 'antique' 19th century almshouses. From here it is possible to walk up a cobbled pathway to the church's south door.

Pilton was a priory church of the Benedictines until the Dissolution in 1536, and although much altered about that time, there are still signs of its 13th century origins. The Chichester family purchased Pilton Priory soon after the Dissolution and evidence of their connection with Pilton is provided by the two splendid monuments to Sir John Chichester (1569) and Sir Robert (1627). See these two monuments and several others; also the ornate font cover, with a canopy similar to that at Swimbridge, the 16th century stone pulpit, and the fine rood screen.

At Pilton Bridge, on the A39 Lynton road, will be found the establishment of S. Sanders and Son, the oldest tannery in the south-west, which has been operating on this site for two hundred years. Visit the works and the showroom. *(Tel: 0271 42335.)* Woodside Gardens are situated just off the A39, 400 yards beyond the Fire Station. Here are two acres of largely south sloping gardens which will appeal particularly to the plantsman. *(Tel: 0271 43095.)*

Porlock (181) (SS 88-46) A large, but picturesque village situated astride the A39, between Exmoor and the sea. It is always busy throughout the holiday season, but its character inns, its restaurants and bright shops, and its colourful cottage gardens make a visit here well worthwhile. It has several attractive buildings, including the Old Ship Inn, a favourite of the poet Southey, who appears to have written some of his verse by its fireside, including the perhaps rather unwelcome lines:

Porlock, I shall forget thee not,
Here by the unwelcome summer rain
confined

The mainly 13th century church of St Dubricius,

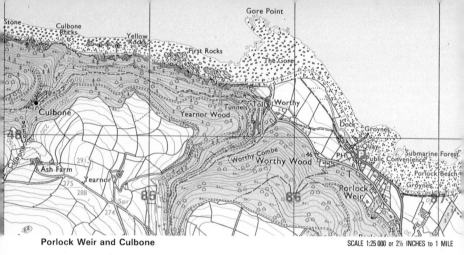

Porlock Weir and Culbone

SCALE 1:25 000 or 2½ INCHES to 1 MILE

with its fine porch and splendidly canopied tomb of Sir John and Lady Harrington, is well worth visiting. St Dubricius was the first Bishop of Llandaff, and the church here no doubt owes its origins to Welsh missionaries who crossed the Bristol Channel to convert the heathen peasants along its southern shores. Close by the church is the 15th century Doverhay Court, which houses a Tourist Information Centre and small museum.

The main A39 road westwards out of Porlock is notoriously steep, but there is a well graded toll road, which branches to the right just beyond the Ship Inn, at the bottom of the hill, with a toll house over half way up the hill. This joins the A39 at Porlock Common. There is a second toll road starting at Porlock Weir, and this joins the A39 at Culbone Stables Inn.

South of Porlock Common, on the west side of a minor road going southwards over the moors to Exford, will be found a small prehistoric stone circle of forty three stones, with about ten still standing (SS 84-44). This almost certainly dates from the Bronze Age, and must have been contemporary with Stonehenge, a stone circle of obviously vastly greater proportions.

Walking possibilities from Porlock are almost limitless: north to the shores of Porlock Bay; north-east to Bossington, Allerford and Selworthy; south-east to Horner and the lush Horner Woods beyond; south to Stoke Pero and the heights of Dunkery Beacon; south-west up through beautifully wooded Hawk Combe; and west to Porlock Weir and Culbone. Our **Walk 3**, page 112, starts from Porlock.

Porlock Weir (181) (SS 86-47) This is Porlock's miniature harbour, lying at the foot of great woodlands about a mile and a half to the west of the main village, which the sea has deserted long ago. There are three hotels including the Ship Inn, one or two attractive shops, and a coarse pebbly beach. To obtain the best view of the quayside and the charming cottages along it, walk out to the end of the little harbour wall. The harbour is a pleasant base for sailing and sea fishing, and there are fine views to be had from the woodland paths above it. Walk west from the Worthy Toll Gate, up through Yearnor Wood, to the little church at Culbone (see page 41). Or walk south-west up via Pitt Farm, Smalla Combe, across the A39 by Culbone Stables Inn, and down to Robber's Bridge (see page 67).

Putsborough (180) (SS 44-40) Pleasant hamlet with a thatched manor house overlooking a small ford. Nearby Putsborough Sand lies at the southern end of the great stretch of Woolacombe Sand. Walk north to Woolacombe, either along the Sand, or along the low cliffs behind; (see Woolacombe, page 86) or walk westwards to Baggy Point, and around to Croyde Bay.

The Quantocks (181, 182) The Quantocks are a hill ridge about three miles wide and about twelve miles in length. Their tops are seldom higher than twelve hundred feet, and are turf covered, with bracken, whortleberry and heather in plenty. Among their gentler eastern slopes are a series of beautifully wooded combes, almost all of which may be explored on foot, and most of which link on to a central spine track running in a north-westerly direction from Lydeard Hill (see page 59) to West Quantoxhead (see page 82). Car parks will be found at both these ends of the 'spine track', and also at the Triscombe Stone (see page 76), and Dead Woman's Ditch (see page 42). There are superlative views from this track, northwards out over the Bristol Channel to the South Wales coast, east to the Mendips, southwards out over the Vale of Taunton Deane to the Black Down Hills, and west to the dark outlines of Exmoor. Red deer were introduced to the Quantocks from Exmoor in the 1860s, but for details see Natural History, page 13.

Quarts Moor (181) (ST 15-16) A small parking area on the north side of the spine road along the Black Down Hills, with fine views out over the Vale of Taunton Deane to the Quantocks. There are pleasant walks in the surrounding woodlands.

Rackenford (181) (SS 85-18) An enviably quiet village in high, rather featureless country, with a welcoming old inn, the Stag, which serves good bar meals. The small 15th century church has a ceiled wagon-roof, with a series of rather rustic carved angels supported on corbels. Walk westwards over rolling countryside to West Backstone, to link on to the Two Moors Way (see page 76).

Raddington (181) (ST 02-25) Here in a remote valley to the south of Heydon Hill, is a solitary church perched on the top of a small hill, which can only be approached by a steep pathway. The rood screen probably dates back to about 1400, but is not in a good state of preservation. See also the 13th century octagonal font, and the ancient south door with its decorated iron hinges.

Rams Combe (181) (ST 16-37) Here in this thickly wooded combe is a car park, a camp site, and a picnic site, with a forest trail close by. The picnic site is in the valley bottom, surrounded by mature Douglas fir and conifers. The nearby Quantock Forest Trail, for which there is a guide leaflet, climbs through mixed woodland, and through remnants of old oak coppice and birch, crossing a stream to a viewpoint at Lord's Ball (not marked on Map 181).

Roadwater (181) (ST 03-38) This is a long thin village straggling up the valley of the little Washford River, with an attractively signed inn, The Valiant Soldier. There are interesting traces of the long vanished iron ore railway, that once ran down from the workings on the Brendon Hills to Watchet (see Brendon Hills, page 31). Walk south along part of the disused track, to Leighland Chapel (ST 03-36), and up over the hills to Treborough, or Comberow.

Robber's Bridge (181) (SS 82-46) A pleasant old bridge across the Oare Water stream in a deep moorland valley. The bridge itself is not exceptional, but the surrounding scenery is some of the loveliest to be found in the whole area. It also provides some indication of the rewards attainable by those who are prepared to walk up some of the valleys away from the roads at many points all over Exmoor. There is a car park at this very popular point of call.

Roborough (180) (SS 57-17) Small village in high watershed country, with a stream in the parish running west to the Torridge, and one not far away, running east to the Taw. The church was heavily restored in 1868, and is not of great interest to visitors. There is a pleasantly wooded road leading westwards down into a steep sided valley, and it is possible to walk southwards from Great Barlington, over a switchback route, to Beaford.

Rockford (180) (SS 75-47) Here are a few houses in the deep, wooded valley of the East Lyn River, with a shop selling local craft-work situated opposite the popular Rockford Inn. Walk down the valley from here, beside the sparkling East Lyn, to Watersmeet and Lynmouth; or walk south, up on to the moors, crossing high Shilstone Hill, before reaching the B3223 at the Dry Bridge car park (SS 76-45).

Romansleigh (180) (SS 72-20) Small hill-top village with a series of neatly thatched cottages, and fine views of Exmoor to its north. The church was rebuilt in the latter half of the 19th century, and is not of great interest to visitors. Just to the north of the churchyard are the fragmentary remains of St Rumon's Well, said to be the site of baptisms carried out in the Dark Ages by the Celtic saint, from whom the village took its name.

Rose Ash (180) (SS 78-21) Delightful little village whose hill-top setting on a long ridge provides distant views of both Exmoor and Dartmoor. There is a village green overlooked by a manor house and church, the latter being largely rebuilt in 1888. Despite this, the interior is still worth visiting, as its contents include a 15th century rood screen, and Jacobean screens on the south and west side of a chancel chapel which incorporates the arms of James I, Anne of Denmark and Prince Henry (1618). There is also a screen of about the same date, enclosing the Southcombe Chapel. No fewer than eight generations of the Southcombe family were rectors here, from 1675 until 1948, and most of them lie in the churchyard. Walk west and south-west from Rose Ash along a bridleway to Meshaw.

Rosemoor Gardens (180) (SS 50-18) Situated in the Torridge valley, on the B3220 about a mile to the south-east of Great Torrington, these delightful woodland gardens include rhododendrons, ornamental trees and shrubs, scree and alpine beds, and a young arboretum. They are now owned and managed by the Royal Horticultural Society.

St Giles in the Wood (180) (SS 53-18) The Hon. Mark Rolle built the great Victorian mansion of Stevenstone, well to the north-west of the village, and he also paid for the rebuilding of the church in the village. Neither building has found favour with later generations, but at least the contents of the church include a series of monumental brasses which are well worth inspecting. Do not expect woodlands hereabouts, apart from a large Forestry Commission wood to the north of Stevenstone, and in a valley well to the east of the village.

Sampford Arundel (181) (ST 10-18) Although not far from the slopes of the Black Down Hills, this small village is isolated from them by the M5 motorway. Its church has a slim 13th century tower, but the rest is a 19th century rebuild. It is however worth visiting to see the sculpture in a niche in the north aisle of a heart held by two hands. This probably indicated the burial of a heart nearby, a practice that sometimes took place when the body of the person concerned could not be brought back for burial in entirety. The village takes its name from the Norman knight Roger Arundel, who led the central part of the Conqueror's army at Hastings, and who was given the manor as part of his reward.

It was on the main railway near here in 1904, that the Great Western Railway's 'City of Truro' became the first locomotive in the world to exceed 100 mph.

Sampford Brett (181) (ST 08-40) Small village in the valley of the Doniford Stream, with views eastwards to the smooth flanks of the Quantock Hills. The undistinguished exterior of the church conceals a stylish early-19th century interior, the contents of which include a battered effigy, believed to be that of Richard de Brett, one of the four knights who murdered Archbishop St Thomas à Becket, at his own altar at Canterbury in the year 1170. The leader of these knights, Sir Reginald Fitzurse, was born at the manor of Orchard, now Orchard Wyndham, which lies to the west of Sampford Brett (ST 07-39). See also, in Sampford church, the bench-end commemorating the macabre story of Florence Wyndham, who is supposed to have come back to life only a short time before she was due to be buried in the family vault.

SAMPFORD PEVERELL

Walk south-west from here, up over the hills to Monksilver, and on to Sticklepath (ST 04-36).

Sampford Peverell (181) (ST 03-14) Once a borough with an annual fair and a weekly market, this village has a church with 13th century nave and chancel, and an ambitious south aisle added in 1498 by Margaret Beaufort, the mother of our first Tudor king, Henry VII. Although heavily restored in the 1860s, it is a fine building, the contents of which include a Norman font, the mutilated effigy of a 13th century knight, thought to be Sir Hugh Peverell, who went on crusade to the Holy Land; and a brass of Lady Margaret Poulett (1602), who was the wife of Sir Amyas Poulett, the 'keeper' of Mary Queen of Scots at Tutbury, Chartley and Fotheringay castles, and who was himself buried in the family chapel at Hinton St George, near Ilminster.

The Grand Western Canal passes right through the village, and several cottages had to be demolished during its construction in about 1811. During the cattle fair held in that year there was a riot by about three hundred navvies, angered by delays in the payment of their wages, and one was shot while they were attacking a house in the village. There is a pleasant enclosed picnic area here, which gives good access to the attractive canal towpath ... all part of the Grand Western Canal Country Park.(See page 48.)

The Grand Western Canal at Sampford Peverell.

Satterleigh (180) (SS 66-22) Here, in undulating plateau country above the deep Mole valley, is a minute hamlet which has a delightful little 15th century church. Once inside the old south door in its original wooden frame, the visitor will find early-19th century inscriptions on its 'tympanum' screen between nave and chancel, a 17th century pulpit and a series of charming Victorian hat pegs. Do not miss a visit here.

Saunton (180) (SS 45-37) Just a few houses and a large hotel, all close to the B3231, with splendid views out over Saunton Sands, which stretch southwards to the mouth of the Taw and Torridge. There is a car park, from where it is possible to walk the three miles to Airy Point (SS 45-33). Watch out for flags marking possible danger areas on the fringes of Braunton Burrows.

Selworthy (181) (SS 91-46) This is delightfully situated beneath the wooded slopes of Selworthy Beacon (see below), looking south towards the bare

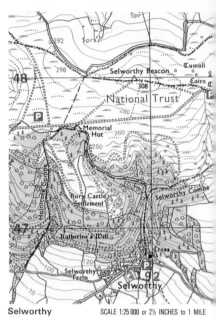

Selworthy   SCALE 1:25 000 or 2½ INCHES to 1 MILE

northern slopes of Dunkery Beacon on Exmoor. Owned by the National Trust, its seven entrancing cottages are grouped around a little green below the church, and are complete with thatch, gabled porches, round painted chimneys and lattice windows. The white-painted church has an interesting interior, the contents of which include a splendid wagon-roof with bosses, shields and angels; an 18th century west gallery and no fewer than three Acland monuments by the sculptor Sir Francis Chantrey. There is a National Trust Information Centre and shop at Selworthy, and a car park at the top of the village, by the church. It is possible to walk north from here, up through woods, above which are the earthworks of an Iron Age settlement, Bury Castle, and beyond, past the 'Wind and Weather' Memorial Hut, erected by John Acland in memory of his father, to Selworthy Beacon and Bossington Hill.

Selworthy Beacon (181) (SS 91-48) This fine stretch of hill country rising to over a thousand feet above sea level, may be reached by a long road westward from Minehead, or by steep paths up from Bossington, Allerford or Selworthy itself. There are fine views northwards, out over the Bristol Channel to the South Wales coast, or inland to the dark outlines of Dunkery Beacon, and other parts of eastern Exmoor. For neighbouring North Hill, see page 63.

Shebbear (190) (SS 43-09) Quiet village in remote countryside to the east of the infant Torridge, with the 17th century Devil's Stone Inn (beer from the wood, bar meals and separate restaurant) looking out over a large square. The name of this inn reminds us that here, on each November 5th, the villagers hold a ceremony to turn over the Devil's Stone, a large rock weighing about a ton, of a type similar to the stones of Stonehenge, and which like them, must have come from the Preseli Hills in

Dyfed (S.W.Wales). The ceremony is intended to ensure that the Devil does not get too much rest. This stone lies on the green, not far from the entrance to the churchyard, and the partly-14th century church standing beyond is worth visiting. Its contents include a pleasantly ornamented Norman south doorway, and an Elizabethan or early Jacobean pulpit with crude carvings of grotesque men and women holding musical instruments, flowers and torches ... perhaps parishioners at their Devil's Stone turning ceremony ?

Shipload Bay (190) (SS 24-27) Small, partly sheltered cove with a little shingly beach, which can best be reached from a car park at the entrance to East Titchberry Farm (SS 24-27), off the minor road between the A39 at Clovelly Dykes and Hartland Point. There is a dramatic and demanding cliff walk eastwards from here to Clovelly, following the course of the North Devon Coastal Path, via Chapman Rock (SS 26-27), Exmanworthy Cliff (SS 27-27), Windbury Point (SS 26-28), and Mouth Mill (SS 26-29) (see page 63). Use the excellent National Trust leaflet, *Clovelly to Hartland Point*.

Shirwell (180) (SS 59-37) Small village lying to the west of the beautifully wooded valley of the Yeo. It was here that Sir Francis Chichester, the first of the great single-handed yachtsmen, spent much of his early life, as his father was rector here. Both father and son are buried in the churchyard. A branch of the Chichester family lived at Youlston, to

Shirwell ... early home and last resting place of circumnavigator, Sir Francis Chichester.

the west of the village, and at Arlington Court, to the north (see page 23), and Shirwell church has many connections with them. The church dates back to the 13th century, and its most unusual feature is a rough-hewn timber pier supporting part of the entrance to the north transept. There is a 15th century effigy of a lady in the chancel, above which is a wall monument to Lady Anne Chichester (1723). Although this church was considerably restored in the 19th century, it has retained a most pleasing atmosphere. Walk north from here, up the Yeo valley to Arlington Court.

Simonsbath (180) (SS 77-39) Situated at the very heart of Exmoor, this beautifully sited village shelters in the valley of the Barle, and is overlooked by hillsides planted with larch and fir. There is an

The River Barle at Simonsbath.

hotel, the hospitable Exmoor Forest, and an interesting pottery and craft gallery. There is also excellent fishing to be had on the Barle. It is possible to walk south-eastwards from Simonsbath, down the valley of the Barle, linking on to the Two Moors Way near the oval Iron Age settlement of Cow Castle (SS 79-37). From here walkers can head west and then north-west, to join the B3358 near Cornham Farm, and return on this road to the village.

Nobody knows for certain why this village is called 'Simon's Bath', but a deep pool in the Barle about a hundred yards above the bridge is the legendary bathing place of a much-feared local brigand called Simon. Simonsbath appears to have been the centre of the Royal Forest of Exmoor since Norman times, and in the 17th century Simonsbath House was built by James Boevey, a Forest Warden during the Commonwealth period. In 1818 all the remaining royal interests were offered for sale, and most of the land was purchased by John Knight, a prosperous Worcestershire iron-master. Vast sums of money were spent by John Knight and his son, upon the reclamation of great tracts of derelict moorland, and much of the pattern of present-day Exmoor farming is due to their persistent pioneer work.

The Knights lived at Simonsbath for most of the 19th century, but by 1900 they had sold their estates to Lord Fortescue, whose family had been Devonshire landowners for many generations. Today however the Fortescues' Exmoor holdings have been sold off and are now fragmented. During the course of the last fifty years many further encroachments have been made upon the surviving wild areas of Exmoor, and the conflict of interests continues between landowners anxious to develop their assets and those who wish to preserve the open spaces.

The cairn on the west side of the road leading south-westwards from Simonsbath (SS 75-38), was erected in memory of Sir John Fortescue (1859-1933), the fifth son of the third Earl Fortescue. He was Librarian at Windsor Castle from 1905 to 1926, and wrote a sixteen volume *History of the British Army*. He should perhaps be best remembered for his moving introduction to the first edition of Henry Williamson's splendid book, *Tarka the Otter*. This edition of only a hundred copies was printed and published privately by the author, and Sir John's introduction must have been a great encouragement for Williamson. For *Tarka the Otter*, see pages 48 & 79.

Skilgate (181) (SS 98-27) An unexceptional village at the head of a valley running south-westwards from Haddon Hill, with a church built as late as 1872. There is a pleasant walk down the valley into Skilgate Wood, but unfortunately this stops short at the Devon county border. The great reservoir of Wimbleball is not far away to the north.

The Somerset and North Devon Coastal Path

This runs from Minehead to the Cornish border at Welcombe Mouth, and is part of the South West Way, which runs on around the Cornish coast, and along the South Devon and Dorset coast, as far as Poole. There is a small break in the area of the Taw and Torridge estuaries, but it otherwise forms an almost complete path along the coastline covered by this guide — a length of 82 miles. The South West Way as a whole covers a distance of 572 miles. See 'Further Reading', page 144.

South Molton (180) (SS 71-25) Lively little town which has had the right to hold a market here on each Thursday since the 14th century, and which was once very prosperous with the woollen industry. The coming of the railways did much to

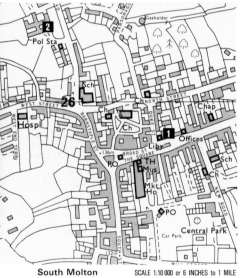

South Molton   SCALE 1:10 000 or 6 INCHES to 1 MILE

1 Tourist Information Centre
2 Quince Honey Farm

undermine South Molton's prosperity, both as a market centre and a coaching halt, but it now bustles with activity once again, especially in the summer. The grandfather of the great painter, J.M.W. Turner, was a saddler here, but Turner's father and mother had left South Molton some time before their son was born.

The town has an extremely handsome Georgian Guildhall, with a 19th century Market House beside it, both of which look across a broad main street towards a prettily overhung pathway leading up to the church. This is a largely 14th century building with a very grand interior. See especially the lovely stone pulpit and font, both 15th century work. There is a **Tourist Information Centre (1)** at 1,

East Street *(tel: 07695 4122/2378).* While in the town do not miss a visit to the **Quince Honey Farm (2)**. Visitors may watch the bees at work producing their honey in a very large indoor apiary, and there are special glass booths which make it possible to watch the fascinating activity from all sides. *(Tel: 07695 2401.)*

Walk north-east from here, following the track of the long-vanished mineral railway, up the valley of the River Mole, to North Molton.

Speke's Mill Mouth (190) (SS 22-23) A small beach in a cove, with a stream falling over the cliff edge into a pool before flowing into the sea. This dramatic waterfall may be visited on foot from the tiny hamlet of Lymebridge, using a path that forms part of our **Walk 11, page 128.** It may also be reached by walking south from the car park at Hartland Quay (SS 22-24).

Stawley (181) (ST 06-22) Here on the eastern slopes of the well wooded upper Tone valley are a few houses and a largely unspoilt little church with Norman origins, looking across to the village of Ashbrittle. Over the west doorway, below the tower, there is a charming frieze of panels dated 1523, asking all who come this way to pray for the

Quiet countryside near Stawley.

souls of Henry Howe and his wife. Beyond the 13th century south door with its ancient iron hinges, ceiled wagon-roofs look down on a delightful interior, the contents of which include a tall 18th century pulpit with domed canopy, and old box pews. While in the village do not overlook the letter box produced in 1857-59 by Smith and Hawkes of Birmingham. Only seven of these original standard wall boxes, known to enthusiasts as WB72s, now survive. If possible, walk down into the valley, and head north beside the Tone, along a path which heads in the direction of Waterrow (ST 05-25).

Stogumber (181) (ST 09-37) An exceptionally beautiful village in undulating country between the Brendon Hills and the Quantocks. It has colour-washed and thatched cottages, and cobbled pavements lining a street sloping up towards a group comprised of 17th century almshouses, the attractive White Horse Inn and a handsome red sandstone church opposite. The church was considerably enriched by Cardinal Beaufort, one of Joan of Arc's judges, who used to come here for the hunting; and it has a spacious and most interesting interior. See

Stogumber . . . in undulating country between the Brendon Hills and the Quantocks.

especially the carved bench-ends, the north aisle roof wagon-roof, the brass candelabra, the elaborate tomb of Sir George Sydenham (1597) and his two wives, and in the south chapel, the handsome monument to George Musgrove (1742) which is probably the work of the fashionable sculptor J.M.Rysbrack. Also do not miss the turret stairway to the rood loft, with its original 15th century door and door handle.

Stoke (190) (SS 23-24) This minute thatched hamlet, less than a mile from the sea, is dominated by the 130-foot tower of Hartland's parish church of St Nectan, the highest in all Devon. A landmark for miles around, this lofty pinnacled tower has an original figure of St Nectan in a niche in its east face. The church dates from about 1350 and has a spacious interior containing the largest screen in the county, fine wagon-roofs, some interesting bench-ends, a beautifully carved Norman font, and an elaborate altar tomb. There is a small museum in the priest's room, above the north porch. Stoke is on our **Walk 11**, page 128. It is also possible to walk north-west from here, close to the little Abbey River, to join the North Devon Coastal Path near its mouth.

Stoke Pero (181) (SS 87-43) A small hamlet high up on the slopes of Dunkery Beacon, looking down over the great woodlands of Holnicote. An oft quoted verse reads:

Culbone, Oare, and Stoke Pero,
Parishes three where no parson'll go.

Culbone is now the only one of the three still inaccessible by car, but it is a long steep road up to Stoke Pero, and on a dark winter day, it still seems very remote up here. The little saddle-back towered church situated close to a farm, has been extensively restored, but there are light oak pews, and a tower-arch opening into a rugged tower interior, in which there is a 15th century doorway. There is also a fine old south door fitted into a frame constructed of only two massive pieces of oak, which seems singularly appropriate in a setting as remote as this.

Stoke Pero is on our **Walk 3**, page 112, coming

up through the Horner Woods, but it is also possible to walk south-east, up a minor road, and then across country, to Dunkery Beacon.

Stoke Rivers (180) (SS 63-35) Small village in high country with wide views westwards out over wooded valleys running towards the Yeo. The tall towered church was much restored in the 19th century, but retains a few items of interest including a pulpit with Renaissance panels, some 18th century panelling, and a font with a delightful 17th century cover. Walk south from here, via Great Beccott, to Gunn, and return northwards after walking a short distance along a road to the west.

Stoodleigh (181) (SS 92-18) Compact little village grouped around its old school, cottages and church. The latter is largely 15th century, and has a fine wagon-roof above its south aisle, and a stout

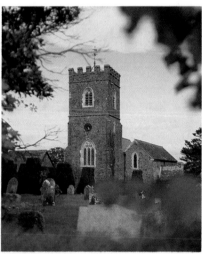

Stoodleigh Church.

Norman font with two primitive faces on its shaft. The village stands in high country to the west of the deep set Exe valley, its steep sides clad with lush woodlands.

Well to the west is Stoodleigh Beacon (SS 88-18), which at 987 feet above sea level, is the highest point between Exmoor and Dartmoor. Risdon, the 17th century Devonshire topographer, states that a beacon was set up here in 1326, on the orders of Edward II, when he was worried about the landing of his queen, Isabella of France, who was plotting against him with the infamous Roger Mortimer. He had every right to be worried as he was subsequently deposed and suffered a horrible death at Berkeley Castle in Gloucestershire. Despite the radio mast, there are fine all-round views from the Beacon.

Stringston (181) (ST 17-42) Small village in dullish country to the east of the Quantocks. There are the remains of a medieval cross in the churchyard with a Crucifixion just discernible, and inside the much restored church, there is a handsome 18th century monument to John St Albyn, a member of the family who once owned Alfoxton Park, the house which they let for a year to William Wordsworth and his sister Dorothy. Fairfield House, well to the east of the village (ST 18-42) is a fine Elizabethan building. It is just visible from the road, but is not open to the public.

Sutcombe (190) (SS 34-11)

Sutcombe (190) (SS 34-11) Situated 500 feet above sea level, in remote country above the little River Waldon, Sutcombe is a small village looking southwards over unspoilt countryside. There are dark grey terrace cottages behind the church and pleasingly lettered tombstones in the churchyard. Although the tower and south doorway are older, the rest of the church is Perpendicular. It was apparently remote enough to escape the more rabid enthusiasms of the Victorian 'restorers', and retains a most pleasing warmth of feeling. There are many fine bench-ends, a well restored screen, and a wide area of Barnstaple tiles with patterns in high relief. See also the gorgeous carved pulpit with its tall Renaissance panels, the simple granite arcading, and the 18th century memorials to Jonathan Prideaux and his son-in-law, Charles Davie, a man 'who really feared God'.

Swimbridge (180) (SS 62-29)

Swimbridge (180) (SS 62-29) Pleasant village in a valley, with some of its cottages attractively sited on hillsides above. The Jack Russell Inn lies close to the churchyard where John ('Jack') Russell is buried. He was rector here for forty eight years from

Swimbridge Church . . . a medieval spire and a fascinating interior.

1833, and apart from being a great hunting man, he was the original breeder of those splendidly bouncy little terriers, the Jack Russells.

Russell's church has one of Devon's three medieval spires, and it also contains a wealth of interesting interior details, including partly ceiled and painted wagon-roofs, and one of Devon's finest rood screens (perhaps a little too completely restored). See also the delightfully coloured stone pulpit (*c1500*) and the fascinating font cover with its richly carved Renaissance detail.

Tamar Lakes (190) (SS 29-11)

Tamar Lakes (190) (SS 29-11) For most of its length the River Tamar marks the border between

Devon and Cornwall, and the northernmost of these two reservoirs on the upper reaches of that river is in fact astride this border. There is a large car park on the shore of this Upper Lake complete with a shop, and there is fly fishing and a dinghy sailing club here. The Lower Lake, with the county boundary on its western shore, is best reached from the road between Thurdon and Soldon Cross, and it offers fine bird watching and coarse fishing. The key to the bird observation hide here is obtainable from the Warden at the Upper Lake, and there is a pleasant nature trail down the western shore of the Lower Lake.

Tapeley Park (180) (SS 47-29)

Tapeley Park (180) (SS 47-29) The home of the Christie family of Glyndebourne, this large Georgian

Tapeley Park . . . Georgian mansion and Italian garden.

mansion has a restored neo-Georgian facing, and contains fine plasterwork ceilings, furniture and porcelain. There is a long drive with rhododendrons, formal 'Italian' gardens complete with statuary and palm trees, and a woodland lake. There are splendid views out across the Taw and Torridge estuary to Appledore and Braunton Burrows. The 'Queen Anne Dairy' tea room is open for refreshments, and there is a craft shop, a plant and produce shop, a putting green and a picnic area. (*Tel: Instow 860528.*)

Tarr Steps (181) (SS 86-32)

Tarr Steps (181) (SS 86-32) These make up a long low bridge of massive stone slabs averaging about seven feet in length and three foot six inches in width, resting on roughly erected piers which project on either side of the slabs. It has sometimes been claimed that this bridge had its origins in the Bronze Age, but it is almost certainly a medieval pack-horse bridge, and similar in origin to the clapper bridges found on Dartmoor.

Tarr Steps span the sparkling River Barle and are overlooked from the north and west by delightfully wooded banks. There is a good car park a short distance to the north-east, and refreshments are available at Tarr Farm overlooking the bridge. Come here if possible early on a summer morning, or at any time in late autumn. But if there are too many crowds about, walk up the valley of the Barle, making use of our Walk 4, page 114, or walk down the valley via Hawkridge and Mounsey Castle (SS 88-29) to Dulverton. Walking enthusiasts will be interested to learn that Tarr Steps are astride the Two Moors Way (see page 76).

Taunton (193) (ST 22-24) Situated in the broad Vale of Taunton Deane, between the southern end of the Quantocks and the long line of the Black Down Hills, this busy and colourful county town is well worth exploring in detail. Its varied roof lines are dominated by two splendid church towers, both carefully rebuilt in the 19th century. The red sandstone tower of *St Mary Magdalene (1)*, which lies to the east of the Market House and to the west of the little footway, *Whirligig Lane*, is especially fine, and the interior of the church contains several items of interest including a memorial to Thomas More (1576) and a full size figure of Robert Graye (1635). The bells of St Mary's are a special feature, and various tunes are rendered, including, 'Oh, We come up from Somerset', which, we are told, tends to be played when the County Cricket Team are playing on the nearby ground.

St Mary Magdalene stands at the end of *Hammet Street (2)*, which was laid out in 1788 by Sir Benjamin Hammet, M.P. for Taunton, and is an early example of conscious town planning, with its terraces of handsome Georgian houses, each with its white portico. The mellow brick 18th century *Market House (3)* has a handsome doorway, but is not otherwise of great interest to visitors. The half-timbered *Tudor House (4)* in Fore Street is dated

1578, and was the home of Sir William Portman, who took the Duke of Monmouth as his prisoner to London, following his defeat at nearby Sedgemoor in 1685 and subsequent capture. The ill-fated Duke was later executed.

Walk from here up *Castle Bow*, through an archway with portcullis, beside the attractive Castle Hotel, into the rather confusing confines of *The Castle (5)* itself. Here may be seen the Gate House and the Great Hall, where Judge Jeffreys held his 'bloody assize' after the Battle of Sedgemoor, the disastrous culmination of a foolhardy venture now referred to as 'The Pitchfork Rebellion'. Even before Jeffreys began his work, the infamous Colonel Kirke and his soldiers (usually referred to as 'Kirke's lambs') slaughtered up to about a hundred fugitives in and around Taunton. As a result of Jeffreys' assize, nearly two hundred prisoners were executed and over six hundred more were transported as slaves to the West Indies. The town was singled out by Kirke and Jeffreys because of its involvement in the proclamation of Monmouth's kingship, and the apparent enthusiasm for Monmouth's cause shown by many of its misguided inhabitants. These included 27 young ladies, the 'Maids of Taunton', one of whom, the unfortunate Mary Blake, had presented the Duke with a sword and a bible, and who was imprisoned in Dorchester Gaol and later

1 Church of St Mary
  Magdalene
2 Hammet Street
3 Market House
4 Tudor House

5 Taunton Castle, Somerset
  County Museum & Somerset
  Military Museum
6 Goodland Gardens
7 Brewhouse Theatre

8 Tourist Information Centre
9 Bath Place
10 Vivary Park
11 High Street

Taunton   SCALE 1:10 000 or 6 INCHES to 1 MILE

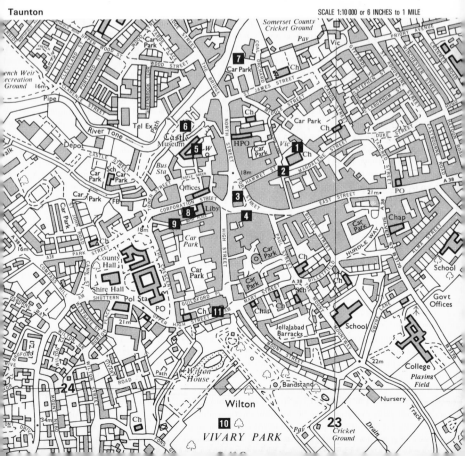

died there.

Here in the castle are also the **Somerset County Museum (5)** and the **Somerset Military Museum (5)**, with the bare frame of a half-timbered building displayed in the old moat, while beyond lie the pleasantly landscaped **Goodland Gardens (6)** with several paths beside the River Tone. One of these heads north-eastwards, going beyond the Bridge and past the **Brewhouse Theatre (7)**.

Further to the north there is a **Tourist Information Centre (8)** at the Central Library opposite the Municipal Buildings in Corporation Street (tel: 0823 274785/270479), while just to its south lies **Bath Place (9)**, a delightful mixture of old shops and cottages, and a market run by the W.I. on Wednesdays and Fridays. Well south from here is **Vivary Park (10)**, beyond the **High Street (11)**, a wide thoroughfare bordered by the many fine Georgian buildings that typify this handsome county town.

Tawstock (180) (SS 55-29) Quiet little thatched village with an 18th century Gothick mansion on a hill above. This is Tawstock Court, and was built in 1787 to replace an earlier house, of which only the splendid gatehouse (1574) survives. This is situated on the small road down to the church, which is itself delightfully sited on the slopes of a small combe overlooking the broad Taw valley. Tawstock church dates largely from the 14th century and has an interior unspoilt by over-restoration. It contains a bewildering quantity of beautiful things, which include a series of splendid monuments to the successive owners of Tawstock ... the Fitzwarrens, the Bourchiers and the Wreys. Do not miss the lovely plastered ceilings of the transepts, the little galleried walk to the tower, nor the carved French Renaissance manorial pew.

Thornbury (190) (SS 40-08) Small village in remote but undramatic countryside in the valley of the River Waldon not far from its confluence with the infant Torridge. The largely 14th century church has retained a Norman south doorway, and there is a substantial 17th century altar tomb, with the alabaster effigies of Sir John Specott and his wife Elizabeth, attended by four smaller kneeling figures, no doubt their children.

Visitors are welcome to look round the Waldon Fish Farm (Tel: Milton Damerel 426) where there is a shop and three acres of still-water fly fishing which is let on a day ticket basis.

Thorne St Margaret (181) (ST 09-21) Small village on a hill overlooking the River Tone, with a church that was rebuilt by the Victorians. They did however spare the 15th century tower, and inside will be found a red sandstone Norman font, and a 17th century brass to John Worth inscribed as follows:

John Worth lies here, and John is grace
And Worth doth virtue sound.
His virtue praise hath left on Earth,
His grace hath glory found.

At Wellisford, to the north of the village, the Grand Western Canal (see page 48) used to drop no less than eighty one feet, and this was dealt with, not by locks, but by an 'incline', with the boats being moved up and down on wheeled cradles. The farm, which incorporates cottages for the incline keepers and an engine house, is still called 'Incline Farm'. There is a right of way along the course of the old canal, which can be followed south-westwards from here to the vicinity of Holcombe Rogus, where the course of the water-filled, 'Country Park' section of the canal begins.

Timberscombe (181) (SS 95-42) Pleasantly sited in a well wooded valley between the great woodlands of Croydon Hill and the lower slopes of Dunkery Beacon, this attractive village has a largely 15th century church. Its door must have been inserted when most of the church was built, and still has its original metal-work, while the finely vaulted rood screen must be of about the same date. The west tower was built in the early 18th century, although the little pyramid-shaped top was added more than a hundred years later.

Walk south-east from here, through the Forestry Commission plantations of Croydon Hill, to Luxborough; or westwards, via Burrow or Wootton Courtenay, up on to Dunkery Beacon.

Tiverton (181) (SS 95-12) A bright and busy town, prosperous both as a market town and an industrial centre. Tiverton stands at the meeting point of the little River Lowman, with the larger Exe. There were fords across both rivers here, the two fords providing the basis for its ancient name 'Twyforde'. Writing in 1724, Daniel Defoe stated that: 'Next to Exeter, Tiverton is the greatest manufacturing town in the County and, next to it in wealth and in the numbers of people'. However its 17th and 18th century prosperity was already on the wane when John Heathcoat, a lace maker from Leicestershire, moved down here in the early 19th century following the destruction of his mill by Luddites. He brought a new surge of activity to the town, and although a number of other industries have grown up in more recent years, and Tiverton continues to thrive as a market centre, the John Heathcoat organisation is still very much the key to its present day prosperity.

The pink sandstone **Tiverton Castle (1)** is an ancient fortress, which once belonged to the powerful Courtenays, the Earls of Devon. Here, high above the River Exe, is a fine medieval gatehouse, a Joan of Arc Gallery, a Norman Tower with an interesting collection of clocks, and the romantic ruins of fortifications dismantled by General Fairfax after the castle's capture in 1645 towards the end of the Civil War. (Tel: Tiverton 253200.) The nearby **St Peter's Church (2)**, also standing high above the Exe, has a large interior, the contents of which include the tombs of two rich merchants, Waldron and Slee, both of whom provided sets of almshouses that may still be seen in the town. The splendid south porch was built in 1517 by another merchant, John Greenway, who also built the **Greenway Almshouses (3)** in Gold Street, to the east. At the end of Gold Street, beyond the bridge over the Lowman are the buildings of **Old Blundell's School (4)**, built by a local wool merchant in 1604, and now in the care of the National Trust. John Ridd of *Lorna Doone* went to school here, and fought Robin Snell on the lawn still known as the 'Ironing Box'. Blundell's moved to new buildings on the east of the town in 1882, but this was many years after R. D. Blackmore, the author of *Lorna Doone*, was a pupil here. The forecourt is open to pedestrians at all reasonable

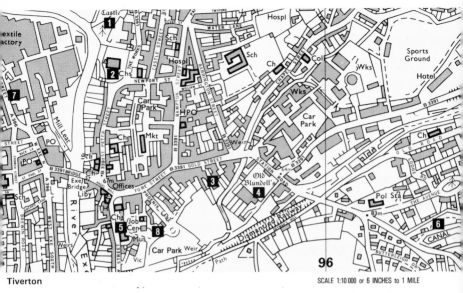

Tiverton

SCALE 1:10 000 or 6 INCHES to 1 MILE

1 Tiverton Castle
2 St Peter's Church
3 Greenway Almshouses

4 Old Blundell's School
5 Tiverton Museum
6 Grand Western Horseboat
  Company

7 John Heathcoat Factory Shop
8 Tourist Information Centre

hours.

See also the **Tiverton Museum (5)** in Andrew Street, which is a comprehensive local folk museum embodying a wagon gallery, natural history, wartime history, a Victorian laundry, Grand Western Canal, lace machine gallery, and many other items of interest, including a G.W.R. locomotive. *(Tel: Tiverton 256295.)*

For details of the **Grand Western Horseboat Company (6)**, which operates from Tiverton on the canal of that name, see page 49. While in Tiverton, visit the **Factory Shop of John Heathcoat & Co (7)**, which retails products of their group. During the summer months there is a **Tourist Information Centre (8)** at the town's main car park, in Phoenix Lane *(tel: Tiverton 255827).*

Tivington (181) (SS 93-45) Pretty hamlet below woodlands, with views south-westwards, out over a broad valley to the wooded lower slopes of Dunkery Beacon. There is a little thatched 15th century chapel which had been used as a cottage until it was restored in 1885. Walk east from here, up through woodlands and down beyond to Dunster.

Tolland (181) (ST 10-32) Compact village snugly situated in a valley below the eastern end of the Brendon Hills. The church overlooks a little stream and has a dumpy 13th century tower, but has otherwise been largely rebuilt. For Gaulden Manor, to its south-east, see page 48.

The Torrington Canal (180) (SS 47-20 etc) This was inspired by the Rolle family, landowners of Torrington. It was opened in 1827, from Torrington to the River Torridge near Bideford, where there was a tide-lock at Pillmouth (SS 46-24). It only

lasted until 1871, when part of its course was utilised by the South Western Railway. The fine five-arched stone aqueduct which carried the canal over the Torridge is still visible near Beam College (SS 47-20). Beyond, near Weare Giffard, there was an inclined plane used for transporting boats sixty feet down to the canal, which from this point ran at a lower level in the valley bottom. For details of the canal's history and its course, read Ronald Russell's excellent book, *Lost Canals & Waterways of Britain*.

Treborough (181) (ST 01-36) This hamlet is quietly situated beneath the northern slopes of the Brendon Hills and has a minute 19th century church containing a Perpendicular font with angels beneath its bowl. Not far from here are the remains of the long deserted iron mines of the Brendon Iron Ore Company, and in Eastern Wood about two miles to the south-east (ST 02-34) there are the remains of 'The Incline', the steepest section of the little mineral railway built in the 1850s between these mines and the harbour at Watchet (see also Brendon Hills, page 31).

Trentishoe (180) (SS 64-48) Here, just below the top of smooth Trentishoe Down, between a small wooded valley and a steep cliffed coast, is Trentishoe church. This is a small building close to a farm, and seemingly quite remote from the sea. It has been over-restored inside, with glossy tiles and pitch pine pews much in evidence. However there is a delightful little 18th century musicians' gallery, so small that a hole was cut into the parapet to accommodate the double-bass! For further details of this area, see the National Trust leaflet, *Heddon Valley and Woody Bay*.

Trentishoe is on our **Walk 8**, page 122, but it is also possible to walk south from here, up the

TRISCOMBE

Heddon valley to Parracombe, and beyond to the Long Stone, in the very heart of Exmoor.

Triscombe (181) (ST 15-35) An unspoilt hamlet beneath the Quantocks' highest point, Wills Neck (1260 feet above sea level). There is a colourful little inn, The Blue Ball, which has a skittle alley, and it is possible to walk from here up to the Triscombe Stone, which is also close to a good car park astride the 'spine track' along the Quantock ridge. This

The Blue Ball Inn, Triscombe.

park makes an especially good base for exploring the wooded combes on the eastern side of the hills. The Triscombe Stone itself is connected with old tales of 'the Devil, and the hounds of death', and in times past Quantock folk would ensure that they did not pass the stone at night, especially if it was a dark and stormy one. Rest assured, it is not too menacing on a bright summer's day.

Twitchen (180) (SS 78-30) Situated high up on the southern boundary of Exmoor, this remote and unspoilt hamlet looks southwards down a thickly wooded valley, out over the rolling hill country of mid-Devon. Its small church dates only from 1844, and apart from its tower and Norman tub font, is not of great interest to visitors.

Twitchen ... quiet hamlet on Exmoor's southern slopes.

The Two Moors Way (180, 181, 191, 202) This is a 'walking clearway' making use of footpaths, bridle-ways, and in certain instances public roads, right

across the county of Devon. It links Ivybridge, near Plymouth, with Lynton on the north coast, and takes in some fine moorland country over Dartmoor and Exmoor, as well as many miles of the less dramatic, but often very rewarding mid-Devon countryside. It enters the area covered by this guide near the village of Witheridge (181) (SS 80-14), and then heads in a northerly direction, past Bradford Mill, Knowstone, West Anstey, Tarr Steps, and, sharing one of its alternative routes with our **Walk 4**, page 114, thence to Withypool. Then up more of the Barle valley as far as Cow Castle (180) (SS 79-37), and westwards round to the south and west of Simonsbath, before heading up over high Exmoor and down into Lynton. For details of this exciting project read the booklet *Two Moors Way*, by Helen Rowett, and published by the Devon Ramblers' Association.

Uffculme (181) (ST 06-12) A large village on the River Culm, with several pleasant Georgian houses providing evidence of Uffculme's prosperity in the 18th century, when its serges were exported as far as Holland. The large church of St Mary has a steeple which was rebuilt in 1849, and inside will be found an unusually wide, early 15th century rood screen, and two interesting 17th century monuments in the Walrond Chapel.

Uffculme's connection with the woollen industry is still much in evidence today, at Coldharbour Mill. There has been a mill on this site since medieval times, and during the 18th century it was first a paper mill and then a grist mill. In 1797 it was converted to the processing of wool by Thomas Fox, but it is sad to relate that, after nearly two centuries, Fox Brothers have now been forced to close it due to the effects of recession. However it is now a fascinating 'Working Wool Museum', complete with massive water wheel, great steam engine, and a wide variety of spinning machinery and looms. There is also a restaurant, shop, picnic site and a riverside walk. *(Tel: Craddock 40960.)*

Walk westwards, up beside the Culm to Culmstock, crossing the river from south to north, at Five Fords (ST 08-13).

Umberleigh (180) (SS 60-23) The attractive Rising Sun Hotel overlooks Umberleigh's bridge over the beautiful River Taw flowing north to Barnstaple. There used to be a chapel here, but it was demolished in the 19th century, and its monuments moved to Atherington (see page 24).

Uplowman (181) (ST 01-15) Small village near the point where the little River Lowman emerges from the hills. The church here is believed to have been built in about 1500 by the mother of Henry VII, Margaret Beaufort, who at times lived at nearby Sampford Peverell, and who added the south aisle to the church there at about the same time. Heavy 'restoration' was carried out by those over enthusiastic Victorians in 1864, who almost rebuilt this church. About a mile to the south-west is Widhayes Farm (ST 00-14), which has a 17th century stone arch in its wall, with a fine old wooden door below.

Upton (181) (SS 99-28) Windy upland parish on Haddon Hill, almost a thousand feet above sea level, with a small Victorian church and the scanty ivy-clad remains of an earlier church, St James's, about a mile to the north-west, overlooking woods bordering Wimbleball Lake.

The Valley of Rocks (180) (SS 70-49) A rock-scattered valley running almost parallel with the coast, The Valley of Rocks inevitably caught the imagination of the Romantic poets, and was well described by the poet Southey. The valley is dominated by the Castle Rock, with its massive blocks of stone piled one upon the other. Other formations are known as the Devil's Cheesewring and Ragged Jack. A herd of wild goats are still to be found in the valley, and they can often be seen on high rocks, silhouetted against the skyline. It was here that Blackmore's John Ridd visited old Mother Meldrum, who lived here in a cave below the rocks.

There is a car park near the western end of the valley, but it is best approached from Lynton via North Walk or Hollerday Hill. Walk west from The Valley of Rocks to link on to our **Walk 7**, page 120, at the Lee Abbey Toll House.

Vellow (181) (ST 09-38) Modest hamlet to the north of Stogumber, and just above the valley of the little Doniford Stream. The Vellow Pottery, at the north end of the hamlet, is worth visiting. *(Tel: 0984 56458.)*

Walford's Gibbet (181) (ST 17-39) For the sad story connected with this place-name, see Dead Woman's Ditch, page 42.

Warkleigh (180) (SS 64-22) Here is a church and farm remotely sited in wooded plateau country between the Mole and Taw valleys. The largely 15th century church has been heavily restored, but its contents include a very rare medieval pyx or tabernacle – a painted wooden box, once used to carry the Blessed Sacrament to the sick. See also the 18th century pulpit, and the tower screen with re-used panels incorporating carved Renaissance detail.

Washfield (181) (SS 93-15) Small village high above the Exe valley, but less than three miles

Washfield Church ... a fine Jacobean screen within.

north-west of Tiverton. A visit to the church is made well worthwhile by the fine, richly carved Jacobean screen (1624) which is surmounted by a Royal Coat of Arms. See also the Norman font, with zigzag decoration, and the brass to Henry Worth in the north chancel. Drive north-east, down into the Exe valley, and then north and north-west along pleasantly wooded roads, to Stoodleigh. Or walk via Courtenay, Windbow, Ennerleigh, and Pylemoor (if possible use Pathfinder Map SS 81/91).

Washford (181) (ST 04-41) Small village astride the busy A39, with tall radio masts and a station on the West Somerset Railway, where there is a most interesting railway museum, run by the Somerset and Dorset Railway Trust. The radio station's old transmitting hall now houses 'Tropiquaria' – a 'tropical jungle' complete with exotic trees, snakes, spiders, etc., while there is an aquarium in the basement, and also a cafe, playground, picnic area and shop.

Watchet (181) (ST 07-43) Busy little town with cliffs on each side of its harbour and a small shingly beach. Early in its history it suffered at least three

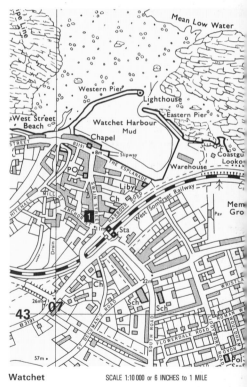

Watchet   SCALE 1:10 000 or 6 INCHES to 1 MILE

1 Tourist Information Centre

disastrous raids by the Danes, but it appears to have recovered from these with ease. There was a royal mint here during the late Saxon and early Norman period, and it also continued to flourish as a port of some consequence throughout the Middle Ages. Daniel Defoe, writing in 1724, described Watchet as 'a small port but of no importance', and its decline was due to the ability of neighbouring Minehead to handle ships of greater size. However in the 19th century, between 1856 and 1883, vast quantities of iron ore from the Brendon Hill mines were shipped from here, and despite the damage wrought over the years by a number of storms, Watchet has fought back with repairs and redevelopment of its harbour facilities. As a result of this tenacity small coasting and foreign cargo vessels are still to be found alongside its snug quay, adding much character to this salty little town. It is widely believed that Watchet harbour was in Coleridge's mind when he wrote his long poem *The Ancient Mariner* and these lines almost certainly refer to it:

> The ship was cheered, the harbour cleared,
> Merrily did we drop
> Below the Kirk, below the hill,
> Below the lighthouse top.

Welsh missionary and subsequent martyr, St Decuman, is said to have crossed the Bristol Channel on a hurdle in the company of a faithful cow, who with great consideration provided him with milk during the journey. On landing he established his cell on the spot where Watchet's fine church now stands, well to the south-west of the town. He was killed here many years later by a bloodthirsty Dane, who cut off his head, and who was then somewhat disturbed to note that the martyr picked up this severed member, washed it in a nearby stream, and then lay down calmly to die with the head beside him.

St Decuman's church has a fine tower overlooking the town from a distance, and a most attractive

St Decuman's Church, Watchet ... an attractive interior and a wealth of legends.

interior including an outstanding rood screen, old ceilings, a Jacobean pulpit and a splendid assortment of monuments in the Wyndham Chapel. St Decuman's Well, marking the place where the martyr is reputed to have washed his head, is a small stone-surrounded spring on a hillside, down a little track beyond the west end of the churchyard. It was in this large churchyard that Lorna Doone's mother was said to have been buried in R. D. Blackmore's story of *Lorna Doone*.

Do not miss a visit to the little Watchet Museum in Market Street, with its collection of interesting local material, including many photographs of 19th century Watchet harbour and the ships that were to be seen there. At least one sea angling boat is based in the harbour, and rods and tackle may be hired from the skipper. The **Tourist Information Centre (1)** will be found in Swain Street.

Waterrow (181) (ST 05-25) Pleasant hamlet in the wooded valley of the infant Tone, with an old bridge over the shallow waters of this attractive river. There is a caravan and camping site here. Walk south beside the Tone, to Stawley, or north, partly using a minor road, and then through woods to

Waterrow ... a pretty hamlet beside the infant River Tone.

Washbattle Bridge (ST 05-28), and on to Huish Champflower.

Watersmeet (180) (SS 74-48) This is an outstandingly beautiful estate belonging to the National Trust, with the fast flowing East Lyn River being joined by the smaller Hoaroak Water at Watersmeet itself. Here in a deep, lushly wooded valley, is Watersmeet House, built as a fishing and shooting lodge in about 1830 by the Halliday family, and now accommodating a National Trust restaurant and shop. The best car park for Watersmeet is at Hillsford Bridge, on the A39, some distance to the south (SS 74-47). Watersmeet is on our **Walk 6**, page 118, but there are a variety of other paths through the surrounding woods and up on to the partly wooded cleaves above, and over the moorland beyond. For further details see the excellent National Trust leaflet, *Watersmeet*. Walk from here beside the East Lyn River, down to Lynmouth, or up to Rockford and Brendon. It is also possible to walk northwards to Countisbury and beyond to Foreland Point.

Sea trout, brown trout and salmon are to be found in the East Lyn River, and the fishing here is organised by the South West Water Authority. *For details of rod licences, contact Combe Park Lodge, Hillsford Bridge, Lynton. Tel: Lynton (05985)3586.*

Weare Giffard (180) (SS 47-21) Long thin village on the quiet eastern side of the wooded Torridge valley, with Weare Giffard Hall and the church close to each other at the northern end. The Hall was rebuilt by the Fortescue family in the 15th century, and is a fine example of a fortified manor house, although its fortifications were partly demolished at the end of the Civil War. The magnificent hammer-beam roof of its great hall is particularly impressive, and the team of craftsmen that constructed it were probably also responsible for the fine roof of the church's chancel. This church, a largely 14th and 15th century building contains much of interest including two effigies of 13th century Giffards, a knight and his lady, several Fortescue monuments, some 15th century bench-ends, and a painting of the martyrdom of St Edmund, which probably dates back to Tudor times.

The River Torridge near Weare Giffard was the setting for much of *Tarka the Otter*, the splendid book by Henry Williamson, who lived for many years at Georgeham, to the north of Barnstaple. The winding, wooded banks of the Torridge provided much of the setting for Williamson's delightful story. Tarka was born in a hollow tree below the Canal Bridge, and finally met his death after the epic fight with the otterhound Deadlock, only about a mile to the north of this bridge, near the village of Landcross. Be sure to read Tarka's story, if you wish to absorb the spirit of the 'Land of the Two Rivers', and the moorland and hill country above and beyond it. This experience will be further enhanced by the outstanding wood engravings of G. F. Tunnicliffe, with which the book is illustrated.

Welcombe (190) (SS 22-18) Scattered little village to the immediate north of the Cornish border, and just inland from the line of dark, wild cliffs that characterise Devon's west-facing coast. A stream flows down a valley between high gorse-covered hills to Welcombe Mouth, where it flows over a small rock-strewn shingly beach. Marsland Mouth, to its immediate south, marks the actual border with Cornwall.

Welcombe church stands above the valley in a churchyard bright in springtime with daffodils and primroses. Inside this small building, which is Norman in origin, will be found one of the oldest screens in Devon, crudely carved, but very pleasing. There is also an attractive 15th century pulpit with early Renaissance panels, and a Jacobean lectern and clerk's desk. This church marks the beginning of our **Walk 12**, page 130. The Old Smithy, in the adjoining hamlet of Darracott, is a pleasantly rural inn, with an attractive garden.

Wellington (181) (ST 14-20) Lying beneath the northern slopes of the Black Down Hills, this bright and busy little market town is now happily relieved of most of its through traffic by the M5 motorway, which passes just to its south. It has had the right to hold a market since the early Middle Ages, and was once an important cloth-making centre. *Fox Brothers' Tonedale Mill (1)* on the north-west side of the town, continues to flourish in the making of high class woollen and worsted cloths, and there is a factory shop that can be visited *(tel: Wellington 2271)*. While here note the square, known as Five Houses, with a group of early 19th century dwellings, built to house the factory workers.

The main shopping streets, High Street, Fore Street and Mantle Street, have many pleasant Georgian buildings, and the 19th century *Town*

Wellington ... a view from the Wellington Monument.

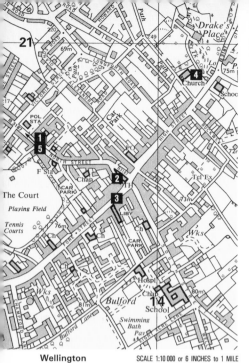

The Wellington Monument ... a windy viewpoint on the Black Down Hills.

Wellington   SCALE 1:10 000 or 6 INCHES to 1 MILE

1 Tonedale Mills (off map, to north-west)
2 Town Hall Buildings
3 Museum and Tourist Information Centre
4 St John the Baptist's Church
5 Sports Centre (off map, to west)

Hall Buildings (2) now form an attractive shopping precinct. There is a small *Town Museum (3)* in part of the former 18th century coaching inn, the Squirrel, and this is run in conjunction with a *Tourist Information Centre (tel: Wellington 4747).* They are however only open during the summer months.

St John the Baptist's Church (4) has a tall, handsomely pinnacled red sandstone tower, and is a largely 15th century building. The best feature in the interior is the splendid 17th century monument to Sir John Popham (1607), who was the Chief Justice who presided at the trial both of Sir Walter Raleigh, and of Guy Fawkes. This is a massive tomb chest on which lie two effigies, and which is surrounded by the kneeling figures of many children.

While in Wellington, do not miss a visit to the fine *Sports Centre (5)* in Corams Lane, which has a wide range of facilities including an artificial ski slope. If walking is preferred to skiing, there is a path south from the town, passing beneath the M5, and up the slopes of the Black Down Hills, to the Wellington Monument (see below).

The Wellington Monument (181) (ST 13-17) The Iron Duke had few connections with the town of Wellington, and it is thought that he may have chosen it as it so closely followed his family name, Wellesley. He only visited the town once, although he held an estate here, and was Lord of the Manor of the Borough. The monument was built in his honour between 1817 and 1854, to the design of Thomas Lee, the architect of Arlington Court (see

page 23).

Standing high on the Black Down Hills, overlooking the town whose name the Duke took for his title, this 175-foot-high, stone obelisk is an outstanding landmark from many points in the West Country. A winding staircase of 235 steps leads to a little chamber at the top, from whence there are spectacular views. This monument is in the care of the National Trust, and there is a pleasant walk to it from the long east-west spine road running to its south along the Black Down heights. Also walk north from here, down to Wellington, or south down to Millhayes and Hemyock on the River Culm. For further details read *The Devon and Somerset Blackdowns*, by Ronald Webber.

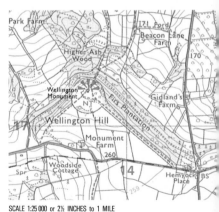

SCALE 1:25 000 or 2½ INCHES to 1 MILE

West Anstey (181) (SS 85-27) Scattered hill parish with a small church standing beside a farm not far from the source of the River Yeo. Lying just to the south of Exmoor, it has distant views of Dartmoor on the skyline to the south, and this perhaps is significant as West Anstey lies astride the Two Moors Way (see page 76). The church of St Petrock is a small 14th and 15th century building with a stout Norman tub font, and some bench- ends with Renaissance details. It unfortunately received the attentions of over-enthusiastic restorers in 1880, just a few years too early for the ideas of William Morris and his friends to have borne fruit, and has a rather stark interior. Walk north from here to Tarr Steps, making use of the Two Moors Way.

West Bagborough (181) (ST 17-33) Pleasant village beneath the Quantocks, with a small pottery, Quantock Design, producing a wide range of stoneware and oven-to-tableware *(tel: Bishops Lydeard 433057)*. There is an elegant late Georgian house with an Ionic colonnade on its south front, beside the 15th century church. The church's interior was enriched in the 1920s by one of our favourite artist-designers, Sir Ninian Comper, who was responsible for the rood screen, font cover and the stained glass. See also the medieval bench-ends.

West Bagborough ... a medieval church enriched in the 20th century.

and the two beautifully carved figures in the porch. Walk north from the vicinity of the Rising Sun Inn, up a steep track beside woodlands, to join the spine track along the Quantock ridge. Walk north-west along this track, and return to West Bagborough by dropping down to Triscombe, and returning via Rock Farm.

West Buckland (Devon) (180) (SS 65-31) Small village in high country above a number of wooded valleys, with a church almost entirely rebuilt in 1860 by the same architect who built the large West Buckland School nearby, R. D. Gould. No other special features.

West Buckland (Somerset) (181) (ST 17-20) Lying below the northern slopes of the Black Down Hills and just to the east of Wellington, this village used to be snugly situated until the arrival of the M5 motorway, which now runs regrettably close by. It is still dominated by the handsome 14th century tower, paid for by the will of a certain John Peryn of Wellington, who died in 1509. Although much

restored in 1891, the rest of the building contains work from the 13th, 14th and early 16th centuries, and renovation carried out in the 1970s has restored much of its medieval flavour. The name of the village is derived from the Saxon word *Bocland*, 'lands in possession of the king', and is recorded as such in the 'Great Book of State' by the Witan, the Saxon parliament. Gerbestone Manor (ST 16-19), beyond the motorway, well to the south-west of the village, is a fine early-Tudor house, with Elizabethan additions and 'improvements'. It is not open to the public, but there is a right-of-way for walkers passing close by.

West Down (180) (SS 51-42) Situated in rolling countryside above one of the many small streams that flow south towards the Taw estuary, this village has wide streets with many white-washed cottages, and a late-16th century manor house close to its church. This cruciform building certainly dates back to the 13th century, although its tower was rebuilt as late as 1712. The chancel was rebuilt in 1675, but in the medieval style. The north transept has a fine wagon-roof, below which will be found the wooden effigy of Sir John Stowford, dressed in his official robes as 'sergeant-at-law'. He was born at West Down in about 1290, and before he died he founded a chantry chapel here. Do not miss the delightful 17th century monument on the nave wall depicting Francis Isaac and his wife, with their children below.

The best walk from here is southwards, down a partly wooded valley, to the hamlet of Little Comfort. Other unusual place names in the area include Crackaway Barton, Snow Ball and Twitching Park Cleaves, the latter only being marked on the Pathfinder Map (sheet SS 44/54).

Westleigh (180) (SS 47-28) Small village to the immediate south of Tapeley Park (see page 72), on a slope above the Torridge estuary, with views across the water to Northam and Appledore. The little streets are dominated by the stout towered church of St Peter, a building that dates back to the early years of the 14th century. The Perpendicular north aisle was added about two hundred years later, and medieval tiles are to be found in the floor of both nave and north aisle. See the painting 'Rizpah', by the fashionable 19th century painter Lord Frederic Leighton, and exhibited by him at the Royal Academy in 1893. There are also a series of monuments to members of the Clevland family, of Tapeley Park, including one to Archibald Clevland, who actually leed the charge of the ill-fated Light Brigade, and survived this fiasco, only to die at the Battle of Inkerman a mere eleven days later.

West Luccombe (181) (SS 89-46) Pretty hamlet on the banks of the little Horner Water, here crossed by a picturesque packhorse bridge, dating back to medieval times. It is possible to walk south, up into the great Horner Wood, north across the fields to Bossington and the sea shore at Porlock Bay, or eastwards to Selworthy, and up on to Selworthy Beacon. There is a caravan and camp site here, and a pleasant road south-westwards, on to the moors at Wilmersham Common (SS 86-42).

West Putford (190) (SS 35-15) A small village with a few pleasantly thatched cottages and an undistinguished bridge over the River Torridge, here little more than a stream. The Elizabethan Churston Manor is situated at the western end of the village, but little of interest can be seen from the road. However the church opposite the manor is full of atmosphere, and is well worth visiting. It lies above and away from the road in a tree-sheltered church-yard, and has a lovely old south door, dated 1620.

The interior is one of the few in Devon to have escaped restoration in the 19th century, and is wholly satisfying. It has delightfully uneven plas-tered walls, a chancel floor almost entirely covered with medieval Barnstaple tiles, a primitive Norman tub font, and an 18th century pulpit and altar rails. There is also an attractive monument to Susannah, 2nd wife of John Avery (1689), and some very early woodwork in the north transept.

While in West Putford, do not overlook its other very different attraction, the Gnome Reserve, to the south of the first cross-roads out of the village, following a sign to Milton Damerel. Here will be found a wealth of gnomes in a woodland garden setting, and gnomes are for sale throughout the year. Whatever your opinion of gnomes, the Reserve provides a light-hearted excuse for an expedition into some unspoilt countryside.

The best walks in the area are in Melbury Woods (see page 60), about two miles to the north-east. In the vicinity of nearby Wrangworthy Cross (190 SS 38-17), there is a group of no fewer than eight Bronze Age round barrows, some of which may be seen from the road.

West Quantoxhead (181) (ST 11-41) Here, at the seaward end of the Quantocks, in a beautifully landscaped valley descending from the A39 towards the sea, is a stylish neo-Gothic church, St Audrie's,

with elaborate carving and rich marble arcading … a real Victorian period-piece. Rock strewn St Audrie's beach, approached by a toll-road, is dominated by holiday camps, both to east and west, and the best activity at West Quantoxhead is walking. There is a good car park at Staple Plain (ST 11-41), well to the south of the A39, and from here it is a short, steep walk up to Beacon Hill, the northern bastion of the Quantocks. There are fine views from here, and just below the summit the track along the spine of the Quantocks passes on its long course south-east-wards to Lydeard Hill (see page 59). These hills and the shore beyond them were well known to Coleridge and the Wordsworths, and Dorothy Wordsworth's *Alfoxden Journal* contains several accounts of walks they made here together.

West Somerset Railway (181) (SS 97-46 — ST 16-29) Regular services now run on this revived twenty-mile privately run line between Minehead and Bishops Lydeard, and there is a bus connection between the latter station and British Railways' station at Taunton. Steam and diesel trains run daily at least from May to September along the coast eastwards from Minehead, and then down below the western edge of the Quantocks to Bishops Lydeard, and apart from the fascination of travelling in an old-style train, this line provides the holiday-maker, and especially the walker, with an invaluable facility. There are refreshments and a good book-shop at Minehead Station. *Tel: Minehead (0643) 4996, or write to The Railway Station, Minehead, Somerset TA24 5BG for further details.*

Westward Ho! (180) (SS 43-29) A development company established this 'settlement' in the 1860s and 70s, naming it after the then popular book by

Westward Ho! … a splendid beach stretching northwards for almost two miles.

Charles Kingsley, which had been published in 1855. Rudyard Kipling was educated at the United Services College, an institution that has long since moved from here. Kipling Tors, eighteen acres of hill country at the western end of the town, and now owned by the National Trust, was the scene of many of the exploits of Kipling's *Stalky and Co.*

From the gorse-covered slopes of Kipling Tors there are fine views out over the dramatic line of sands stretching northwards to the mouth of the Taw-Torridge estuary. These sands are backed by Pebble Ridge, nearly two miles in length and twenty feet high in many places. For Northam Burrows Country Park, which lies behind the ridge, see Northam, page 63.

Having grown up as a Victorian speculative venture and having been enlarged in the 1920s and 30s, Westward Ho! does not have a great deal to offer those in search of architectural stimulus, but it does cater ideally for the seaside family holidaymaker.

West Worlington (180) (SS 76-13) Small village on the northern slopes of a valley through which the Little Dart River flows, with old thatched cottages, one of which, the former Church House, has an archway beneath it. This archway shelters part of a cobbled pathway up to the 14th and 15th century church, an attractive building with a little crooked spire on a short dumpy tower. The contents of this pleasant little building include 16th century bench-ends and screen, and a tablet in memory of Sir Thomas Stucley (1663), one of the Stucleys of Affeton. This was a large fortified manor house well

West Worlington Church . . . with crooked spire and dumpy tower.

to the west of the village (SS 75-13), the only surviving medieval part of which is a 15th century gatehouse tower. There is a pleasant road westwards past Affeton Barton, and down through a wooded valley on its way to Cheldon.

Wheddon Cross (181) (SS 92-38) A windy hamlet at the point where the road coming from the Brendon Hills in the direction of Exford and Simonsbath crosses the A396, Dunster to Dulverton road. This is in high watershed country between the north-flowing Avill and the south-flowing Quarme, the latter a tributary of the Exe. There is a cheerful inn here, the Rest and be Thankful, which

serves bar meals and steaks. There is also a public car park, from which there are good walking possibilities north over a shoulder of Dunkery Hill, down to Horner Wood, or west to Luckwell Bridge, and then south to Winsford.

Williton (181) (ST 07-41) Cheerful little town about two miles inland from Watchet, with several hospitable inns and hotels, and a varied selection of shops. Do not miss a visit to Orchard Mill, with its water-mill machinery intact, its 'Mill Museum', Craft Shop, 'Miller's Pantry' Restaurant and Orchard Tea Garden *(tel: Williton 32133)*.

The church is almost entirely Victorian, although it does include a fragment of a chantry chapel erected by his brother for the soul of Sir Reginald Fitzurse, the local knight who was the leader of the party that murdered Archbishop Becket by the high altar of Canterbury Cathedral in the year 1170. (See also neighbouring Sampford Brett, page 67, for details of Fitzurse's friend Richard de Brett, another member of this infamous gang.)

Wimbleball Lake (181) (SS 97-30) Situated in attractive hilly country, the southern half of which is delightfully wooded, this large man-made reservoir has been formed by a 160-foot-high concrete dam

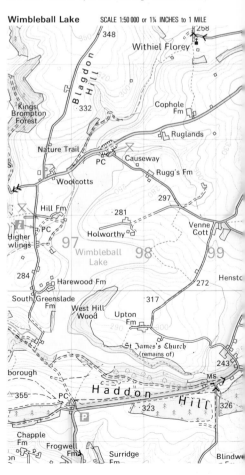

Wimbleball Lake SCALE 1:50 000 or 1¼ INCHES to 1 MILE

Wimbleball Lake . . . a view northwards from Haddon Hill.

across the River Haddeo, a tributary of the Exe. There is a car park, information centre, picnic area and toilets at the Cowlings Recreation Area (SS 96-30), to the south-east of Brompton Regis. There is also a car park and toilets at Frogwell Lodge, just off the B3190 (SS 97-28), and a car park, picnic area, nature trail and toilets at Bessom Bridge (SS 97-31), near the north end of the reservoir. There are opportunities for walking with many way-marked walks, fishing, rowing, sailing and camping. *For detailed information, tel: Brompton Regis (03987) 372, preferably between 10 and 10.30 a.m., or call at the Information Centre.*

Winsford . . . a village with no fewer than seven bridges.

Winsford (181) (SS 90-34) This village shelters in the Exe valley, with the high moorland of Winsford Hill only a mile to the south-west (see Winsford Hill, below). With no fewer than seven bridges, including an attractive packhorse bridge, Winsford is probably Exmoor's most beautiful village. The delightfully thatched Royal Oak Inn looks across the road to a small stream, and a few yards below this, there is a ford. Beyond the ford there is a road leading up a steep narrow lane to the church, the fine stout tower of which dominates the village most decisively.

There is a pretty niche above the church's south door, itself a splendid piece of woodwork, probably dating back to the 15th century. The interior has wonderfully lofty proportions, with light flooding in through plain glass upon early 19th century black and white chequered tiling. See also the Jacobean pulpit, the Norman tub font, and the varicoloured arcade columns with their predominantly grey stonework relieved by layers of red sandstone.

Ernest Bevin, the great pioneer of modern trade unionism, and one of the Labour Party's most respected figures, was born at Winsford in 1881.

Winsford Hill (181) (SS 87-34) An unspoilt stretch of high moorland country in the care of the National Trust, with many fine open views. There are several lay-bys and pull-offs on the B3223 which intersects this area, and with its gorse, heath, bracken and thorn trees, it provides good opportunities for wildlife spotting (stonechats, whinchats, buzzards and wheatears). There is a group of Bronze Age barrows, known as Wambarrows, and the Caratacus Stone (see page 34) is worth inspecting.

Wistlandpound Reservoir (180) (SS 64-41) An attractive man-made lake in the hills to the west of Exmoor, about a mile to the south of Blackmoor Gate, with tree clad banks and fine views over rolling country westwards. There are opportunities for bird watching here, and study of Landranger Map 180 will reveal the course of the long-dismantled Lynton and Barnstaple Railway running above the north shore. Fishing permits (fly fishing for trout) are usually available from a hut by the car park.

Witheridge (181) (SS 80-14) This large village in upland country above the headwaters of the Little Dart River was once a thriving town with a weekly market and an annual three-day fair. It still has a large market place overlooked by attractive

thatched cottages, late-18th and early-19th century houses and the colour-washed Hare and Hounds Inn. The Aston House Hotel and the Angel Inn also offer accommodation to walkers on the Two Moors Way (see page 76), the long distance footpath that passes through Witheridge. The church of St John Baptist has an early 14th century chancel and a nave with a ceiled wagon-roof, but it was considerably restored in the later years of the 19th century. However do not miss the 16th century stone pulpit, with its carved figures in narrow panels and carved crucifix, nor the Perpendicular font.

Make use of the Two Moors Way (see page 76), to walk north-eastwards from here, up the valley of the Little Dart River, to Bradford Mill.

Withiel Florey (181) (SS 98-33) Here, in a remote valley on the southern side of the Brendon Hills, and to the north east of Wimbleball Lake, is a single farm and a small over-restored Perpendicular church, the contents of which include a Norman font. Walk south-west to Bessom Bridge, at the head of the lake, linking with a nature trail that starts from the road to the west of the bridge; or walk north-east over the Brendon Hills, to Treborough and Roadwater.

Bridge over the Barle at Withypool. See page 86.

WITHYCOMBE

Withycombe (181) (ST 01-41) This pretty village shelters in a small combe below the partly wooded slopes of Withycombe Hill, which is itself not far to the east of Dunster's deer park. The small 13th and 14th century colour-washed church has a circular Norman font, a fine 15th century fan-vaulted screen, and below a window on the north side, the effigy of an early 14th century lady. On the south side will be found an effigy of a man, who probably died some fifty years earlier than the lady. Both hold heart cases in their hands, possibly indicating that they were buried abroad, and that only their hearts were brought home for burial ... a usual arrangement in medieval times, when it was impractical to take corpses on a journey of more than a day or two.

Sandhill Farm, to the east of the village, was said to be haunted by the ghost of a witch, Joan Carne, who was reputed to have murdered no fewer than three husbands. She was buried in Withycombe churchyard in the year 1612, but her neighbours were rather put out, on their return from her funeral, to find her at home, quite unconcerned, and reputedly frying eggs and bacon. She was eventually placed in a nearby pond, but she then reckoned to be returning ever nearer to the house by a 'cock-stride' each year. A dull story, but the eggs and bacon add a nice West Country flavour!

Church tower, Wiveliscombe.

Withypool (181) (SS 84-35) A largely unspoilt village in the very heart of Exmoor, with an interesting old bridge over the River Barle, below which is a long pebbly 'beach' looking out across the river to the church. This has a squat tower and a sensible porch. Inside all is white-washed, even the well proportioned arcading. There is an interesting Norman font with chevron decoration and other deeply incised carving, and some pleasant old panelling at the foot of the tower arch. Was the wall monument to Dorothy Adams originally intended for the churchyard? It certainly resembles a normally shaped tombstone, with its semi-circular top.

It is believed that R. D. Blackmore wrote much of his book *Lorna Doone* while staying at Withypool's hospitable Royal Oak Inn. Some of the best of Exmoor country can be found to the immediate west of the village, on Withypool Common, with its heather, bracken, gorse and thorn trees. There are several Bronze Age barrows here, and just to the south of Withypool Hill, there is a Bronze Age stone circle, with thirty seven stones still remaining (181) (SS 83-34).

Walk west beside the Barle, to Landacre Bridge (see page 56) and return over the Common to Withypool. Not only is this village on our **Walk 4**, page 114, but it is also on the Two Moors Way (see page 76).

Wiveliscombe (181) (ST 08-27) Small but most attractive market town below the south-eastern slopes of the Brendon Hills, and on the western edge of the Vale of Taunton Deane. Its name is pronounced *Wivvel-is-cum*, but is usually shortened locally to *Wivvy*. There is an Iron Age settlement on Castle Hill to the east of the town, and the earthworks of a Roman fort to the south east, but otherwise most of Wiveliscombe's buildings date from the late 18th and early 19th centuries. The best of these are grouped around the area covered by its Square, the hub of the town, and the nearby Church Street, Russells, Rotten Row, Silver Street, and Golden Hill. See especially the tile-hung Court House in the Square, which now houses the town's library. While in Wiveliscombe, visit the Wilscombe Design Factory Shop in Ford Road (B3188, Watchet road), just to the north of the B3227, where there are a variety of melamine and textile products made in the adjoining factory, available for sale. *(Tel: Wiveliscombe 23047.)*

The red sandstone church was rebuilt in 1829, and further changes were made later in the 19th century, but its contents include box pews installed in 1829, and a handsome 17th century monument to Humphrey Wyndham and his wife. Do not overlook the plaque listing the art treasures stored for safe-keeping in the 1939-45 War, in the extensive catacombs below the church. This list includes some of the country's finest art treasures.

Walk north from here, on a small road to Langley (divert here to Langley Marsh, just to the west, where there is a lively inn, the Three Horseshoes, serving beer from the wood and good bar meals), and then duly fortified, up the wooded Combe Bottom, to Brompton Ralph (ST 08-32).

Woody Bay (180) (SS 67-49) Mostly in the care of the National Trust, there is dramatic coastal scenery here. This is made up of high bracken-covered moors, delightful woodlands, complete with stream, and below it a curving rock-strewn shore. There was once a wooden pier here, and holidaymakers used to come ashore from paddle steamers from Bristol, Weston-super-Mare, or South Wales, to take tea in a refreshment hut. However this enterprise did not flourish and now all that remains of the pier is a concrete stump. The shore may only be reached on foot from the National Trust's car parks above, and the long steep pull up is not recommended to elderly people or parents with young children. All others should ensure that a visit here is not missed. For further information see the National Trust leaflet *Heddon Valley and Woody Bay.*

The narrow, often steep little road from Hunter's Inn eastwards to Martinhoe, Woody Bay, and The

Woolacombe.

Valley of Rocks should be tackled when visitor traffic is likely to be light, or perhaps preferably it should be walked (see our **Walk 7**, page 120).

Woolacombe (180) (SS 45-43) A holiday village, which despite later developments, has retained a strong Edwardian flavour. It lies in a wide combe at the northern end of the splendid two mile long Woolacombe Sand, which offers superb sandcastle building, swimming and surfing, and which is backed by dunes known as The Warren. Above The Warren is the Marine Drive which stretches behind the sands almost as far south as Vention, and which allows motorists to park behind the whole length of beach. Behind the Marine Drive is gorse- and heather-covered Woolacombe Down, and the whole area is owned by the National Trust. To survey this fine prospect try to climb Potter's Hill which is above the Drive at its northern end. It is not possible to drive from here to Vention, for Putsborough Sand (see page 66), but there is a path for walkers starting from the end of the Drive (for further details see the National Trust leaflet *Woolacombe to Croyde Bay).* There is an Information Centre at Hall '70, Beach Road. *(Tel: 0271 870553.)*

Woolfardisworthy (190) (SS 33-21) Not to be confused with Woolfardisworthy near Crediton, this village of thatch and cob stands in undramatic plateau country about three miles south of Clovelly, and not far from the headwaters of the River Torridge. Ask for 'Woolsery' if seeking for route directions locally. The church is a largely 15th century building, but its Norman origins are revealed in the south transept and the fine late-12th century south doorway. Inside will be found a Norman font, a good series of early-16th century

bench-ends, one of which shows the Crucifixion, and an interesting wall monument to Richard Cole (1614). For good forest walks not far away, see Hartland Forest, page 50, and Melbury Woods, page 60.

Wootton Courtenay (181) (SS 93-43) Long straggling village beautifully situated in a valley between the wooded hills of Wootton and Tivington Commons, and the eastern slopes of Dunkery Beacon. The church dates from the 13th century, but incorporates some finely detailed Perpendicular work, notably the canopied niches in the north arcade pillars. Do not miss the ceiled wagon-roofs to the nave and north aisle, with their fine bosses.

Walk up through the woods, and over to Minehead or Dunster; or walk south-westwards, up to high Dunkery Beacon, and return via Cloutsham and Webber's Post.

Yarde (181) (ST 06-39) Modest hamlet on the B3188 in a valley below the Brendon Hills, about two miles north of Monksilver.

Yarnscombe (180) (SS 56-23) Minute village in remote, rolling country well to the west of the Taw valley. The church is largely 15th century, although parts of the tower are of Norman origin. The contents of the church include some medieval Barnstaple tiles in the south aisle, and a 15th century tomb in one of two recesses in the north wall of the chancel, this being to John Cookworthy and his wife. There is also a monument to John Pollard (1667), one of the influential Pollard family of Langley Barton (SS 56-24), a farm well to the north of the village.

Motor and Cycle Tours

Tour 1
Quantock Journey

35 miles. Reasonable for cyclists.

Our route starts from Watchet and with the object of encircling the lovely Quantock Hills, first runs eastwards to Quantockhead, lying at their seaward end, here dominated by the bracken-covered Beacon Hill. It then heads south-eastward through villages where the poets Wordsworth and Coleridge once stayed, below the gentler, more thickly wooded eastern slopes of the hills. At least one foray is made, up a wooded combe to the Quantocks' high whale-back ridge, before the route calls at The Quantock Visitor Centre at Fyne Court, an important destination for those who wish to learn more about these lovely hills, and the wildlife to be found there. It then descends at the southern end of the hills into Kingston St Mary, before heading north-westwards to return below the steeper western side of the hills, through the delightful villages of Cothelstone, West Bagborough and Crowcombe. From the latter, our route runs westwards across the valley of the little Doniford Stream to beautiful Stogumber, nestling at the foot of the Brendon Hills, and then north again, up the Doniford valley, through Sampford Brett and Williton, to return to Watchet.

Leave the bright little harbour town of **Watchet** on a minor road heading eastwards from X-rds in the vicinity of the **West Somerset Railway** Station. Views of the Welsh coast over to the left. Through Doniford hamlet, and eventually bear left at diagonal X-rds, on to A39 by **West Quantoxhead** entry sign (but go straight ahead if you wish to use Staple Plain car park; good base for exploring northern end of Quantocks). St Audrie's church down to left. After one mile, large car park on right. Walk from here, up to Beacon Hill, northern bastion of the Quantocks.

Now keep on A39 unless you wish to visit **East Quantoxhead**, or **Kilve** by taking turns to the left. Both worth exploring if you have time. Turn right off A39 in **Holford**, to visit this attractive village, with its associations with William Wordsworth and his sister Dorothy, who in 1797-8, stayed for a year at Alfoxton Park (now a hotel), and possibly to link on to **Walk 1**, page 108. Now re-join A39 heading south-eastwards, passing beautiful National Trust woodlands and the Castle of Comfort. Turn right at X-rds on to minor road and start to climb up into woodlands covering eastern slopes of the Quantocks, passing **Walford's Gibbet** and arriving at **Dead Woman's Ditch**. Good car park here.

Turn sharp left at **Dead Woman's Ditch**. (But go straight ahead if you wish to link on to **Walk 1**, at Crowcombe Park Gate.) Now drop down from Quantocks, over small X-rds, and into pretty **Nether Stowey**, to visit Coleridge Cottage where this poet lived for three years between 1796 and 1799, and to explore the village. Take minor road south from **Nether Stowey**, over X-rds in Marsh Mills hamlet (unless you wish to explore **Rams Combe** by turning right), bear left at next two junctions (unless you wish to divert right, up wooded Cockercombe to the Triscombe Stone car park), and head through hamlets of Lower Aisholt and Courtway, to wooded five-way cross by garage at Timberscombe.

Over five-way cross at Timberscombe following sign to Broomfield. Eventually turn left for **Broomfield**, with its unspoilt 14th and 16th century church and Fyne Court where there is an interesting **Visitor Centre for the Quantocks** (see under Broomfield, page 32). Turnabout in **Broomfield**, turn left re-joining road heading south-eastwards, and soon turn right, following signs to **Kingston St Mary**. This attractive village at the southern end of the Quantocks has a fine church and an interesting weaving workshop and gallery, Church Farm Weavers.

Leave **Kingston St Mary** westwards, and pass through hamlets of Fulford, Yarford and Cushuish, skirting around the southern end of the Quantocks. Turn right in minute village of **Cothelstone**, with its fine Elizabethan manor house and 16th century church, both in red sandstone. Two of Monmouth's supporters were hung from the manor gatehouse here. Now climb back on to the Quantocks, through woodlands, and turn left at Park End. Then turn left, following sign to West Bagborough. (But go straight ahead for Lydeard Hill car park, which lies at southern end of the 'spine track' running from here to Beacon Hill, at the northern end of the Quantocks.)

Drop steeply down into quiet village of **West Bagborough**, which has a pleasantly restored church and a small pottery. Go straight, not left in West Bagborough, and later turn right in Heathfield hamlet, and head northwards, beneath the Quantock slopes to the minute hamlet of **Triscombe**, with its colourful little inn, the Blue Ball. It is possible to walk up into the Quantocks from here to visit the Triscombe Stone, and to link on to the 'Spine Track', but parking space at Triscombe hamlet is restricted. Now move along only possible road to the most attractive village of **Crowcombe** situated below the wooded Quantock slopes. This was a

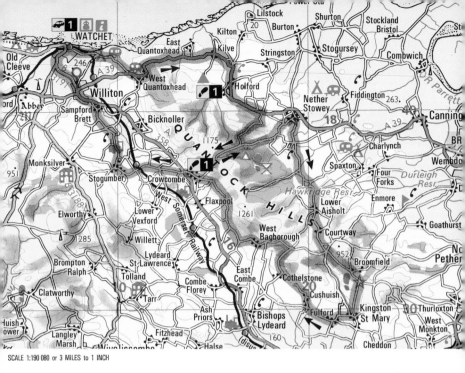

SCALE 1:190 080 or 3 MILES to 1 INCH

borough town in medieval times, and has a handsome and very interesting church, a restored Church House, and an elegant 18th century house in its own park, Crowcombe Court.

Near the end of Crowcombe's village street, beyond the Carew Arms, fork left, cross the A358 with great care, and follow signs towards Stogumber. Pass the site of the **Heddon Oak**, from which the mutilated bodies of six of Monmouth's supporters are believed to have been hung in 1685, a few days after the Battle of Sedgemoor. Pass Stogumber Station, a useful stopping point on the **West Somerset Railway**, and enter the delightful village of **Stogumber**. Here will be found a friendly inn, the White Horse, and groups of colour-washed, cob and thatched cottages, looking out over cobbled pavements to a handsome red sandstone church, where Sir George Sydenham, father of Sir Francis Drake's second wife, is buried. He lived at **Combe Sydenham**, a fine Elizabethan manor house, less than two miles to the west. Although off our route, a diversion to **Combe Sydenham**, with its 'Country Park Trout Farm', would be well worthwhile if time allows. It is also on our Tour 2.

Now head north from Stogumber, through hamlet of Wayshill, where there is an interesting workshop, Stogumber Woodwork, and through **Vellow**, to arrive at the small village of **Sampford Brett**. The church here has an effigy thought to be that of Richard de Brett, one of the infamous gang of knights

who in 1170 murdered Archbishop Thomas à Becket at his altar at Canterbury Cathedral, in response to Henry II's angry but indiscreet cry, 'Who will rid me of this turbulent priest?' Sampford's other story concerns Florence Wyndham, a lady who, by great good fortune, showed signs of life only a few seconds before she was due to be buried.

Bear left on to A358 beyond Sampford Brett and enter the lively little town of **Williton**, with its wide choice of shops, restaurants and inns. The Victorian church has memories of Richard de Brett's friend, and fellow thug, Sir Reginald Fitzurse, who appears to have led the knights who killed Becket (see Sampford Brett, above).

Join the A39 briefly in Williton, and then leave it to head north on B3191 in the direction of Watchet. Bear right on to B3190, and shortly turn down left if you wish to visit St Decuman's which is Watchet's church. This is an interesting building, and was founded by Decuman, an enthusiastic missionary from South Wales, who is reputed to have drifted across the Bristol Channel on a hurdle, in the company of a cow from whom he was able to obtain milk during their rather precarious journey together. Read more about St Decuman on page 78. R. D. Blackmore sited the grave of Lorna Doone's mother in the churchyard, and Coleridge is widely believed to have had Watchet in mind when his *Ancient Mariner* referred to 'the kirk below the hill'.

Return to the B3190 and into **Watchet** thus completing Tour 1.

89

Tour 2

Dunster, the Brendons and Dunkery

40 miles. Reasonable for cyclists between Minehead and Monksilver. The country beyond this is more demanding.

Our route sets out eastward, parallel with the coast, calling first at the delectable little town of Dunster, and then has a brief encounter with the seaside at Blue Anchor. It then heads inland passing the atmospheric ruins of Cleeve Abbey, and beyond Monksilver, the fine Elizabethan manor house of Combe Sydenham, with its various family leisure facilities. The route now climbs up into the Brendon Hills, and before tackling the road along their long whale-back ridge, it drops down to the southern side of these hills to look at Clatworthy Reservoir at the head of the little River Tone, with its attractive visitor facilities. And now back on to the Brendon ridge, to move past the remains of long-vanished iron mining activities, and extensive Forestry Commission woodlands, with two picnic sites provided. From Wheddon Cross where the Brendons end and Exmoor begins, it is only a short distance to the open moorland of Dunkery, and from here to the Horner woodlands there is a stretch of grand open country with superlative views and a wealth of walking opportunities. Dropping down into the Horner valley, we pass through the picturesque hamlets of Horner and West Luccombe, before reaching the busy A39. Before completing the tour, there are three pretty villages to be explored — Allerford, Bossington and Selworthy — but these are all so delightful that they should perhaps be the subject of a special extra visit. And so we move back along the A39 to complete Tour 2 at Minehead.

Leave the bright and busy holiday resort town of **Minehead** south-eastwards on the A39, and after about two miles, turn right on to A396, and enter the exceptionally pleasing little town of **Dunster**. Use car park on left near entry to town. Luttrell Arms on left, Yarn Market on right, ahead is Dunster Castle, looking out over town. Do not miss a walk round Dunster, at least visiting castle, Yarn Market, water mill and church. Link in Dunster with our **Walk 2**, page 110. Turn-about at car park, and re-join A39 again heading eastwards. At far end of **Carhampton**, where there is a fine 16th century rood screen in the church, turn left on to B3191, to reach modest beach resort of **Blue Anchor**, which has a long open beach, many caravans, and a useful station on the **West Somerset Railway**.

At the far end of **Blue Anchor**, turn right off B3191, and move through Chapel Cleeve to **Old Cleeve**. Keep straight through village, unless visiting factory shop of John Wood (sheepskin products), or handsome Perpendicular period church, with an amusing epitaph in its churchyard. Turn left on to A39, and enter unexceptional **Washford**. Turn right at X-rds in village, following sign to Cleeve Abbey. **Cleeve Abbey** soon on left. Do not miss a visit to the fascinating ruins of this Cistercian abbey founded in the 12th century, and much added to in the 15th and early-16th centuries. Well-mown lawns, sparkling stream, and a strong sense of the past here.

Bear left by the White Horse Inn in Hungerford hamlet, and bear left at end of Torre hamlet. Straight, not right, immediately fork right, and over X-rds crossing B3190, on to B3188 which starts here (Sign — Monksilver). Keep on B3188 into **Monksilver**, a small village in a wooded valley below the **Brendon Hills**, with interesting church. Keep on B3188 beyond Monksilver and the fine Elizabethan manor house of **Combe Sydenham** on right. Interest and amusement for all the family here, see page 39.

Now high up on the eastern end of the

Higher Town, Minehead.

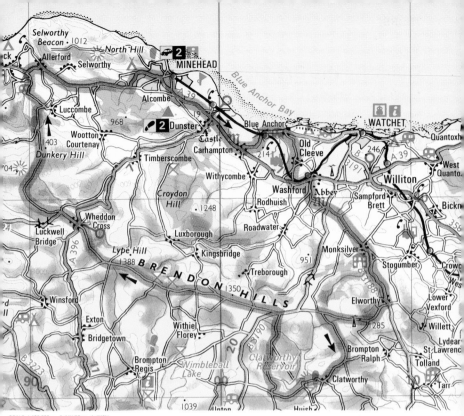

SCALE 1:190 080 or 3 MILES to 1 INCH

Brendon Hills, through hamlet of **Elworthy**, fine views, simple church. Beyond the village, turn right at X-rds, on to road which runs along the top of the Brendon Hills all the way to Wheddon Cross. However our route, after passing Elworthy Barrows on left, complete with radio mast, turns sharp left well beyond Holcombe Water Farm (on left). Long narrow road heads south, and our route turns right at X-rds (Sign — Clatworthy). Through minute village of **Clatworthy**, another simple church here. Bear right at end of village.

Dam of Clatworthy Reservoir visible up valley to right. Straight, not right. But turn right to visit **Clatworthy Reservoir**. Good facilities for visitors. See page 37. Turn right well beyond reservoir entrance and head westwards, to arrive at small X-rds. Turn right at this X-rds, and head northwards to join B3190 briefly, by turning left on to it near Huish Champflower Barrow (181 SS 02-34). Almost immediately, fork right, off B3190 (Sign — Wheddon Cross). Path down to Treborough on right passes close to 'The Incline' in Eastern Wood (see **Brendon Hills**, page 31, and Landranger Map 181, ST 02-34). Now head westwards on this whale-back road along the Brendon Hills, in the direction of Wheddon Cross, passing scanty remains of the West Somerset Mineral Railway, of

which 'The Incline' was an important part, (see Landranger Map 181), and beyond these, the two Forestry Commission Picnic Sites at Chargot and Kennisham, both near road. See Brendon Hills, page 31.

At **Wheddon Cross**, over X-rds by the Rest and be Thankful Inn, joining B3224 (Sign — Exford). After three quarters of a mile, go over X-rds, leaving B3224 (watch for this with care). Over cattle-grid at Dunkery Gate. Path to **Dunkery Beacon** on left. Car park and second path to Dunkery Beacon on left. Fine views ahead out over woodlands and beyond to Porlock Bay. Straight, not left at Webber's Post, Cloutsham. Large car park area here. Good picnic opportunities.

Down through Horner woodlands, and turn left at X-rds (Sign — Horner). Through **Horner** hamlet. Tea garden, gift shop, car park, packhorse bridge, stream, walks in Horner Wood. Straight, not left in **West Luccombe**, beyond another packhorse bridge. Turn right, with care on to A39. But turn left if you wish to link on to **Tour 5**, page 96, at **Porlock**. Follow into **Minehead** on A39, but divert to the left to the three attractive villages of **Allerford**, **Bossington** and especially **Selworthy** if time allows. There are car parks at all three places. Now keep into **Minehead** on A39, thus completing Tour 2.

91

Tour 3
Quiet Country twixt the Exe and the Tone

30 miles. A demanding route for cyclists, especially when away from the A roads.

Our route starts from Tiverton, and straight away heads into unspoilt hilly country parallel to, but well above the Exe valley. An early call is made on the stylish Victorian house of Knightshayes, with its splendid gardens, both now in the care of the National Trust. After a few miles of quiet, hilly roads, we descend into the Exe valley, and after a climb up through lush woodlands, we cross the Exe once again, and head up the Batherm valley to the little town of Bampton. Now going eastwards, we cross a watershed between the Batherm and the Tone and drop down into Somerset, to cross the Tone at the charming hamlet of Waterrow. From here we head south, over hilly country just to the east of the Tone, calling at the delightful villages of Stawley and Holcombe Rogus. From the latter, our route runs south and west, parallel with the Grand Western Canal, to return to Tiverton through Sampford Peverell and Halberton, two villages now much relieved by the A361.

Depart northwards from the busy market town and interesting tourist centre of **Tiverton**, from the vicinity of the hospital, up the successive minor roads of Bampton Street, Park Street, Park Road and Brickhouse Hill. Beyond end of town, go straight not left and head for Chettiscombe, (but turn left and then up drive to right, if you wish to visit the National Trust's **Knightshayes Court** and its delightful gardens). Main route keeps to left in Chettiscombe hamlet, up wooded valley of the Town Leat, and over steep sided Hone Hill. Keep straight, past Longhayne and Landrake, and then turn sharp left at diagonal X-rds (marked 'Van Post' on Landranger Map 181, ST 97-18).

After one mile, drop steeply down into the Exe Valley, through Cove hamlet, and over X-rds crossing A396 with great care. Over River Exe and just beyond, over small X-rds before climbing steeply up through woods. At edge of woods turn sharp right, and along open road through more woods before dropping down to re-cross the River Exe. Over X-rds re-crossing A396 with great care, and take minor road into little market town of Bampton.

In Bampton, turn right with care on to B3227 and large 13th and 15th century church with over-restored interior is soon on right. Straight, not right, in centre of town, keeping on B3227 (Sign — Taunton).

SCALE 1:190 080 or 3 MILES to 1 INCH

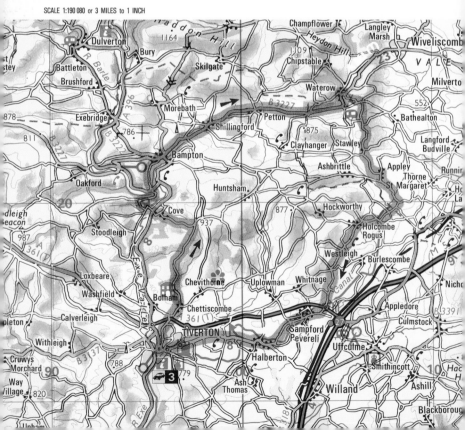

Holcombe Court, Holcombe Rogus ... one of Devon's finest Tudor buildings.

Straight, not left, keeping on B3227 where earthworks of a Norman castle are visible up to left. Keep on B3227 for 7 miles until reaching charming hamlet of **Waterrow**, which lies in the wooded valley of the infant River Tone.

In **Waterrow** turn right, off B3227 immediately after crossing bridge over River Tone, and climb steeply out of valley. Drop down again partly and bear left at Y-junction. Now turn right at X-rds, and follow small hilly road southwards, following signs to Stawley. Bear left and then right, in minute village of **Stawley**. But bear right at entry to village, to visit delightfully unspoilt little church, with its origins in Norman times. Also keep an eye open for an early pattern letter-box here; there are only a very few of these venerable WB72's left now.

Bear left well beyond Stawley, turn right in Appley hamlet, and turn left just beyond. Over River Tone in Greenham hamlet, and turn sharp right just beyond. Over two small X-rds following signs to Holcombe Rogus, then turn right at T-junction, and cross the attractive **Grand Western Canal**, a water-way with a fascinating history, and which is now a linear Country Park stretching south and west to Tiverton. Fork left well beyond canal, and bear left at entry to the delightful village of **Holcombe Rogus**.

Bear right twice in **Holcombe Rogus**, up village street with attractive vicarage and 'priest's house', and at the end, a beautiful Tudor house, Holcombe Court, close to a fine Perpendicular church, both below wooded, sloping parkland. Now return down village street, turn right, and head south-westwards, through several junctions following signs to Sampford Peverell.

Through part of **Sampford Peverell** and turn right beyond canal bridge if you wish to visit church built partly by Margaret Beaufort, mother of Henry VII, or to linger beside the **Grand Western Canal**. Now move westwards to large village of **Halberton**, turning right onto B3391. Pass pond that is reputed never to freeze up, due to its being fed by a warm spring, and a large sandstone church dating back to the 14th century. From here move westwards on B3391 to return to Tiverton, thus completing Tour 3.

Tour 4
Dulverton and South-East Exmoor

38 miles. Hard work for cyclists, but well worth the effort.

Starting from Dulverton our route follows the course of the lovely River Barle for a short while, before heading westwards over the Anstey Commons, the southern fringe of Exmoor, and a foretaste of more pleasures to come. On Molland Common, having possibly first diverted to visit the interesting little church at Molland, we start to turn northwards, and near the lonely Sportsman's Inn the route starts to head north-eastwards, partly over moorland roads, dropping down to cross the Barle at beautifully situated Landacre Bridge. Soon turning southwards, we head for Withypool and Tarr Steps, both astride the River Barle; before heading up over the moors and dropping down into the Exe valley at the pretty village of Winsford. For a contrast, we now leave the moorland country and head first south and then west, to encircle the beautiful man-made Wimbleball Lake, with its host of recreational facilities. And so, past the delightful hamlet of Bury, before re-crossing the Exe valley to return to Dulverton.

Leave the Square of the delightful little town of **Dulverton** northwards on B3223 (Sign —

The Royal Oak, Winsford.

Lynton), but not before a visit to the helpful and very interesting National Park Information Centre at Exmoor House. Up wooded road beside the River Barle, then fork left off B3223 and turn left, crossing bridge over the Barle (Sign — East Anstey). Climb steeply out of valley, keep straight at next three junctions, and over X-rds at 'Five Crosses' (Sign — Molland). Now on **Anstey Common**, the southern fringes of Exmoor, with fine views on both sides of the road. Large boulder on left is a memorial to Philip Hancock, hunting man and great lover of Exmoor.

Turn right at X-rds (but turn left if you wish to divert to the fascinating little church at **Molland**). Over X-rds at 'White Post', and turn right at next X-rds. Turn right at third (off-set) X-rds, and now head north-eastwards, very soon passing the lonely Sportsman's Inn. Fork left at Withypool Cross, and eventually drop down over open moorland, to cross the River Barle at fine old **Landacre Bridge**, a popular port of call for Exmoor visitors, and which was also the place where Jeremy Stickles escaped from an ambush by the Doones in the story *Lorna Doone*.

Climb steeply out of the Barle valley, soon passing the line of the **Two Moors Way**, and then straight, not left, at Y-junction. Turn right, at X-rds on to B3223, at Chibbet Post, once the site of a gibbet where sheep stealer Red Jim Hannaford was supposedly hanged, in *Lorna Doone*. After a short distance, fork right, off B3223, and eventually drop steeply down to **Withypool**, attractive village com-

fortably situated in the Barle valley. R. D. Blackmore is believed to have written much of *Lorna Doone* while staying at the pleasant Royal Oak Inn here. It is possible to link with our **Walk 4**, page 114, at this village.

Turn left in **Withypool** and climb steeply out of valley before turning right, re-joining B3223 at Comer's Cross. Follow this pleasant moorland road over Winsford Hill, noting Bronze Age Wambarrows, on left near 'summit'. Turn right at Spire Cross and move to car park beyond Liscombe hamlet. Park here and walk down to **Tarr Steps**, a fine packhorse bridge over the lovely River Barle, which should on no account be missed. Our **Walk 4**, page 114, starts from here. Refreshments available at Tarr Farm.

Turnabout at Tarr Steps car park, and bearing left at entry to Liscombe hamlet, retrace route to Spire Cross, and cross B3223 (Sign — Winsford). Immediately beyond X-rds stop to look at the **Caratacus Stone**, a three foot high relic of the Dark Ages, standing beneath a small stone shelter well over to right of road. Over moorland road before dropping down into the Exe valley at **Winsford**, one of Exmoor's prettiest villages. This has a picturesque inn, the Royal Oak, an interesting church, no fewer than seven bridges, and a ford over the little Winn Brook. Link here with **Tour 5**.

Bear right beyond Royal Oak Inn, and bear right again, on to wider road, and leave **Winsford** on road running south and east, down the Exe valley. Turn right with care, on to A396, and head south, keeping on A396 for two miles. Tower of **Exton** church visible up to left. Wood on left, River Exe on right. Turn left, off A396 just after entrance to Kents Farm on right (Sign — Brompton Regis), **watch for this with care**. Now climb steeply out of the Exe valley, and beyond top of hill, over X-rds, and turn left at T-junction (Signs — Brompton Regis).

Enter **Brompton Regis**, small village which was a market town in medieval times, and which is built around the four sides of its churchyard. Turn right by churchyard, and after leaving village, turn left at Mill Cross, and pass Pulhams Mill where there is a woodworking studio. After less than a mile, turn right to visit the Cowlings Recreation Area, to learn all about the great man-made **Wimbleball Lake**, and the wide variety of leisure facilities that are offered (see also, page 84).

Turnabout at the Cowlings Recreation Area, and turn right to re-join main route; and straight, not left just beyond. Over Bessom Bridge, near head of Wimbleball Lake, fork right just beyond, car park on right with picnic area, nature trail and toilets. Now over causeway, crossing another arm of the lake. Turn right at next two junctions, bear left at entry to unexceptional **Upton**, and turn right on to B3190 (Sign — Bampton). Straight, not left, keeping on B3190 (Sign — Bampton). After just over a mile, entry to Frogwell Lodge car park on right, with toilets. Walk to Wimbleball Dam and possibly down the wooded Haddeo valley from there to Bury.

Turn right at next X-rds, leaving B3190 (Sign — Dulverton). Turn left at entry to the attractive hamlet of **Bury**, but try to walk down right to look at ford and packhorse bridge. Turn right with care, on to A396, and cross River Haddeo. Turn left, on to B3222 (Sign — Dulverton), and cross River Exe. Complete Tour 4 by returning to **Dulverton**.

SCALE 1:190 080 or 3 MILES to 1 INCH

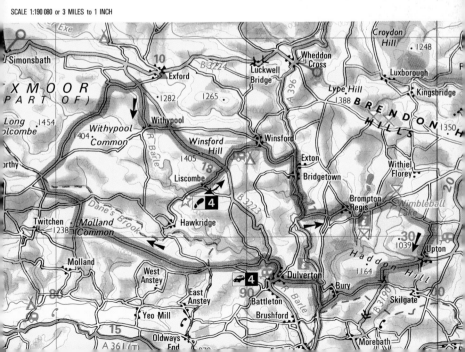

Tour 5
Porlock and North-East Exmoor

33 miles. Only for the most dedicated of cyclists.

This route starts from the north coast at Porlock, and immediately tackles a series of steep and adventurous hills, to climb up through lush woodlands on to the high moors skirting around the great bastion of Dunkery Beacon. Leaving the moors for a time, it heads southwards to meet the River Exe, which it then follows up past the attractive villages of Winsford and Exford. It then veers away from the Exe, and heads north once again, making a fine moorland run over Exford Common and beyond, to meet the A39 a mile or so to the west of this road's steep climb up Porlock Hill. We now head west for a short time, on the busy A39, before turning at Culbone Stables Inn, down a quiet road that provides access to paths

leading to what is usually regarded as England's smallest church, at Culbone. Our road now drops down into woodlands, and after paying a modest toll, we pass the entry to pretty Porlock Weir, before returning to Porlock.

Leave the popular and attractive village of **Porlock** southwards from the car park by Doverhay Court. Fork left immediately beyond 'Unsuitable for Heavy Vehicles' sign, and soon climb steeply. Now turn very sharp right and again climb very steeply on to open moorland road above woods to right. Straight, not right, and eventually drop down to cross stream in wooded valley. Fork left beyond Pool Farm (Sign — Wilmersham), through Wilmersham farmstead and down into another wooded valley before climbing up to **Stoke Pero**, with its little church on left.

Turn left at T-junction, and through Cloutsham farmstead into more wooded country, with fine picnic opportunities. Turn sharp right near Webber's Post. Good car parking here. Now climb steadily southwards up

At Porlock Weir.

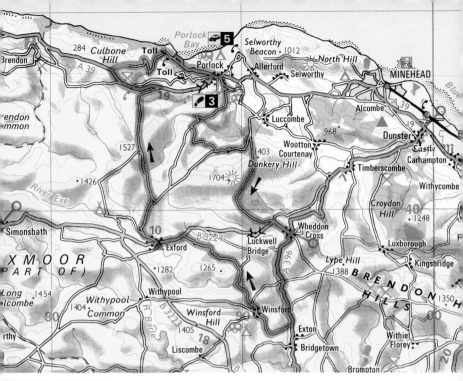

SCALE 1:190 080 or 3 MILES to 1 INCH

Dunkery Hill. Car park with path to **Dunkery Beacon** on right. Second car park and path to **Dunkery Beacon**, at Dunkery Gate, where road leaves moorland. Over small X-rds, on to B3224, and turn right with care, on to A396 in windy upland hamlet of **Wheddon Cross**. Good car park. Rest and be Thankful Inn.

Now head south on A396 for **three** miles, take **third** turn right, off A396 (Sign — Winsford), and follow Exe valley up to **Winsford**, one of Exmoor's prettiest villages. This has a picturesque inn, the Royal Oak, an interesting church, and no fewer than seven bridges, and a ford over the little Winn Brook. Link here with **Tour 4**. Explore this village, and then head up Exe valley, keeping village on left. Straight, not right twice after leaving village, keeping to wider road, and following signs to Exford.

Turn left on to B3224, and drop down into Exe valley, to **Exford**, bright little village with an inn and a hotel, and the kennels of the famous Devon and Somerset Stag Hounds. Turn right, off B3224 before bridge, and fork right in Edgcott hamlet just beyond village, to climb northwards out of the Exe valley. Fork left at Hillhead Cross, and soon bear left on to the open moorland of Exford Common. Now heading north on a fine open moorland road. Straight, not left at Lucott Cross. After one mile note remains of small Bronze Age stone circle over to left of road (see Porlock, page 65).

Turn sharp left, with great care, on to A39. Good car parking here. Also good car park half mile beyond, with fine views out over the coast. Straight, not right, keeping on A39. Picnic site on right. Straight, not left at Oare Post, keeping on A39. (Road to left goes down to Robber's Bridge, Oare and Malmsmead ... see **Tour 6**.) Turn right off A39 at Culbone Stables Inn, on to road which eventually becomes a toll road (Sign — Culbone). (But go straight ahead on A39 if you wish to visit **County Gate** National Park Information Centre, under three miles.)

Turn right at T-junction. It **may** be possible to park down to left, and to then walk to **Culbone**, with its minute church in a lovely woodland setting; but if possible park near the Ashley Combe Toll Gate (see below), and walk through woods. This is a longer walk, but a much more rewarding one. Turn sharp left at Y-junction. Toll road commences at entry to wooded area. Car Park on left. Walk from here, to **Culbone** (see above). Ashley Combe Toll Gate just beyond.

Straight, not left at entry to Porlock Weir, and then bear right on to B3225 which starts here. But turn left if you wish to visit delightful **Porlock Weir**, with its little harbour and pebbly beach overlooked by hotels and an inn, all beneath the great woodlands that here cover the steep northern slopes of Exmoor. Now through hamlet of West Porlock to return to **Porlock**, thus completing **Tour 5**.

Tour 6

Lynmouth, the Doone Country and North-West Exmoor

40 miles. Many grand moorland and coastal runs on this route, but cyclists will find a number of hills that might make them at least briefly appreciate the merits of car travel!

This route starts from Lynmouth and after a long climb, runs eastward for a time just behind the coast. It then turns abruptly and dives down into the gentle valley of the west-running Oare Water and East Lyn River, to explore some of the country immortalised by R. D. Blackmore in Lorna Doone. *After this valley run, the route heads southwards across the heart of the moor crossing that part which is so decisively marked 'Exmoor Forest' on our map, grand open country which was once a Royal hunting preserve. It turns again at Simonsbath in the lovely Barle valley, and leads away to the western confines of the moor at Blackmoor Gate, before heading almost due north to the coast again, this time at Hunter's Inn and Heddon's Mouth. From here we follow glorious coastal country eastwards past Woody Bay, Lee Abbey and The Valley of Rocks to return to Lynmouth via its hill-top neighbour Lynton.*

Starting from the delightful 'fishing village' of **Lynmouth**, which shelters beneath high cliffs at the mouth of the East and West Lyn Rivers, this route follows the A39 eastwards. It first climbs the long Countisbury Hill, and through the minute village of **Countisbury** beyond its top, and we are reminded of the epic journey made by the people of Lyn-

mouth, on one stormy night in January 1899. For details see page 40. Fine walking opportunities and coastal views.

Keep on A39, eastwards to **County Gate**, where there is a car park and an Exmoor National Park Information Centre from Easter to September. Walk from here, north to the coast at Glenthorne, or south to Malmsmead in the valley of the East Lyn River, which will be reached by road later on this tour. Keep on A39 by Culbone Stables Inn (but link with **Tour 5** here if you wish to move to Culbone and Porlock). Turn sharp right with care, off A39 at Oare Post and descend steeply into the Oare Water valley. Good car park on right, just before **Robber's Bridge**.

Now move down valley and go straight, not right by **Oare** church, scene of the shooting of Lorna in Blackmore's *Lorna Doone*. Apart from this connection, Oare church is worth visiting in its own right. See page 64 for other *Lorna Doone* associations. Pass roadway to Cloud Farm on left, Exmoor Natural History Centre opposite on left hand side of road. Just beyond this, over bridge and turn right in **Malmsmead**. Souvenir shop, and refreshment facilities here. Car park and picnic site just beyond. Our **Walk 5**, page 116, starts from here, running southwards, up through 'Doone Country'.

River in valley now known as East Lyn and no longer the Oare Water. Over X-rds in little village of **Brendon**. Enter narrower, thickly wooded part of valley beyond Stag Hunter's Hotel on left. Walk from here down beside the East Lyn River to Lynmouth. Rockford Inn on right. Now climb steeply out of valley, with Brendon church on right. Turn left at T-junction, fork right, turn left, and finally bear left on to B3223.

Now head southwards over grand moorland country, with at least three good car parks, from the last of which, Dry Bridge, it is

The Valley of Rocks, near Lynton.

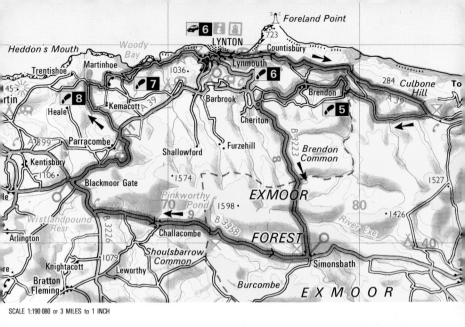

SCALE 1:190 080 or 3 MILES to 1 INCH

possible to walk eastwards, over to Malmsmead and the Doone Country, but only if properly equipped and experienced. Over cattle-grid into county of Somerset at Brendon Two Gates. Turn right, on to B3358 in **Simonsbath**, small village beautifully sited in the Barle valley, in the very heart of Exmoor. But turn left on to B3223 for nearby car park and picnic site. Walk from here down the Barle valley to Withypool, linking on to the **Two Moors Way** just beyond Cow Castle (180 SS 79-37).

Head westwards along B3358, passing across the line of the **Two Moors Way**, which uses a short section of our road at this point. Pass good car park and picnic site on right, below Goat Hill. Bleak moorland area to the north of here is known as **The Chains**, and represents a challenge only to the hardier and more experienced walker. Straight, not left, in **Challacombe**. Beyond Barton Gate (180 SS 68-41) there is a bridleway northwards running close to **Chapman Barrows** and not far to the west of the **Long Stone**. Advisable to use Landranger Map 180, or preferably Pathfinder Map SS 64/74, and to accept that this is not terrain for the faint-hearted, or the inexperienced.

Turn right at T-junction, on to B3226 (but turn left and take first right if you wish to visit the Exmoor Bird Gardens at South Stowford, see **Blackmoor Gate**, page 30). Straight, not right, keeping on B3226 (but turn left if you wish to visit **Wistlandpound Reservoir** — bird watching and fishing). Turn right on to A39 at **Blackmoor Gate**, and keep on A39 going straight, not left, above **Parracombe** village, observing slight remains of the old **Lynton and Barnstaple Railway**.

(But turn down left into village, and then up to right, if you wish to visit the interesting old church.)

Keep on A39 over first X-rds beyond **Parracombe**, and then turn left off A39 (Sign — Hunter's Inn). Drop down steeply and move with care down the Heddon valley to **Hunter's Inn**. Car park, hotel, shop, refreshments. Our **Walk 8**, page 122, starts from here. Turn sharp right by Hunter's Inn (Sign — Martinhoe) and up very steep hill. At Mannacott Farm, on left, there is the Exmoor Farm Animal Centre (see **Hunter's Inn**, page 53).

Turn left at T-junction, and then bear right through **Martinhoe**; splendid setting, but itself unexceptional. Small car park on left. Our **Walk 7**, page 120, starts from here, but if full, use next park. Straight, not right, and large car park on right; if you wish to walk down to Woody Bay, please park here. Fine views out over **Woody Bay**. Turn left at next junction (Sign — Woody Bay). Bend sharply round to right, road ahead is cul-de-sac with no parking. Now enter woods, path to **Woody Bay** beach soon down to left. Straight, not right, at Y-junction beyond hotel.

Beyond **Woody Bay**, through woods above the shore, and through Toll Gate near Lee Abbey. Car park, picnic site, toilets. Now enter dramatic '**Valley of Rocks**', a rock-scattered valley that first caught the imagination of the Romantic poets, and which has been highly popular ever since. Good car parking. Enter **Lynton**, a lively hill-top resort, complete with the Lyn and Exmoor Museum, and splendid views out over its smaller neighbour Lynmouth, in the valley below. Move through the town, and down to **Lynmouth**, thus completing Tour 6.

99

Tour 7
The Moltons and South-West Exmoor

35 miles. Not recommended for cyclists.

Our route sets out westwards from South Molton along the A361 Barnstaple road, and after passing the large mansion of Castle Hill, heads north through quiet and hilly countryside to the Bucklands, and north again to the little hamlet of Charles, where the uncle of Lorna Doone's creator was once rector. It then crosses the deep Bray valley to Brayford and starts a gradual climb, up on to the south-western fringes of Exmoor. Once on the moor near quaintly named Mole's Chamber, it starts a long run south-eastwards along the border between Devon and Somerset, before dropping off the moor to visit the little church of Molland. From the moors to the north of Molland we then head westwards through partly wooded countryside passing the hamlets of Twitchen and Heasley Mill, before returning through North Molton, to our journey's end at South Molton.

Start from the lively little market town of **South Molton**, with its handsome Georgian Guildhall, and its fascinating Quince Honey Farm. Move north-westwards, first on B3226, then keep on the old road towards Barnstaple. Cross River Mole at Stag's Head hamlet, and pass the fine 18th century mansion of Castle Hill (see **Filleigh**, page 47). Do not miss distant view of the Triumphal Arch at the end of an avenue on a hill well to the left.

Fork right with care about a mile beyond **Filleigh** church, and over small X-rds at Heddon, and soon over bridge crossing the A361. Over small X-rds at Buckinghams Leary, and keep straight through **West Buckland**, small village with no special features. At end of village, turn right (Sign — East Buckland), and West Buckland School soon on left. Over X-rds in **East Buckland**, drop into valley, turn left in Charles Bottom, and climb steeply up hill. Bear left, then turn right at X-rds and turn left in **Charles**, minute village where the young R. D. Blackmore used to stay with his uncle, who was rector here. Church not of great interest to visitors.

Head north from Charles, going straight, not left near Welcombe, and then drop very steeply down into the Bray valley. Turn left on to B3226, and very soon turn right, off B3226. Now go straight, not left, immediately beyond bridge into **Brayford** and climb up beyond village. Straight, not right (but turn right if you wish to visit Brayford church, at High Bray). Turn left, and up hill, going over junction of 'Cross Gate'. Now head northwards along road forming the western boundary of the Exmoor National Park.

SCALE 1:190 080 or 3 MILES to 1 INCH

South Molton's elegant Town Hall.

Turn right at Five Cross Way and climb steadily north-eastwards up towards the moor. Earthworks of Shoulsbury Castle over to left (see **Challacombe**, page 34). Turn right at Mole's Chamber, and head south-eastwards along the edge of Exmoor, following the Devon-Somerset boundary in parts. Many Bronze Age round barrows to left of road. Straight, not right at junction. Now following county boundary for some miles. At Comerslade, a wild moorland area to the left, ponies are usually to be seen grazing. More Bronze Age barrows ('Five Barrows') over to right.

Over X-rds at Kinsford Gate. Gradual rise to fine all-round viewpoint near Fyldon Common, with panoramic views of Exmoor over to left. Straight, not right twice, and turn right at Sandyway Cross (lonely Sportsman's Inn just up to left). Almost immediately turn left, and then bear left at diagonal X-rds. Over X-rds at 'White Post', and head south over open moorland. Over X-rds near Round Hill, leave moorland, and take first turn to right (but go straight ahead if you wish to visit interesting little **Molland** church). On to open moorland, and straight, not right, at entry to the remote hamlet of **Twitchen**, which is in a delightful setting, but is not itself very interesting.

Straight, not right, and straight not left in **Twitchen**, and bear left beyond church. Over five-way X-rds at Headgate (Sign — North Molton), and over second X-rds (Sign — North Molton). Through Millbrook hamlet, and eventually turn very sharp right (Sign — Sandyway). Now turn left at T-junction (Sign — Heasley Mill), and well beyond, over small stream entering wooded area along open road. Sharp turn left, down hill at T-junction, and over stream entering attractive hamlet and old mining centre of **Heasley Mill**.

Take first turn left in **Heasley Mill**, and climb out of valley. Head south, going straight not right three times, and enter **North Molton**, also a mining centre and once the fictional home of Tom Faggus, highwayman cousin of John Ridd in *Lorna Doone*. Largely unspoilt by tourism, it does have a pottery and craft centre and an interesting church. There is a good walk south from here, partly along the course of the old mine railway, to South Molton. Turn right by North Molton church and right again, and follow road southwards to South Molton, thus completing Tour 7.

Tour 8

Ilfracombe Country ... sandy beaches and secret inland valleys

35 miles. Good cycling, but very hilly in places.

This route starts from Ilfracombe, and heads eastward on an often dramatic coast road, before turning inland beyond Combe Martin. From here there is a diversion further along the coast to Hunter's Inn, but the main route heads southwards to the delightful National Trust property of Arlington Court, before plunging into quiet hill country punctuated by a series of deep wooded valleys. Here will be found a number of unspoilt villages including Shirwell, once the home of circumnavigator, Sir Francis Chichester. Moving westwards, with views south over the Taw estuary, the route eventually reaches the open coast beyond Braunton, and passes just behind a succession of magnificent beaches, and rock-girt peninsulas ... Saunton, Croyde, Baggy Point, Putsborough, Woolacombe, and Morte Point ... before arriving at journey's end at Ilfracombe.

Leave the bright and colourful resort town of **Ilfracombe** eastwards on A399 (Signs — Combe Martin), passing Hele Mill, a well restored 16th century watermill on right, after about a mile. Watermouth Castle (see **Berrynarbor**, page 27) up to right, entry to Watermouth Cove on left. Keep on A399 into **Combe Martin**, long village, and lively little holiday resort, complete with beaches and Motor Cycle Collection. Straight, not right by

church, keeping on A399, and straight not left at Y-junction keeping on A399. But fork left off A399, up Buzzacott Lane, if you wish to visit **Trentishoe** and **Hunter's Inn**. **If you do not wish to take the diversion, please skip next paragraph.**

To follow this diversion, climb steeply beyond **Combe Martin**, over X-rds at Stony Corner, and sharp turn left just beyond. Car parks with paths to **Holdstone Down** soon to left. Trentishoe Down to right. Much of this attractive area open to the road, with good walking opportunities. Now partly owned by National Trust, it was saved from housing development due largely to the lack of available water. Fork left keeping to higher road, and pass delightful little **Trentishoe** church. Drop down from **Trentishoe** into wooded valley, and bear left on to slightly wider road to arrive at **Hunter's Inn**. Link here with our **Walk 8**, page 122. **This ends our diversion. Now re-join main route by returning to A399.**

Now back on main route, leaving **Combe Martin** south-eastwards on A399. After almost two miles, over X-rds leaving A399, on to B3229. At Kentisbury, bear slightly right with care, on to A39. Now take second turn left off A39 (Sign — Arlington Court). Entry to **Arlington Court** on left, car park on right. Do not miss a visit to this outstanding National Trust property, home of the Chichester family from the 14th century until 1947. Delightful interior, and beautifully wooded park, with nature walk, carriage rides, Shetland ponies and Jacob sheep.

Bear left at T-junction beyond **Arlington Court**, but turn right if you wish to visit Arlington church. Bear right at Y-junction well beyond. Straight not right, unless you wish to visit **Loxhore** church. Straight, not

Ilfracombe Harbour ... in a splendidly romantic setting.

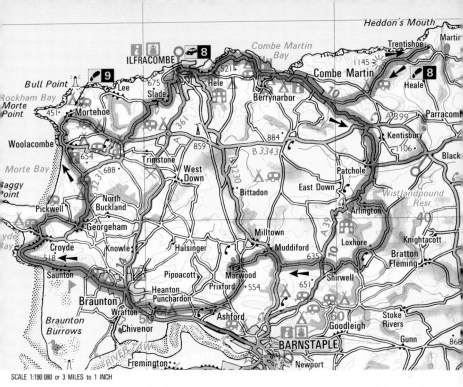

SCALE 1:190 080 or 3 MILES to 1 INCH

left, and then bear right, dropping steeply down into Yeo valley. Bear left in valley bottom, at Loxhore Cott, and then turn right beyond woods. Cross River Yeo, and climb steeply out of valley, to **Shirwell**. Church on right has associations with Sir Francis Chichester and his father, and both are buried in the churchyard.

Turn right beyond **Shirwell** church, and over X-rds crossing A39 with great care. Drop into small valley, up the other side and then bear right on to B3230, after dropping into second valley. Turn left, off B3230 in **Muddiford**. Visit Blakewell Fisheries. Turn left at X-rds, but go straight over if you wish to visit **Marwood**. Interesting 14th century church, and extensive gardens at Marwood Hill opposite. Having turned left at X-rds, over next X-rds in Guineaford, and eventually bear right in Prixford. Then bear left and turn right at Springfield Cross, and over diagonal X-rds before entering **Ashford**.

Keep straight, not left in **Ashford**, unless you wish to visit church, and heading west, eventually over X-rds at Windy Cross. Straight, not right and straight, not left in **Heanton Punchardon**, and past fine Perpendicular church, with interesting interior. Bear left by phone box, over minor road at off-set X-rds in Wrafton, bear right with care on to A361, and enter busy **Braunton**, a village which claims to be England's largest. Turn left at traffic lights, on to B3231 (Sign — Saunton). But go straight ahead on A361 if you wish to visit the fine church.

Well beyond **Braunton**, over offset X-rds, keeping on B3231. But turn left if you wish to visit Braunton Burrows and Braunton Marsh. Good car parks behind Burrows (SS 46-35) and on shore of Taw estuary (SS 46-32). Enter **Saunton**, passing **Somerset and North Devon Coast Path** to left. Car park for Saunton Sands on left. Enter **Croyde**, good car park to right. Turn left off B3231 (Sign — Croyde Bay). Straight, not left. But turn left if you wish to visit Croyde Beach or walk to **Baggy Point**. Turn right, but turn left if you wish to visit Putsborough Sand. Through small ford in **Putsborough**, and eventually turn left on to B3231 in **Georgeham**.

Pass **Georgeham** church, and keep on B3231 for two miles, before turning left following sign to Woolacombe. Drop steeply down hill towards **Woolacombe**, Woolacombe Warren car park on left below Potter's Hill. Marine Drive runs south from here, below Woolacombe Down, giving access to glorious stretch of Woolacombe Sand. Turn left in centre of Woolacombe, following sign to **Mortehoe**.

In **Mortehoe**, bear right by church. Our **Walk 9**, page 124, starts from Mortehoe car park. Over X-rds at Borough Cross. (Turning to left is start of very narrow road to **Lee Bay**, but it is preferable to visit this on our **Walk 9**.) Straight, not right, on to B3343, and almost immediately turn left on to B3231, and follow this into **Ilfracombe**, thus completing Tour 8.

Tour 9

Barnstaple, Bideford and the Taw and Torridge Country

42 miles. Rather hilly. Cyclists would be advised to select quiet, alternative, river valley roads shown on accompanying map.

This route starts from Barnstaple, southwards along the Taw valley, but soon heads into the hills to the east to visit the unusual Combat Vehicles Museum at Cobbaton, and the pretty thatched village of Chittlehampton. It then moves south-east, and later south-west, through Chittlehamholt and down to cross the Taw valley at Kingford. After climbing up through woodlands it calls first at High Bickington, whose church has a fine set of bench-ends, before heading westwards to the attractive little town of Great Torrington, with its fascinating Dartington Glass works, and fine views out over the Torridge valley. Now west again, through pretty Frithelstock and Buckland Brewer, before turning north to visit the fine old seaport town of Bideford. Beyond here, the route heads eastwards over quiet rolling hills, through Horwood and Tawstock, both of which have delightful churches well worth visiting, to return finally to Barnstaple.

Set out from the centre of the busy market town and holiday centre of Barnstaple, first going southwards on the B3138 following signs to Exeter. Then join A377 at busy interchange and head south into **Bishop's Tawton**, long village with fine church, pleasant views across Taw valley to Tawstock, and a good walk up to neighbouring Codden Beacon. At end of village bear left, off A377 and head east below Codden Hill. Take third turn to right (Sign — Cobbaton), and follow signs to Cobbaton. Bear right at second X-rds in Cobbaton hamlet, and beyond next small X-rds, **Cobbaton Combat Vehicles Museum** on left. Return to X-rds and now turn right (eastwards).

Now follow signs to **Chittlehampton**, large village with sloping square dominated by tall-towered church, and with a chilling tale of martyrdom here in the 8th century. Turnabout in square, turn left at X-rds, and over next X-rds crossing B3227. Head southwards over rolling hill country to **Chittlehamholt**, situated on a ridge with well afforested slopes on either side. Fork right in Chittlehamholt, then fork left and turn right,

SCALE 1:190 080 or 3 MILES to 1 INCH

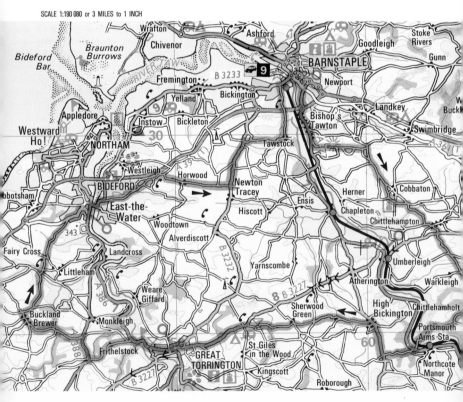

Tawstock Church, with Bishop's Tawton in view across the Taw Valley.

dropping down to cross River Taw, and just beyond cross A377 with great care at Kingford hamlet. Up hill through woods, and turn right at X-rds on to B3217.

Into **High Bickington**, small village with a church of Norman origin and a fine series of bench-ends. Take second left, off B3217, and leave village past church. Fork right in wooded valley, and climb steeply up beyond. Over X-rds, and over second X-rds, bearing partly left in Sherwood Green. Now bear right, on to B3227, and enter pleasant little market town of **Great Torrington**. Bear left at roundabout on to B3232, and almost immediately straight, not left, joining A386. Turning to right, down School Lane, leads to interesting Dartington Glass works which are well worth visiting. Church on left. Keep through town on A386.

Straight, not left at end of **Great Torrington**, keeping on A386. Car park and picnic area on right. Pleasant bracken-covered country. Over Rothern Bridge, crossing River Torridge, and soon fork left, off A386, and straight not right (Signs — Frithelstock). Enter **Frithelstock**, pleasant village with hospitable inn, interesting church and remains of a 13th century priory. Fork right and turn right with great care, on to A388 at Frithelstock Stone hamlet. Turn left at X-rds, off A388, and eventually into deep wooded valley, following signs to Buckland Brewer.

Bear right, into hill-top village of **Buckland Brewer**. Church has Norman south doorway and interesting 17th and 18th century monu-

ments. Turn right at X-rds beyond village, fork left in Burrough hamlet, and turn right to cross little River Yeo beyond Hooper's Water Farm. Now straight, not right twice, up steep hill, and over small X-rds. Straight, not right, and drop into a deep valley beyond Littleham Court. Climb up and eventually bear right on to old main road, and follow signs marked **Bideford.**

Into attractive old town of **Bideford**, with its quays and fine bridge over the River Torridge. Cross this bridge, into East-the-Water. Turn left at end of bridge and after short distance, fork right off A386 (Sign — 'Old Barnstaple Road'). But go straight ahead on A386 then B3233 if you wish to visit attractive **Tapeley Park** and **Instow**. Now head north-eastwards, straight across open country to Eastleigh hamlet, where route turns right (Sign — Horwood). Through little village of **Horwood**, with its small but interesting church.

Over X-rds in Lower Lovacott hamlet, and turn left at X-rds, on to B3232. After two miles turn right at X-rds in St John's Chapel hamlet, off B3232, and head eastwards to **Tawstock**, pleasant little thatched village with a splendid 16th century gatehouse and beyond it, a fine church with many attractive features. Turn-about at **Tawstock** church, take first turn to right, and follow minor road into **Barnstaple**. Bear right, on to main road, follow down on this road, and cross bridge over the River Taw to arrive at **Barnstaple** town centre, thus completing Tour 9.

Tour 10

Clovelly, Hartland and the western cliffs

43 miles. An exhilarating, but sometimes tiring run for cyclists.

This route starts from Bideford, and for a reason that will soon become apparent, it runs in an anti-clockwise direction, unlike the other nine tours. It heads west along the A39, and after calling at delightful Buck's Mills, it suggests the use of the outstandingly beautiful Hobby Drive (hence the anti-clockwise route). After visiting Clovelly, probably the West Country's most popular attraction, our route heads further west, to Hartland Point and Hartland Quay, but not before providing further diversions to explore the rugged coastline behind which it passes. And now southwards, behind the high western cliffs that run beyond our turning point at Welcombe Mouth, along the dramatic coast of North Cornwall. We now turn inland, passing small unspoilt villages, and through an undramatic farming landscape punctuated in places by woodlands and small stretches of wilder country, and enlivened from time to time by distant views of Dartmoor and Exmoor. Pausing perhaps for a visit to the Gnome Reserve at West Putford or a walk in Melbury Woods, the route returns northeastwards to the rather busier world of Bideford, thus completing Tour 10.

Starting from the fine old seaport town of **Bideford**, this route soon joins the A39 and

heads westwards for almost ten miles, passing through two hamlets, Horns Cross and Hoops, both with welcoming inns. Beyond these it passes through Buck's Cross, and it is possible to turn right here to visit the pretty coastal hamlet of **Buck's Mills**, where there is a car park, which is the starting point of our **Walk 10**, page 126. On the right, just under a mile beyond Buck's Cross, is the entrance to the Hobby Drive (see Clovelly, page 38), a three-mile toll road running through coastal woodlands. This is not shown on the accompanying map and its surface requires slow and careful driving, but the views make it well worthwhile. It ends at Clovelly car park — see below.

If you have kept on A39, and not used the Hobby Drive, move a further two miles westwards, and then turn right, on to B3237 at **Clovelly Dykes** (Sign — Clovelly). Drive to Clovelly car park, and walk down to the outstandingly beautiful village of **Clovelly**. If you cannot manage the walk back up the very steep village street, use the Landrover service, but the experience is far more rewarding if you can cope unaided. While here, look at the church and also try to walk westward to **Mouth Mill**.

Turnabout at Clovelly car park, and take first turn to right, off B3237, and turn right again, by **Clovelly Dykes**. Fork right (Sign — Hartland Point). Straight, not right. But turn right if you wish to use National Trust car park at Brownsham Farm as a base for a walk to **Mouth Mill**, and Gallantry Bower. Continue to head westwards, following signs to Stoke and Hartland Quay, but turn to right if you first wish to visit **Shipload Bay**, north

Hartland Point . . . Devon's north-western extremity.

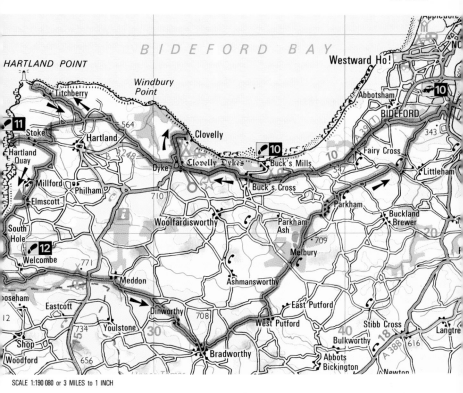

SCALE 1:190 080 or 3 MILES to 1 INCH

of Titchberry (park at entrance to East Titchberry Farm), and **Hartland Point**.

Beyond Pattard Cross and Downe Farm, turn left, cross deep little valley over the Abbey River, and turn right beyond hill, to move to **Stoke**, small thatched hamlet with a tall-towered church, well worth visiting. Move west from here to visit **Hartland Quay**, which is the start of our **Walk 11**, page 128. Fine coastal scenery here, with several walking opportunities. Turnabout at Hartland Quay, and return to Stoke, forking right at end of this hamlet, taking two turns to right, and then turning left at small X-rds to head south to Lymebridge. Walk right from here to visit the rocky coast at **Speke's Mill Mouth**, which is also on our **Walk 11**.

Move south to Elmscott, and turn right at X-rds here (Sign — Welcombe). Straight, not left twice, and bear round to left near Welcombe Mouth, which is on our **Walk 12**, page 130 (see **Welcombe**, page 79). (Walk from road to Welcombe Mouth, and beyond to **Marsland Mouth**, which marks the border with Cornwall.) Now head inland, eastwards through Darracot hamlet, and bear right at T-junction.

Eventually at Welcombe Cross, over X-rds with great care crossing A39. Turn right in Meddon hamlet, straight, not right just beyond Brinford Bridge and head south-eastwards, through Dinworthy hamlet to large and unspoilt village of **Bradworthy**. Turn left at X-rds in square, turn right at T-junction beyond village, and follow signs to West Putford; but turn right at X-rds before reaching village if you wish to visit the Gnome Reserve (see **West Putford**, page 82).

Turn left at X-rds in West Putford, but turn right if you wish to visit unspoilt little church. Now heading northwards, going straight not left twice, and over Kismeldon Bridge, crossing infant River Torridge. Over X-rds at Powler's Piece. **Melbury Forest** picnic site in the vicinity, with two forest trails starting from it. Through extensive woodlands, fork left and through further woodlands and straight not left, before entering **Parkham**. Church has Norman south doorway and medieval Barnstaple tiles.

Fork right by **Parkham** church and descend into deep little wooded valley. Turn right, cross bridge, turn left just beyond, and head along road parallel with little River Yeo. Eventually bear right at T-junction, keeping on wider road, then turn left near Hooper's Water Farm and over bridge crossing River Yeo. Now straight not right, twice, up steep hill and over small X-rds. Straight, not right, and drop into deep valley beyond Littleham Court. Climb up and eventually bear right on to the old main road, and then follow signs into **Bideford**, thus completing Tour 10.

Walks

Walk 1
Quantock Uplands ...
'Poet's Country'

Approximately 6 miles. Allow 4 hours.

This walk follows a series of well defined tracks and pathways, up deep wooded combes, and out over a typically beautiful stretch of Quantock hill country. A short length at the beginning and end of this walk is on a minor road, and almost all the remainder is on a hard stony track, which is a public bridleway. Here on the central spine of the hills are wide expanses of bracken, gorse and heather, providing a gently coloured foreground to distant views out over the often sunny waters of the Bristol Channel. There are also views out over the surrounding valley country, with its patchwork of fields and woodlands, towards the Black Down and Brendon Hills, and on the skyline over to the west, the darker outlines of Exmoor itself. This Quantock countryside was much loved by Wordsworth and his sister Dorothy, who lived for a time at Alfoxton (Alfoxden) Park, and by their friend Coleridge, who lived at Nether Stowey. For an account of the happy

and formative months they all spent in and around these hills, read Berta Lawrence's excellent book, Coleridge and Wordsworth in Somerset, *and the* Alfoxden Journal of Dorothy Wordworth, *edited by H.Darbishire.*

Drive to the village of **Holford** (181) (ST 15-41), which is situated about 11 miles west of Bridgwater, just off the A39, and which is on **Tour 1**, page 88. After passing church and row of thatched cottages, fork right towards Hodder's Combe, cross stream to the Green, and **car park** is on left.

(A) Start walk by re-crossing the stream and turning right, thereby heading towards Holford Combe. After passing Combe House with its attractive waterwheel and old cottages, the road becomes a gravel track, crossing and re-crossing a stream with oak woodlands on each side.

(B) Leave stream after one and a half miles, where it divides into two or three smaller ones and five other paths meet (this is the junction of Holford Combe with Frog Combe and Lady's Combe). Take the centre path, which is quite steep and stony, in a southerly direction. In a quarter of a mile reach open hill country, typical of the Quantock uplands, with heather, gorse and bracken. Look **backwards** for view of **Dowsborough** (Iron Age settlement) over to right, the distant waters of the Bristol Channel ahead, and Hare Knap (small hill with

Alfoxton Park Hotel ... the Wordsworths' 'Alfoxden' for a brief year.

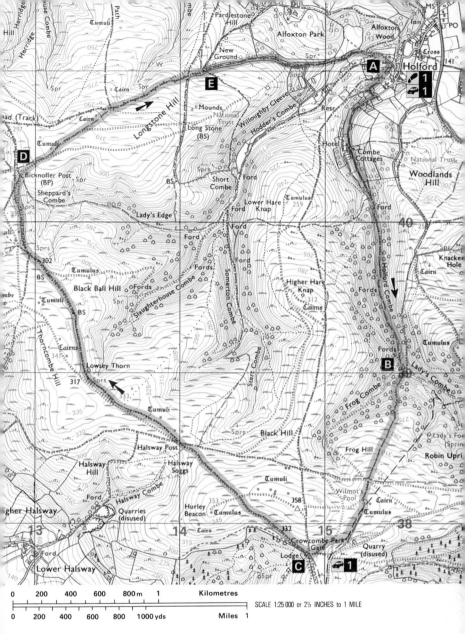

cairns) over to left. Continue in a southerly direction, crossing a well used track and then over the brow of a hill, where a tarred road comes into view. At the road a path turns to a westerly direction and Crowcombe Park Gate is soon reached.

(C) At Crowcombe Park Gate make a half turn right in a north-westerly direction, and follow a track, with Hurley Beacon on left, and continue along ridgeway with fine views over to left of the Brendons, and the dark outline of Exmoor beyond. After a short distance, good views down to right of the wooded Stert, Somerton and Slaughter-

house Combes. At two miles beyond Crowcombe Park Gate, arrive at Bicknoller Post, a meeting point of many Quantock pathways.

(D) Now leave Bicknoller Post by well worn track, bearing right (north-eastwards), over the ridge of Longstone Hill. Picking up a track en route, head towards New Ground where there is a clump of trees known as Holford Beeches.

(E) Beyond Holford Beeches walk in an easterly direction, following a rough lane between Alfoxton Park and Hodder's Combe, down to the Dog Pound and Holford Green **(A)**, thereby completing Walk 1.

Walk 2
Dunster Deer Park and Woodlands

Approximately 5½ miles. Allow 4 hours.

This walk starts from the delightful little town of Dunster, with its great castle overlooking a broad street, in which stands the quaint 17th century Yarn Market. It leaves the town over a medieval packhorse bridge, and climbs up beside a deer park, through splendid woodlands. Dropping down into a valley it passes through quiet farmland, before taking to the woods once more. There is a picnic area on Luxborough Lane, at Croydon Hill (181) (ST 97-42), and this would make an ideal meeting point with any members of the family who do not wish to do the whole walk. From this point, the walk goes up through Towns Wood and Whits Wood, and down into the valley of the little Avill stream, before climb-

ing up into yet more woodlands. Once above these woods, beyond Hole's Corner, there are fine views south and east, out over the valley to the Iron Age settlements of Gallax Hill and Bat's Castle, and beyond to the coast. From here it is downhill all the way, back into Dunster, which has inns, and restaurants in plenty.

Drive to **Dunster** (181) (SS 99-43), which is situated just to the south of the A39, 3 miles south-east of Minehead, and which is on **Tour 2**, page 90.

(A) Start from the small car park at the end of Park Street, Dunster, having turned down from the main road at the Forester's Arms. Head southwards, over Gallox Bridge, a medieval packhorse bridge, passing final cottages on right. Take the Withycombe path over the stile, following red way-marked path up hill through woods, forking left at one point.

(B) Towards top of the hill reach way-marked finger posts and turn left through

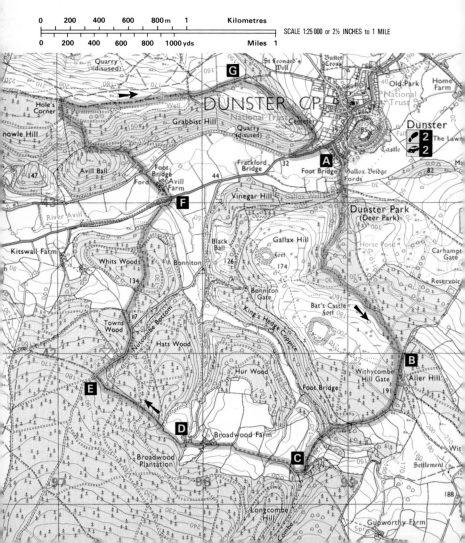

Gallox Bridge, Dunster . . . near the start of Walk 2.

Withycombe Hill Gate, immediately forking right, leaving the Withycombe path on left. Pleasant track continues downhill, until very sharp left turn on to blue way-marked Luxborough path, where route curves right, then left and then straight.

(C) Leave track when it turns sharp left, and turn right, down over a stream, where there is a tree stump on right. The route now follows a grassy track and bears right up through a gate into a field with hedge on right. Pass through another gate, proceed along a farm track, and then finally through gate, turning left on to farm track with Broadwood Farm on right.

(D) After a very short distance, just past a green painted water pumping unit on left, turn left off the lane and enter narrow, rather obscure path into woods, leaving a gate and field on right. The path curves up hill through woods, and crossing over a broad track, continues up a grassy path between woods and ferns. When reaching a further boundary track, turn left for about 400 yards before turning sharp right into fir tree plantation. This area is not way-marked, but after a short while pass through a hunting gate into Luxborough Lane.

(E) Turn right into Luxborough Lane and continue for about one third of a mile. Pass Croydon Hill picnic area on left, and ignoring a green footpath sign on left, turn left on to yellow way-marked route into Towns Wood. Shortly afterwards, turn right into Whits Woods, the path not being way-marked. Continue along left fork of track, and then bearing left along grassy path, leave woods through gate into field.

(F) Cross A396 at Avill Farm, and continue along track across footbridge over stream. Now cross over minor road and continue on right of way across and into Avill Ball woods. The path here has nearly been obliterated in parts due to tracks of timber extraction vehicles, but follow carefully, bearing left and then turning right before reaching the top of Grabbist Hill slightly to the right of Hole's Corner. Turning right along hill-top track, there are fine views ahead of the coastline, with the Iron Age settlements on Gallax Hill clearly visible on the Deer Park hill-top on right beyond valley.

(G) Using yellow way-marked path, fork right at the National Trust sign, down path back into Dunster, turning right on the final stretch before meeting the road by the bridge. Continue along the A396 for a short distance before turning right at the Forester's Arms, down Park Street to the car park **(A)**, thus completing Walk 2.

Walk 3
Exmoor's Wooded Northern Flanks

Approximately 7½ miles. Allow 4½ hours.

This walk starts from the busy and colourful village of Porlock, and heads up a steep road leading to open moorland below Ley Hill, before dropping down into deep woodlands that clothe the valley of the little Horner Water stream. After crossing the Horner Water, the walk heads up through Stoke Wood to the little church of Stoke Pero, which is situated high above the woods, but below open slopes leading to the summit of Dunkery Beacon (not on our route, but well worth a diversion). It now follows a small road from Stoke Pero, down past Wilmersham and Pool Farms, before re-crossing the stream and climbing steeply out of its wooded valley. Leaving the road, the walk heads for Lucott Farm along a ridge above the stream it has recently crossed, before dropping down into yet another beautifully wooded valley, Hawk Combe, which it then follows down into Porlock.

(A) Start from the village of **Porlock** (181) (SS 88-46), which is situated about 6 miles west of Minehead on A39. Leave the Dover-hay car park, off the High Street, with the old pink-washed Museum and Information Centre on the corner, and proceed up Dover-hay, the road soon rising steeply. On reaching the junction signpost, keep left towards West Luccombe, and then take a right hand path signed *'Ley Hill 1½ miles, Stoke Pero 3*

miles'. Pass through gate on to a broad grassy track which eventually leads to a narrow zig-zag path up through Doverhay Plantation to Ley Hill, passing through another gate adjoining the road.

(B) Turn right on to the road for a short distance, then take path on left signposted *Flora's Ride to Horner Gate*, which leads over heathland with fine sweeping views of the Bristol Channel to the right and the villages of Horner, Allerford and Selworthy to the left. This path, narrow at first, broadens into a bridleway. Follow this across the moor, skirting the edge of Horner Woods until the track turns sharp left to enter the wood. Now continue downward through Horner Woods as far as a junction marked *Granny's Ride/ Horner Gate/Stag's Path. Granny's Ride* is shown both to left and right, but the path to the **right** should be taken, descending eventually to a footbridge over Horner Water, the sound of which can be heard well before it comes into view.

(C) Cross this footbridge, on the other side of which is a signpost to *'Stoke Pero'.* The path initially follows the stream on the right and then climbs up through Stoke wood, to Church Farm at Stoke Pero, passing through two gates at the top, and then through the farmyard on to the Cloutsham-Pool Bridge road. Stoke Pero church is now on left. Standing at 1013 feet above sea level, this is the second highest church on Exmoor – only Simonsbath's being higher. Take road to right, downhill towards Wilmersham Farm. Keep on road, past Wilmersham Farm.

(D) Bear right at Pool Cross still keeping on road, past Pool Farm, down to Pool Bridge. Cross the bridge following the road as it turns

Porlock.

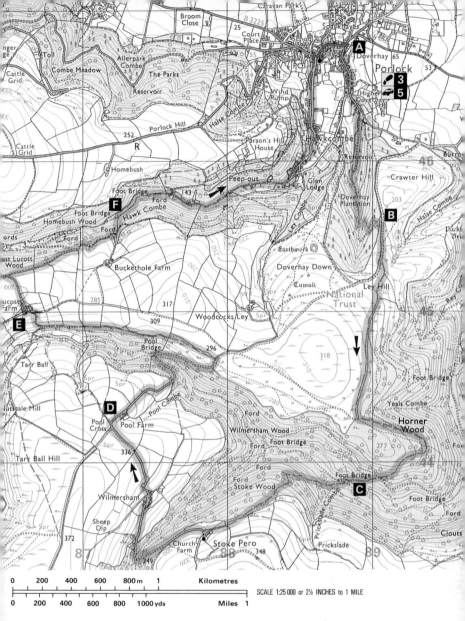

sharp right and then climbs steeply towards the entrance to Lucott Farm at the top of the hill. But just before this is reached, take the path to the left, which follows the farm's boundary fence, and continue along this, passing through two gates until reaching a third gate, which opens on to a narrow stony track. Turn right along this track, which, after a short stiff climb, emerges at Lucott farm buildings.

(E) Take the farm road past Lucott farm buildings (being careful to keep to the 'permissive path'), which leads to a gate signed (in the direction from which we have come) *Horner Valley via Lucott Farm*.

Through gate and turn right, following yellow way-marked path along edge of wood to Buckethole Wood. Bear left down into Hawk Combe, at point where path comes in from right, from Buckethole Farm.

(F) Bear right near stream and follow 'central path' down Hawk Combe towards Porlock. This develops into a lane bordered by houses and cottages (the first being *The Stables, Coombe Garden* and *Peep-Out*), as the village of Porlock is approached. Now into Parson Street with St Dubricius Church on right. Turn right along High Street, and return to car park **(A)**, thus completing Walk 3 .

Walk 4
Tarr Steps and the Upper Barle

Approximately 6½ miles. Allow 4 hours.

This walk runs in a northerly direction, up the valley of the lovely River Barle, from the ancient clapper bridge of Tarr Steps, to the pretty moorland village of Withypool. This village also has a fine old bridge, this one carrying an attractive moorland road, part of which we follow, along the eastern flank of Withypool Hill, running parallel with the Barle on our return to Tarr Steps. We reach these by taking a pleasant way-marked path across the fields from Westwater Farm, ending our journey by crossing the great stones spanning the sparkling river.

(A) Start from the car park above and just to the east of **Tarr Steps** (181) (SS 87-32), which is about 3 miles north-west of Dulverton, off B3223. Go downhill from car park to Tarr Steps. Do not cross the River Barle, but

turn right into a meadow and follow the clear, yellow way-marked path up the valley. Now following one of the routes of the Two Moors Way (see page 76), keep as close as possible to the Barle on the left. This valley has great scenic value and is rich in wildlife.

(B) About 2 miles above Tarr Steps, there is a right of way using stepping stones across the river, but these have been damaged and are usually impassable. (However if it is possible to cross here, the lane on the opposite bank provides a short-cut across to the route returning southwards below Withypool Hill.) The main route, on this section a 'permissive path' waymarked by Exmoor National Park, continues, twisting, climbing away from the river, crossing several stiles to a road. Turn left on to road, and down hill into attractive village of **Withypool**.

(C) Leave Withypool by fine old bridge over the Barle. Straight, not right shortly beyond bridge, and keep straight on up steep hill, on to unfenced moorland road across eastern flank of Withypool Hill. After a mile the road drops between hedges to Westwater Farm.

(D) Beyond Westwater Farm, cross West

Tarr Steps ... the beginning and the end of Walk 4.

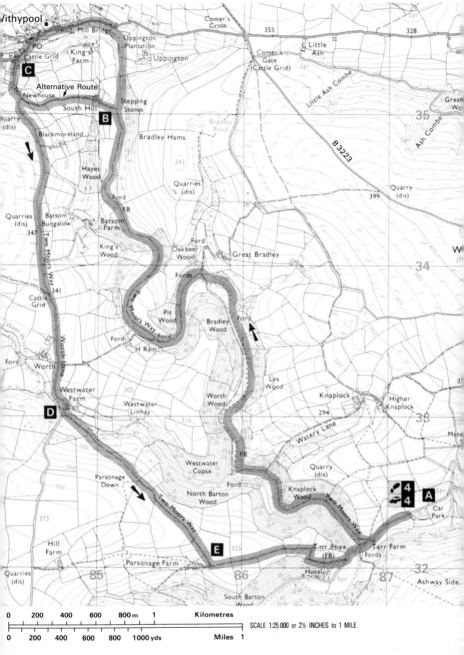

Water stream and turn left on to yellow way-marked path, signed *Tarr Steps*. Cross first field low down to a gate, then continue in same direction uphill, with a gully on left and a wire fence on right, to a gate and stile. Follow the left path at the next field to another gate, then the right hand edge of two more large fields. There are fine views from here over the Barle to Winsford Hill.

(E) In the far corner of the second field turn left with the hedgerow on the right, to another gate. The path follows the right hand edge of the next field and the left of another. In the far corner of this last field, turn right, down a rough sunken track which emerges close to **Tarr Steps**. Cross the river by the great stones and climb steeply back up to the car park **(A)**, thus completing Walk 4.

Walk 5
The Doone Country and Brendon Common

Approximately 6 miles. Allow 4 hours.

This walk will surely be considered a 'must' for any enterprising Exmoor visitor, as it takes one deep into the Doone Country, with its isolated combes surrounded by open heather covered moorland. Starting from Malmsmead, it heads up the lovely Badgworthy Water valley, passing a memorial to R. D. Blackmore, the author who immortalised this countryside in his much loved book, Lorna Doone. *It then passes the entrance to Lank Combe, before heading further up the valley to the site of a medieval village. From here the walk leads over high moorland country, with fine views on every side, before fording a little stream near the head of Lank Combe. It then heads north-eastwards over more high country, crossing over another ford, and taking in distant views over to the coast, before returning to Malmsmead by a short length of road. (See also Doone Country, page 42.)*

(A) Start from **Malmsmead** (180) (SS 79-

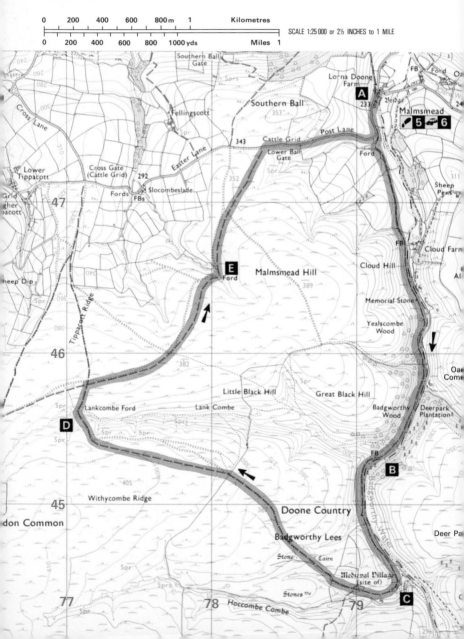

SCALE 1:25 000 or 2½ INCHES to 1 MILE

Lorna Doone Farm, Malmsmead ... a welcome sight at the end of Walk 5.

47), which is situated in the valley of the East Lyn River, about four miles east of Lynton. Use the car park, with its picnic and toilet facilities. Walk to the road junction by the shop and cafe which overlook the bridge and ford crossing Badgworthy (pronounced *Badgery*) Water, a short distance above its confluence with the Oare Water. From this point follow southwards, up the tarred road for about 300 yards. Then branch off to the left through an iron gate on to the way-marked path. Follow the yellow waymarks, eventually passing Cloud Farm, on your left on the opposite bank of the river. Note, a little upstream from the footbridge, the remains of the old bridge swept away by the floods that devastated Lynmouth in 1952. Continue along this path with Badgworthy Water on your left and eventually come to the *Richard Doddridge Blackmore Memorial Stone*, which was erected at this spot in 1969, in memory of the author who will always be best remembered for his classic story, *Lorna Doone*. In rhododendron time, the blossom here is delightful. The path and the river then continue through oak woodlands to a footbridge over Lank Combe.

(B) At this point a short diversion up the attractive Lank Combe is rewarding. Retrace your steps, cross the footbridge and continue southwards, up the path which hugs the side of the river until reaching the site of a medieval village in Hoccombe Combe. A halt here for a picnic and for enjoyment of the scenery and solitude (on all but the busiest days), is well worthwhile.

(C) Now bear right, out of the combe, following the signpost's direction to *Brendon Common* and climb steadily up on to the moor. Look back over your shoulder occasionally in order not to miss the views which unfold as you climb. Pass through way-marked gate at the top, and continue to Lankcombe Ford.

(D) Beyond Lankcombe Ford there is a multiplicity of tracks, but go straight ahead and look for the signpost on the horizon ahead, as the hill is climbed. At the signpost, turn right to Malmsmead, which is 2 miles from this point. In about one third of a mile, the paths splits into three indistinct and unmarked tracks, so be sure to bear left, and in a few yards, bear left again. The route leads to another ford, about one third of a mile ahead.

(E) Beyond this ford below Malmsmead Hill, the path continues on to the moor road two thirds of a mile beyond. On this stretch glance occasionally to the left for distant glimpses of the South Wales coast, and views of The Valley of Rocks at Lynton, and the Great Hangman hill above Combe Martin. On joining the road, turn right and walk downhill for half a mile, to return to the starting point at Malmsmead **(A)**, thus completing Walk 5.

Walk 6

Lynmouth, Watersmeet and the Cleaves

Approximately 4 miles. Allow 3 ½ hours.

This walk takes the rambler through some of the most spectacular landscape in North Devon. It is an area of deep, steep sided, and lushly wooded valleys, with fast flowing rivers always below. Some sections of the walk are therefore steep. Our path follows up the beautifully wooded, north bank of the sparkling East Lyn River as far as the point where it is joined by the Hoar Oak Water. This is Watersmeet, where there is a picturesque early 19th century fishing lodge, now owned by the National Trust, but which has been a favourite destination for visitors for well over a hundred years. Climbing steeply out of the valley, our walk heads back along the more sparsely wooded moorland country of the Cleaves, from whence there are often spectacular views, before dropping down again to return to Lynmouth.

Lynmouth Harbour.

Drive to the village of **Lynmouth** (180) (SS 72-49), which is situated on the A39, about 17 miles west of Minehead, and 18 miles north-east of Barnstaple, and which is on **Tour 6**, page 98.

(A) Start the walk from the car park upstream from the river bridge. Take path from the car park, walk upstream and shortly cross footbridge. Turn right onto small road on far bank. In about 300 yards join the footpath and keep straight on, turning off left at sign to *Arnold's Linhay*. Climb up steep path through woodlands, but bear right when reaching sign towards *Watersmeet and Rockford*. Later keep left following sign *Watersmeet*, and after a short distance enjoy the view below right, of the East Lyn River and Myrtleberry House. Path now follows bend in the valley until it joins another from a combe on left.

(B) Follow main path, where our route is signed to *Watersmeet, half mile*. Now drop down to river level with rough scree on hillside to the left, and rewarding views of dippers working on the right for those who are prepared to linger quietly here. Pass below Horner's Neck Wood, up to left, and imposing new stone bridge on right. This was

built to replace old one, the remains of which can still be seen farther up stream, washed away by the Lynmouth Flood of 1952. Our path continues on same side of river and soon reaches Watersmeet House, built in 1830 by the Halliday family as a fishing lodge, and now a National Trust property, with a pleasant restaurant and shop which are open throughout the holiday season (approximately from Easter to the end of October). This is a suitable place to take a break for a meal or picnic, and to enjoy the scenery, which includes the waterfalls of Hoar Oak Water, which joins the East Lyn River here, hence the name *Watersmeet*.

(C) Now leave Watersmeet and cross the two footbridges. Climb the path beyond signed *Lynton over the Cleaves, County Road A39*. Cross the A39 with great care and join the path signed *Lynmouth and Lynbridge via the Cleaves*. This climbs steeply for about a quarter of a mile, to the top of the hill, but stop from time to time to enjoy the fine views, especially down right to Lynmouth.

(D) Bear right at the top of hill, on to a path which is later signed *Lynton and Lynmouth*. Cross little Lyn Cleave by steep zig-zag paths, from which there are further spectacular views. Continue to a point overlooking Lynmouth and turn right at the sign marked *Lynmouth, half mile*. Now descend a steep twisting path, to the starting point **(A)**, which is opposite the point where our path emerges on to the main road at the bottom of Lynmouth Hill, thus completing Walk 6.

Watersmeet.

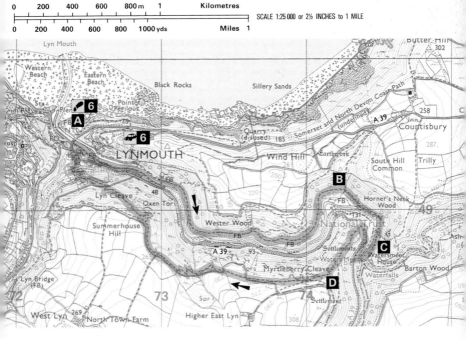

Walk 7
Martinhoe and Woody Bay

Approximately 5 miles. Allow 4 hours.

This walk passes through the beautiful and tranquil Woody Bay area, the character of which might have been vastly different if better fortune had favoured the developers, who built a pier here at the turn of the century to encourage steamer traffic from Bristol and South Wales. Happily for us, stormy seas demolished most of the pier within only five years of its completion, and since then Woody Bay has remained largely undisturbed by tourist pressure. There is access at Woody Bay to the curving rock-strewn shore, and there are delightful woodlands complete with stream and waterfall. There are also attractive coastal views from

the wooded road between here and Lee Abbey, where our walk turns inland up a wooded combe following a quiet path to Croscombe Barton. From here we return over the fields of Martinhoe Common to our starting point, passing a large group of Bronze Age round barrows in the final stages.

(A) Start from small parking area (180) (SS 671-485) to east of **Martinhoe**, which is on **Tour 6**, page 98, and situated just over a mile to the north of the A39, at Martinhoe Cross (itself three miles south-west of Lynton). If there is no space here, use larger car park a little way to the east (SS 674-485). Leave the small parking area, taking the path alongside the National Trust sign marked *Woody Bay*, and shortly re-join the road at a hairpin bend. Almost immediately turn left through gate on to bridleway signed *Coast Path Hunter's Inn* (but see below). After about 200 yards, turn right on to an unsigned, sharply descending

Lee Bay, near the Lee Abbey Toll House.

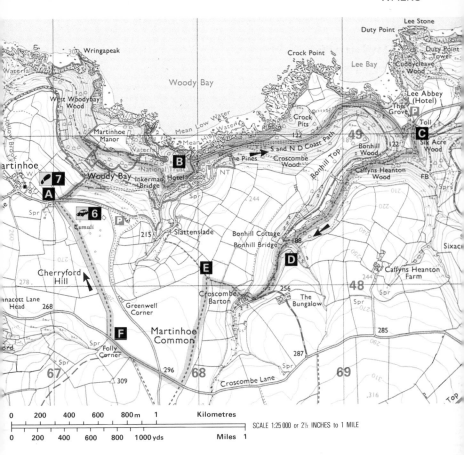

```
0    200   400   600   800m   1         Kilometres
|----|-----|-----|-----|-----|
0    200   400   600   800   1000 yds   Miles   1

SCALE 1:25 000 or 2½ INCHES to 1 MILE
```

track which again joins the road below. As this section of the walk is a steep descent and could be difficult in wet weather, it may be avoided by **not** turning left at sign *Coast Path Hunter's Inn*, but taking the road down towards Martinhoe Manor. This joins the end of the steep track just above Wringapeak House, which is passed lower down. Continue down the twisting road following signs to *Woody Bay Beach*, and shortly afterwards, bear right up an unsigned track. This leads again, after a quarter of a mile, to the public road near the Woody Bay Hotel.

(B) Turn left on to road by Woody Bay Hotel and follow this through a wooded area with sea down to left, until reaching Lee Abbey Toll House. There is a suitable picnic point here, with a cafe open during summer, and parking and toilet facilities.

(C) Turn right, off the road here, between the Toll House and a stream, taking path signed *Public Footpath*. Climb up through woods for about a mile, following occasional signs marked *Croscombe*. Keep stream on your right and be careful not to be misled by tracks carved into the hillside for forestry work.

(D) Eventually cross a small footbridge over stream, leading to Bonhill Bridge and Cottage, and a bridleway. Take the bridleway following sign *Croscombe Barton, quarter mile*. Just before reaching Croscombe Barton, our path turns off right, over a wall, down wooden steps to *Slattenslade*. It then crosses a field to similar steps on the far side. Turn right here on to a track, but after a short way, turn left through gate into a field. Follow in the direction indicated by the signpost and skirt the farm to a stile and signpost directing us to the right. Follow the hedge to a stile at the top of the field.

(E) Turn left after crossing stile, and keep the wall/hedge on left for half a mile until reaching the public road (Croscombe Lane) through a gate. Turn right on to this road, and go straight over cross-roads, following sign to *Hunter's Inn*.

(F) In about a quarter of a mile, at Folly Corner, take the unsigned path to right, through a gate into a field, and follow the hedge on left for about half a mile, noting extensive group of Bronze Age round barrows over to right. Now arrive at our starting point **(A)**, thus completing Walk 7.

121

Walk 8

Hunter's Inn, Trentishoe and Heddon's Mouth

Approximately 5 miles. Allow 4½ hours.

This is a relatively level walk, with only one significant ascent, and takes the walker through woodlands and down a steep-sided valley to some dramatic coastal scenery. There are gift shops, public toilets and refreshments near the Hunter's Inn car park. We first explore up a gentle, wooded valley beside a small stream, and then head up over the bare moorland of Trentishoe Down to visit the delightful little church of Trentishoe. Then down into the wooded Heddon Valley, and beside the river on its final dash to the sea, with every chance of spotting dippers and grey wagtails. Reaching the beach at Heddon's Mouth, we can see the old lime kiln, with its memories of coasting trade with South Wales, and ports along the Bristol

Channel, and we then return up beside the river to our starting point at Hunter's Inn.

Start from **Hunter's Inn** car park (180) (SS 65-48), which is just over 2 miles north of the A39, 15 miles north-east of Barnstaple, and 6 miles west of Lynton. Hunter's Inn is on **Tour 6**, page 98, and on **Tour 8**, page 102.

(A) Leaving the car park, turn left and follow the road past Hunter's Inn, with its attractive gardens and peacocks, over two bridges and on, just past a road to the right. Turn left here down a lane signed *Trentishoe Mill*. Bear left off lane on to path running almost parallel with it. Our path runs through woodlands, largely of oak, keeping stream on left. As path begins to climb note an upright stone once used as a gatepost, and the ancient boundary bank running uphill. Where a path forks uphill, keep left and soon observe the top of Trentishoe Down ahead.

(B) At the road junction turn left, then almost immediately turn right uphill, over a stile. Climb steeply through oaks and bracken, on to open hillside, and straight up for Trentishoe Down. Nearing the top, bear right round the side of the hill, and up to the

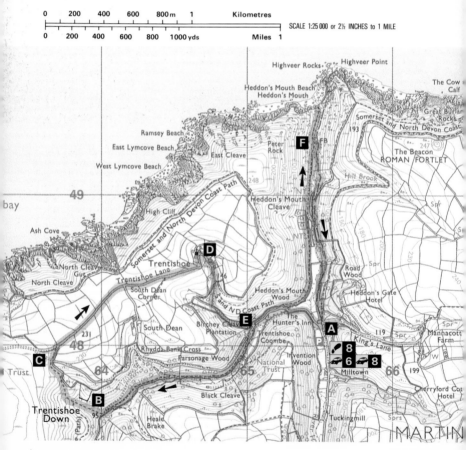

Hunter's Inn ... deep in the Heddon Valley.

road. Pause here for a fine inland view.

(C) Cross the road and go straight ahead to another minor road. In fine weather there are splendid views of the Bristol Channel and the Welsh coast from here. Turn right, along a little used road for just over half a mile, and drop down to the tiny hamlet of Trentishoe. The church on the left, one of the smallest in Devon, is well worth visiting. A delightful little musicians' gallery, erected in 1731, survives at the west end, and the hole cut into its balcony was for the express purpose of accommodating the movement of the double bass player's bow. It is said that the tower was once used by smugglers as a hiding place for their contraband.

(D) Leave Trentishoe down the lane, past the few remaining houses, to the road. Turn left, and in about 30 yards, just before a bridge **(E)**, turn left through a gate marked *Footpath to Heddon's Mouth*. (Alternatively, if you wish to shorten the walk, follow the road for a quarter of a mile, back to the car park starting point at Hunter's Inn. The car park will be on your right).

(E) Follow the level track, with the River Heddon on your right. Presently the steep slopes of Heddon's Mouth Cleave, rising to nearly 700 feet, will appear on the left. Our path detours to the right, through a gap in a stone wall, to avoid scree that has spilled across, but it is possible to go straight across.

(F) Passing a footbridge, climb left towards the beach. The scenery here is spectacular, especially when the waves are high. There are the remains of a lime kiln, in which limestone, brought here in coasters from South Wales, was once burnt with coal, also brought here from across the water, for use on the land, to counteract soil acidity. In return the coasters used to take pit props back to Wales for use in the coal mines. In high summer the further slopes are vivid with gorse and heather.

(F) Now return to the footbridge, cross it, and follow the path upstream, climbing slightly, until passing through a gate to emerge on the road beside Hunter's Inn. Turn right and then left, up the road to return to the car park **(A)**, thus completing Walk 8.

Walk 9
Cliff Country of Mortehoe and Lee Bay

Approximately 5 miles. Allow 4 hours.

This walk takes the rambler along one of the most pleasant scenic stretches of the North Devon Coast Path, with a return across quiet farming country providing a pleasant contrast. There are a few fairly steep gradients. We head north from Mortehoe, soon passing into National Trust owned land which extends around the coast from here to Lee Bay. On reaching the attractive Rockham Beach, we join the North Devon Coastal Path coming in from Morte Point. Then on northwards to Bull Point Lighthouse, built in the 1970s to replace an earlier building. From here our walk follows behind Damage Cliffs, bright with primroses in spring, to descend over the old golf course, into the pretty village of Lee. We then climb gradually up from the coast, over a small stream and

through woodlands, before returning via the attractive 17th century farmstead of Damage Barton, and over the fields to Mortehoe.

(A) Start from the car park at **Mortehoe** (180) (SS 45- 45), which is about 4 miles west of Ilfracombe, and which is on **Tour 8**, page 102. Leaving the car park, turn left and then immediately right, along the road signed *Footpath to Lighthouse and Lee*. Continue for about 400 yards until passing some cottages on left. Turn left down a lane signed *Rockham Beach*. Pass through a wicket-gate on to National Trust land and follow the footpath which runs along the right hand side of the valley, and eventually follows the coast northwards.

(B) The Coast Path from Morte Point joins our path at a stile. Notice the slide-up gate for dogs. Our path drops down to Rockham Bay, where steps lead down to the beach itself (good sand at low tide). Go over the stile and climb the steep slope ahead. From the top there are fine coastal views westward as far as Hartland Point. Lundy may sometimes be visible on the western horizon. Now turn right, drop downwards, and bear left where

Morte Point, near Mortehoe.

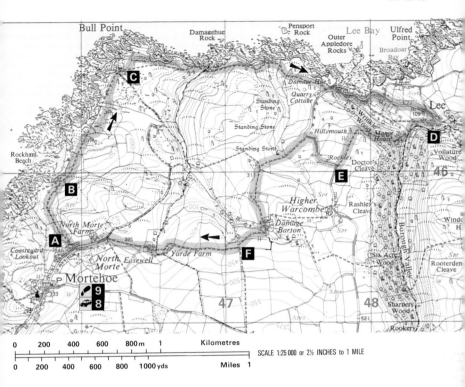

finger-post points. Then climb up straight ahead, until Bull Point Lighthouse comes into view. Descend a flight of steps, then follow the path as far as the lighthouse gates.

(C) Cross the lighthouse road, follow the path that runs up beside the wall, then bear left and continue along the Coast Path, which now runs eastwards, descending into, and climbing out of, two valleys where small streams run into the sea. Damage Cliffs, to our left are noted for their primroses in springtime. On all sides there are splendid views, and on a clear day the Welsh coast is clearly visible. Eventually our path passes through a wicket-gate on to a narrow road. Turn left and descend to the beautifully situated village of Lee, much loved by those who enjoy quiet beaches and rocky pools. Turn right opposite the slipway to the beach, and take the path signed *Lee and Toilets*, which runs alongside the car park. Beyond this, a wire mesh fence protects a field in which rare breeds of sheep are sometimes to be seen.

(D) Turn right with the fence, go through a gate into the field, pass alongside the wall and leave the field by a wicket-gate. Immediately cross a stream by a footbridge, and follow the path signed *Hr. Warcombe*. This path now climbs steeply up through Wrinkle Wood, presently crossing the access track to the Manor House on our right. Continue up through the wood, emerging at a stile at the

top. Bear right, as indicated by yellow marker, and skirt the hilltop on our left, presently bearing left at a view-point over Lee Bay. Cross the field towards *Rockley*, keeping the house on your right, and cross a stile on to a road.

(E) Turn right here, on to road, and descend the hill for about 300 yards, then turn sharp left on to the farm track leading to Damage Barton. The stile at the end of this track leads on to a field track and then on to a further farm track. Keep to the left here and shortly enter Damage Barton itself (keeping strictly to the public right of way). Notice how modern farming practice inevitably requires new structures to replace old farm buildings. Pass across in front of the attractive, largely 17th century farmhouse, and follow the lane uphill.

(F) Go through gate on the right marked *Footpath to Mortehoe*. Keeping hedge on right, go through two fields, then down a lane which leads to Yarde Farm. Turn left, around farm buildings, then right, over a stile beside an outbuilding. Bear diagonally left to the corner of the field, pass through a small gate and turn right across a minute stream by paving stones. Follow the signs for *Mortehoe* through the farm buildings of Easewell Farm and straight across the field used as a camping and caravan site. Turn left at the entrance and follow the road back to Mortehoe car park (A), thus completing Walk 9.

125

Walk 10
Buck's Mills Coast and the Pine-Coffin Country

Approximately 5 miles. Allow 3 hours.

This walk starts from Buck's Mills, a pretty fishing hamlet situated at the foot of a wooded combe, with thatched cottages lining a little road down to a rock-strewn, shingle beach. The old lime kiln just above the shore was once used for the burning of Welsh limestone, which was brought here by coaster from across the Bristol Channel. From Buck's Mills, we head eastwards, making use of the North Devon Coastal Path, before heading southwards, across country, to a quiet valley through which flows the infant River Yeo. Much of this area was owned by the Coffin (latterly Pine-Coffin) family who had lived at nearby Portledge (190) (39-24) since the time of Henry II, but Portledge is now a hotel. Beyond the Yeo we pass through the attractive hamlet of Broad Parkham. Regrettably we have had to use roads for much of this southern portion of our walk, but apart from a short stretch of the A39 in its latter stages, these roads, which are well away from the sea coast, should

prove comparatively quiet. Beyond them our route returns down a delightfully wooded length of path, to our starting point at Buck's Mills.

Drive to the little village of **Buck's Mills** (190) (SS 35-23), which is just to the north of the A39 at Buck's Cross, 7 miles west of Bideford, and which is on **Tour 10**, page 106.

(A) Turn right, out of the Buck's Mills car park entrance, and follow down road, passing cottages on each side, and a converted chapel and roadside stream on right hand verge. Turn right at the telephone kiosk, on to the North Devon Coastal Path, and as you ascend, stop at the bend for views across the bay, westwards to Clovelly nestling at the foot of high cliffs, and, weather permitting, the distant outline of Lundy Island, out to the north-west. Now soon passing the Coast Guard Lookout Station, continuing up well defined path. When reaching gate, go through it, round it, or rest on it to admire the sea view. After passing next stile, the path now continues on an easier climb, and there are glimpses through hedge gaps across Bideford Bay towards Saunton Sands and the large white hotel just above them.

(B) When reaching gate with stile at right hand side, ignore the Coastal Path's direction, and walk straight, on to a narrow road. Continue for about a quarter of a mile, passing Sloo Cottage on left. Road slowly

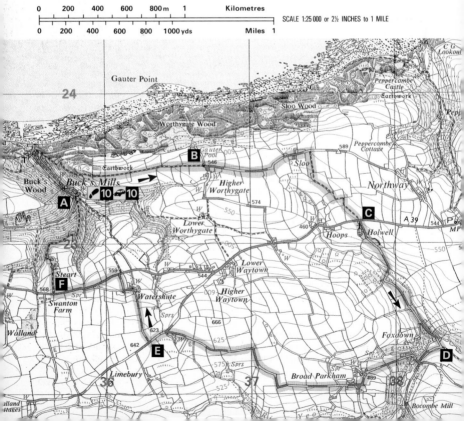

Buck's Mills, near the start of Walk 10.

rises and a concrete lookout shows above hedge on right hand side. Go through gateway on right **well before** this, and follow down with hedge on right. Keep along hedge to reach wide opening on right, go through this, turn right and right again, keeping hedge on right. At fifth corner, directly opposite a cream coloured building which is on the road, go through a small gap in the hedge and cross the field towards the house and road.

(C) Cross this road (the busy A39) with great care, on to a minor road, which passes a disused quarry on left, and goes down to a bridge over a stream. Pass entrance to Foxdown Hotel on right, and over another stream (the infant River Yeo).

(D) Turn to right, keeping on road, and then turn right at cross roads following sign marked *Broad Parkham*. Immediately re-cross River Yeo, by small mill house on left. Now make a short climb along road, first through high trees, later changing to hedges.

Enter Broad Parkham hamlet, and keep right at triangular junction, on to visible long stretch of road, with row of cottages on right. Nearing the top of a gentle rise, look back to see the outlines of Exmoor on the distant skyline, to the left of the television transmission mast.

(E) Turn left on reaching road junction, and then turn right after about 150 yards, at second road junction. As this road wends downhill, a large area of bay is again visible. Cross the busy A39 with great care, and walk left along the wide grass verge until reaching Steart (caravan site).

(F) Turn right, off A39 at Steart, down roadway into caravan site. After passing building on left, go through iron gate on right hand side, turn diagonally across bank, and then across paddock to corner stile. Cross stile and into woodland. Follow well defined path downwards, and eventually enter the rear of our starting point car park at **Buck's Mills (A)**, thus completing Walk 10.

127

WALKS

Walk 11
Hartland Quay Coastal Country

Approximately 4½ miles. Allow 3 hours.

This walk starts from the rugged western coast at Hartland Quay, and explores inland to the little village of Stoke, with its splendidly towered St Nectan's church, before heading southwards, along a pleasantly undulating 'green road' to the little hamlet of Lymebridge. Here will be found a beautifully restored mill, just beyond a small bridge over a stream, which we then come across at its most dramatic conclusion as it plunges over high cliffs into the sea at Speke's Mill Mouth. From here our walk follows the North Devon Coastal Path, past St Catherine's Tor, and St John's Well, before returning to Hartland Quay. This last section of the walk provides dramatic coastal views, both along the Devon coast itself, but also out across the water to distant Lundy Island, and to the long and equally dramatic cliffs of neighbouring Cornwall.

Drive to car park at **Hartland Quay** (190)

(SS 22-24), which is 15 miles west of Bideford, via A39 to Clovelly Cross, and then by a minor road through Hartland village. **Hartland Quay** is on **Tour 10**, page 106.

(A) Start walk by taking the road on which you have just arrived, back towards Stoke. At the gateway entrance on the left is the Rocket Apparatus House, used at times for rescue operations; and on the ridge of the adjoining field is a square stone building, a 'folly' known as 'Squire Orchard's Pleasure House', where this local worthy used to entertain visitors and guests to the delightful surrounding views, over tea, or other appropriate liquor. Continue along this road with Stoke church tower directly ahead. The road here has taken in the old line of footpath, but when reaching signpost a small section remains on the left, passing behind hedge and in front of dwellings, to emerge in front of a row of Coast Guard houses.

(A) Follow road keeping **Stoke** church on left. The handsomely pinnacled church tower, at about 130 feet, is amongst the highest in North Devon. At its entrance gate is a very old tree, with its branch limb now supported on a steel post. The interior of the church is well worth a visit, but for details, see page 71. Here also is a splendid view eastwards along the valley of the little Abbey

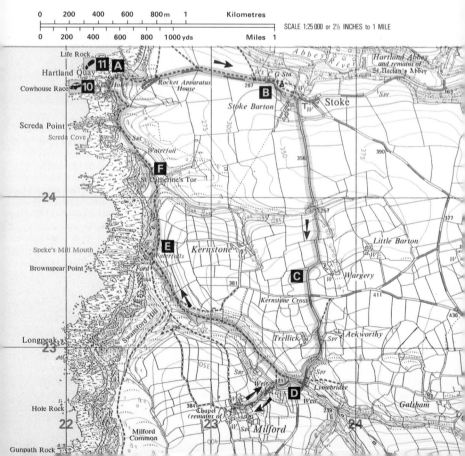

Coastline at Hartland Quay.

River, to the long line of Pattard Wood, which covers the northern valley slopes. Our road now curves around tightly to the left, and in a short distance turns sharp right. At this point there is another entrance to the churchyard on the left, and also toilets. A few yards along this road to the right, turn right between two cottages, one of which has a front door facing us, on to a 'green lane'. Now climb up this 'green lane' over a small ridge, when Wargery Farm will soon be seen almost directly ahead.

(C) At Kernstone Cross, beyond Wargery, the 'green lane' ends and we join a small road, which soon begins to drop quite sharply, passing Ackworthy on the left. Turn right at cross roads just before Lymebridge. Note well preserved cottages on two corners. In a few yards the road crosses the stream, and immediately to the right is the lane along the valley bottom to Speke's Mill Mouth, but before taking this path (which will be used later **(D)**), continue on road to the very charming Docton Mill. A mill has been on this site from the time of the Domesday Book, and since 1979 an imaginative restoration programme has been carried out, including a now working water-wheel, and delightfully landscaped grounds in which many rare plants are to be seen. Further on up the climbing road is the small community of Milford and the remains of an old chapel, now with an iron roof.

(D) Now turn back to the mill and, well beyond it and the bridge, take the valley floor path to which we referred above, and which is now on our left. After about a quarter of a mile, high hedges drop away and the path

ascends, with the sea thereby coming into view.

(E) Now arrive at Speke's Mill Mouth, where a waterfall drops some 54 feet, from 160 feet above sea level, then runs along a trough for about 130 feet, before finally dropping to the sea in three separate falls. This is an ideal picnic spot. Continue north along the way-marked Coastal Path. This starts quite steeply, but soon eases. Near the top there is (on clear days) a good view slightly west of north, to Lundy Island, with the prominent St Catherine's Tor in the foreground.

(F) When reaching the base of the Tor, the path is in a 'sea dissected valley', a rare example of this geographical phenomenon. In medieval times, when a river flowed through it, the monks of nearby Hartland Abbey used this valley as a swannery, and parts of the enclosing walls remain here to this day. On St Catherine's Tor are the very fragmentary remains of a 14th century chapel. Through gate to the left there is another small waterfall and examples of rock strata twisting from horizontal to vertical at sea level, making this coast even more hazardous in the powerful seas that prevail here.

As our route begins to ascend on a gravel track, water seeping from the rock face is still known as St John's Well, which was reputed to have healing properties for eye ailments in times past. Still climbing, turn occasionally to look south-westwards along the magnificent panorama of the Cornish coast. At a stile and wire fence, turn left for Hartland Quay's lower car park, or continue on Coastal Path for upper area **(A)**, thus completing Walk 11.

Walk 12
Welcombe Mouth, Marsland Mouth and the Cornish Border

Approximately 5 miles. Allow 4 hours.

This walk starts from the delightful little Welcombe church, well worth visiting for its crudely carved, but very pleasing 14th century rood screen (one of Devon's oldest), its attractive 15th century pulpit and Jacobean lectern. We drop down into a valley sheltering the small stream that marks the border between Devon and Cornwall, and turn west, parallel with it, to meet the sea at Marsland Mouth. Both this and Welcombe Mouth, which we head for next, shelter beneath great dark cliffs, with high gorse-covered hills rising behind them. As to be expected from their names, both 'mouths' witness the outpourings of small streams across their shingly, rock-strewn beaches, and are as unspoilt as any West Country beaches we

know. The walk north from Marsland Mouth follows the often steep route of the North Devon Coastal Path, and from Welcombe Mouth onwards we have provided an alternative route back to the church by way of an easier road; but if you are sound in wind and limb, do not miss the varied experience of the cliff walk that is taken by the 'main route', with its fine views, wild flowers and varied bird life.

Drive to the small village of **Welcombe** (190) (SS 22-18), which is just over two miles west of the A39 at Welcombe Cross, itself about 19 miles south-west of Bideford, and 10 miles north of Bude. It is on **Tour 10**, page 106.

(A) Take the road eastwards from the church, soon passing 'Down Barton' on right, 'St Morwenna' and village hall, with entrance to Linton on left. At cross roads (King's Cross) keep to road directly in front, which is a very minor one, at the end of which is a small triangle beyond Tredown (on left).

(B) Immediately beyond Tredown (on left), bear right at the triangle, on to a more used

Walkers on the North Devon Coastal Path.

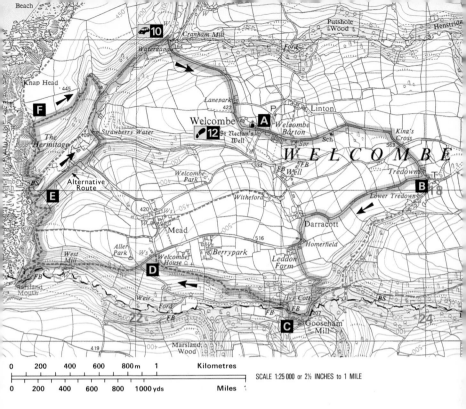

road, and continue until junction is reached at Darracott. Turn left here and go around bend in road, at the end of which is a wide opening into a farmyard (Leddon Farm) on left. Turn left down this now neglected and very minor road into valley and cross bridge by Gooseham Mill.

(C) At road junction near mill, turn right through gate towards 'Tall Trees', over wooden plank bridge and after a few yards turn sharp left by footpath sign in bush. Go along stream bank and over stile to enter woodlands. Keep right at forks and start to climb hill. After passing some small conservation clearings, the track widens and the sea comes in to view across a large clearing. After crossing stile, the path now keeps to right, close to the hedge, with a disused quarry on the right, near the top.

(D) Through gate and turn left on to car track, and cross stile immediately in front, to Marsland Mouth. When this long downward path nears entrance to cottage, turn right on to path in gorse bushes. At wooden barrier join North Devon Coastal Path by going to right up steps. (But go straight ahead if you wish to visit Marsland Mouth, with stream marking the very border with Cornwall, and then return to this point.) Now begins a climb northwards up the cliffs, with a lookout post at the top (not open). Over stile and turn left, with fine view, on a clear day, due north to distant island of Lundy. Beyond the edge of

the rock-face cross another stile, and then drop down to Welcombe Mouth, with its cascade of water over the rocks as the stream drops to the sea.

(E) (If you wish to make a less tiring return to Welcombe church, avoiding some very steep gradients, take the gravel track up, out of the Mouth, and on reaching road junctions, keep left, re-joining the more arduous route beyond the aptly coloured 'Strawberry Water' building.) Our 'arduous path' continues over round stepping stones across the stream and then ahead and left is a slightly less steep climb than the one out of Marsland Mouth. We soon turn partly right, across a shallow valley and then on upwards to a signpost at 400 feet. Here we turn left, alongside a gorse hedge.

(F) Near the top we leave the Coastal Path, which turns left into the gorse, and we follow the edge of cultivated ground, turning right when reaching signpost. Now begins a very steep descent through hawthorn and bramble at a gradient of about 1 in 3 for most of the way.

Eventually we reach a stile, crossing it and turning left when reaching road (where we are joined by the 'easy option walkers', who have come up the road from Welcombe Mouth at **(E)**). Continue along this road and at junction, turn right, over bridge and climb steeply back up to **Welcombe** church **(A)**, thus completing Walk 12.

CONVENTIONAL SIGNS   1:250 000 or 1 INCH to 4 MILES

ROADS
Not necessarily rights of way

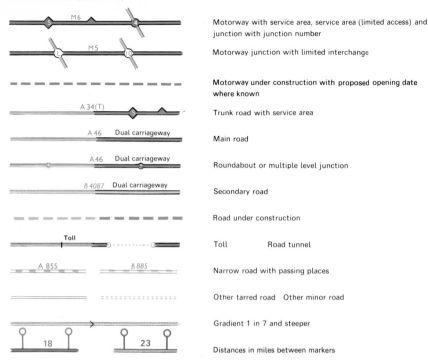

	Motorway with service area, service area (limited access) and junction with junction number
	Motorway junction with limited interchange
	Motorway under construction with proposed opening date where known
A 34(T)	Trunk road with service area
A 46 Dual carriageway	Main road
A 46 Dual carriageway	Roundabout or multiple level junction
B 4087 Dual carriageway	Secondary road
	Road under construction
Toll	Toll Road tunnel
A 855 B 885	Narrow road with passing places
	Other tarred road Other minor road
	Gradient 1 in 7 and steeper
18 23	Distances in miles between markers

The representation of a road is no evidence of the existence of a right of way

PRIMARY ROUTES

These form a national network of recommended through routes which complement the motorway system.
Selected places of major traffic importance are known as Primary Route Destinations and are shown thus BIDEFORD
Distances and directions to such destinations are repeated on traffic signs which, on primary routes, have a green
background or, on motorways, have a blue background.
To continue on a primary route through or past a place which has appeared as a destination on previous signs, follow
the directions to the next primary destination shown on the green-backed signs.

RAILWAYS

	Standard gauge track		Road crossing under or over
	Narrow gauge track		Level crossing
	Tunnel		Station

WATER FEATURES

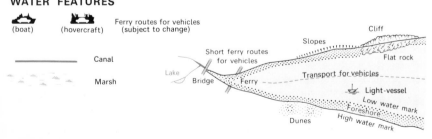

(boat)   (hovercraft)   Ferry routes for vehicles (subject to change)

Canal

Marsh

Lake   Bridge   Ferry   Short ferry routes for vehicles

Slopes   Cliff   Flat rock

Transport for vehicles

Light-vessel

Low water mark   Foreshore   High water mark

Dunes

ANTIQUITIES

✳ Native fortress	✗ Site of battle (with date)	----- Roman road (course of)	CANOVIUM · Roman antiquity
Castle · Other antiquities			

𝔪   Ancient Monuments and Historic Buildings in the care of the Secretaries of State for the Environment, for Scotland and for Wales and that are open to the public.

BOUNDARIES

 National

 County, Region or Islands Area

GENERAL FEATURES

Buildings

Wood

Lighthouse (in use)

Lighthouse (disused)

Windmill

Radio or TV mast

▲ Youth hostel

⊕ } Civil aerodrome { with Customs facilities

✛ } without Customs facilities

Ⓗ Heliport

☎ Public telephone

☎ Motoring organisation telephone

+ Intersection, latitude & longitude at 30′ intervals (not shown where it confuses important detail)

TOURIST INFORMATION

✝ Abbey, Cathedral, Priory

🐟 Aquarium

Ⓧ Camp site

🚐 Caravan site

🏰 Castle

Cave

Country park

Craft centre

❀ Garden

▶ Golf course or links

🏠 Historic house

ℹ Information centre

Motor racing

🖼 Museum

Nature or forest trail

Nature reserve

☆ Other tourist feature

✕ Picnic site

Preserved railway

Racecourse

🎿 Skiing

Viewpoint

Wildlife park

🐘 Zoo

WALKS, CYCLE & MOTOR TOURS
Applicable to all scales

 Start point of walk

➡ Route of walk

Featured walk

 Start point of tour

➡ Route of tour

Featured tour

FOLLOW THE COUNTRY CODE
Enjoy the countryside and respect its life and work

Guard against all risk of fire

Fasten all gates

Keep your dogs under close control

Keep to public paths across farmland

Leave livestock, crops and machinery alone

Use gates and stiles to cross fences, hedges and walls

Take your litter home

Help to keep all water clean

Protect wildlife, plants and trees

Take special care on country roads

Make no unnecessary noise

CONVENTIONAL SIGNS

1:25 000 or 2½ INCHES to 1 MILE

ROADS AND PATHS

Not necessarily rights of way

M I or A 6(M)	M I or A 6(M)	Motorway
A 31 (T)	A 31(T)	Trunk road
A 35	A 35	Main road
B 3074	B 3074	Secondary road
A 35	A 35	Dual carriageway

Narrow roads with passing places are annotated

Road generally more than 4m wide

Road generally less than 4m wide

Other road, drive or track

Unfenced roads and tracks are shown by pecked lines

.... Path

RAILWAYS

	Multiple track	Standard gauge
	Single track	
	Narrow gauge	
	Siding	
	Cutting	
	Embankment	
	Tunnel	
	Road over & under	
	Level crossing; station	

PUBLIC RIGHTS OF WAY

Public rights of way may not be evident on the ground

- - - - - } Public paths { Footpath / Bridleway

+ + + + + Byway open to all traffic

- - - - - Road used as a public path

The indication of a towpath in this book does not necessarily imply a public right of way

The representation of any other road, track or path is no evidence of the existence of a right of way

DANGER AREA

MOD ranges in the area
Danger!
Observe warning notices

Mountain Rescue Post

BOUNDARIES

— · — · — County (England and Wales)

— — — — District

—∘—∘—∘— London Borough

.... Civil Parish (England)* Community (Wales)

— — — — Constituency (County, Borough, Burgh or European Assembly)

Coincident boundaries are shown by the first appropriate symbol

*For Ordnance Survey purposes County Boundary is deemed to be the limit of the parish structure whether or not a parish area adjoins

SYMBOLS

Church or chapel { with tower / with spire / without tower or spire

Glasshouse; youth hostel

Bus or coach station

Lighthouse; lightship; beacon

Triangulation station

Triangulation point on { church or chapel / lighthouse, beacon / building; chimney

Electricity transmission line
pylon   pole

VILLA   Roman antiquity (AD 43 to AD 420)

Castle   Other antiquities

Site of antiquity

⚔ 1066   Site of battle (with date)

Gravel pit

Sand pit

Chalk pit, clay pit or quarry

Refuse or slag heap

Sloping wall

Water   Mud

Sand; sand & shingle

National Park or Forest Park Boundary

NT   National Trust always open

NT   National Trust opening restricted

FC   Forestry Commission

VEGETATION
Limits of vegetation are defined by positioning of the symbols but may be delineated also by pecks or dots

Coniferous trees

Non-coniferous trees

Coppice

Orchard

Scrub

Bracken, rough grassland
In some areas bracken (∙) and rough grassland (·····) are shown separately

Heath

Shown collectively as rough grassland on some sheets

Reeds

Marsh

Saltings

HEIGHTS AND ROCK FEATURES

50 · } Determined { ground survey
285 ·   by   air survey

Surface heights are to the nearest metre above mean sea level. Heights shown close to a triangulation pillar refer to the station height at ground level and not necessarily to the summit

Vertical face

Loose rock   Boulders   Outcrop   Scree

Contours are at 5 metres vertical interval

ABBREVIATIONS
1:25 000 or 2½ INCHES to 1 MILE also 1:10 000/1:10 560 or 6 INCHES to 1 MILE

BP,BS	Boundary Post or Stone	P	Post Office	A,R	Telephone, AA or RAC
CH	Club House	Pol Sta	Police Station	TH	Town Hall
F V	Ferry Foot or Vehicle	PC	Public Convenience	Twr	Tower
FB	Foot Bridge	PH	Public House	W	Well
HO	House	Sch	School	Wd Pp	Wind Pump
MP,MS	Mile Post or Stone	Spr	Spring		
Mon	Monument	T	Telephone, public		

Abbreviations applicable only to 1:10 000/1:10 560 or 6 INCHES to 1 MILE

Ch	Church	GP	Guide Post	TCB	Telephone Call Box
F Sta	Fire Station	Pole or Post	TCP	Telephone Call Post
Fn	Fountain	S	Stone	Y	Youth Hostel

Maps and Mapping

Most early maps of the area covered by this guide were published on a county basis, and if you wish to follow their development in detail R. V. Tooley's *Maps and Map Makers* will be found most useful. The first significant county maps were produced by Christopher Saxton in the 1570s, the whole of England and Wales being covered in only six years. Although he did not cover the whole country, John Norden, working at the end of the 16th century, was the first map-maker to show roads. In 1611-12, John Speed, making use of Saxton and Norden's pioneer work, produced his *'Theatre of the Empire of Great Britaine'*, adding excellent town plans, battle scenes, and magnificent coats of arms. The next great English map-maker was John Ogilby, and in 1675 he published *Britannia, Volume I*, in which all the roads of England and Wales were engraved on a scale of one inch to the mile, in a massive series of strip maps. From this time onwards, no map was published without roads, and throughout the 18th century, steady progress was made in accuracy, if not always in the beauty of presentation.

The first Ordnance Survey maps came about as a result of Bonnie Prince Charlie's Jacobite rebellion of 1745. It was however in 1791, following the successful completion of the military survey of Scotland by General Roy, that the Ordnance Survey was formally established. The threat of invasion by Napoleon in the early 19th century spurred on the demand for accurate and detailed mapping for military purposes, and to meet this need the first Ordnance Survey one-inch map, covering part of Essex, was published in 1805 in a single colour. This map was the first numbered sheet in the First Series of one-inch maps.

Over the next seventy years the one-inch map was extended to cover the whole of Great Britain. Reprints of some of these First Series maps, incorporating various later 19th century amendments, have been published by David & Charles. The reprinted sheets covering our area are Numbers 74, 75, 82 and 83.

The Ordnance Survey's First Series one-inch maps evolved through a number of 'Series' and editions, to the Seventh Series which was replaced in 1972 by the metric 1:50 000 scale Landranger Series. Between the First Series one-inch and the current Landranger maps many changes in style, format, content and purpose have taken place. Colour, for example, first appeared with the timid use of light brown for hill shading on the 1889 one-inch sheets. By 1892 as many as five colours were being used for this scale and at one stage the Seventh Series was being printed in no fewer than ten colours. Recent developments in 'process printing' — a technique in which four basic colours produce almost any required tint — are now used to produce Ordnance Survey Landranger and other map series. Through the years the one-inch Series has gradually turned away from its military origins and has developed to meet a wider user demand. The modern detailed full colour Landranger maps at 1:50 000 scale incorporate rights of way and tourist information and are much used for both leisure and business purposes. To compare the old and new approaches to changing demand, see the two map extracts of Lynton on pages 136 & 137.

Modern Ordnance Survey maps of the area.

To look at the area surrounding our Landranger Sheets 180, 181, 182 and 190, the O.S. 1 Inch to 4 miles, **Routemaster** Sheet 8 (South West England and South Wales) will prove most useful. An alternative will be found in the form of the O.S. Motoring Atlas, at the larger scale of 1 Inch to 3 miles.

The Ordnance Survey publishes a One-inch to the mile Tourist Map of Exmoor which covers an area from Bideford in the west to Cullompton in the east, and from Ilfracombe and Minehead in the north to North Tawton in the south.

To examine our area in greater detail and especially if you are planning walks, the Ordnance Survey publishes a modern Pathfinder map at 1:25 000 scale (2½ inches to 1 mile) which carries public rights of way information. The Pathfinder series is gradually replacing the old 1:25 000 First Series (which does not show rights of way). Most of our area is covered by Pathfinder series maps. Ordnance Survey maps are available from officially appointed agents (local agents are shown on page 21, under 'Useful Addresses'), and from most booksellers, stationers and newsagents. To place the area in an historical context the following O.S. **Archaeological and Historical maps** will also be found useful: **Roman Britain, Britain in the Dark Ages, Britain before the Norman Conquest,** and **Monastic Britain.**

See following pages for extracts relating to Lynton, taken from the First Series one-inch map, and the latest Landranger map.

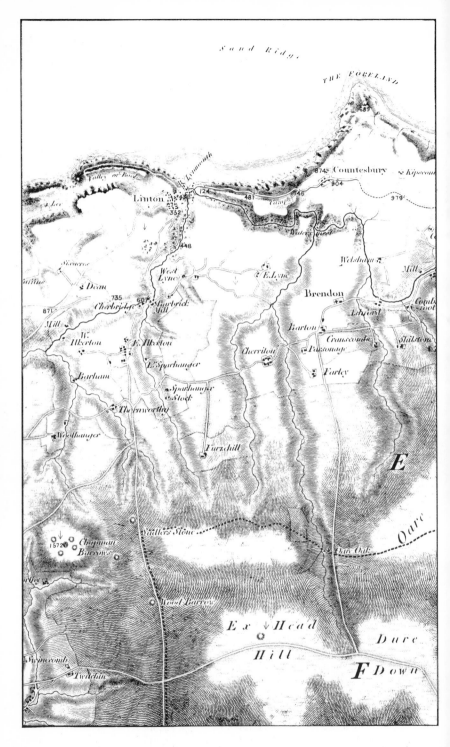

Scale of one Inch to a Statute Mile

0   1   2   Miles 3

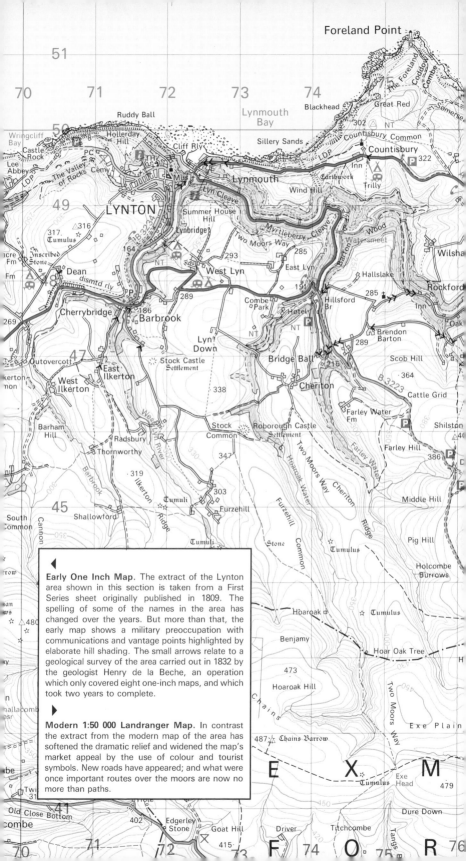

Early One Inch Map. The extract of the Lynton area shown in this section is taken from a First Series sheet originally published in 1809. The spelling of some of the names in the area has changed over the years. But more than that, the early map shows a military preoccupation with communications and vantage points highlighted by elaborate hill shading. The small arrows relate to a geological survey of the area carried out in 1832 by the geologist Henry de la Beche, an operation which only covered eight one-inch maps, and which took two years to complete.

Modern 1:50 000 Landranger Map. In contrast the extract from the modern map of the area has softened the dramatic relief and widened the map's market appeal by the use of colour and tourist symbols. New roads have appeared; and what were once important routes over the moors are now no more than paths.

Index

INDEX

INDEX

Further Reading

General

Delderfield, E.R. *The Lynmouth Flood Disaster.* E.R.D.Publications
Exmoor National Park. *Enjoying Exmoor.* E.N.P.A.
Hoskins, W.G. *Devon.* Collins
Hoskins, W.G. *The Making of the English Landscape.* Pelican
Hutchings, M. *Inside Somerset.* Abbey Press, Sherborne
Hutton, E. *Highways and Byways in Somerset.* Chapman & Hall
Jellicoe & Mayne, *Shell Guide to Devon.* Faber & Faber
Langham, A.& M. *Lundy.* David & Charles
Mee, A. *Devon.* Hodder & Stoughton Queen's England Series
Mee, A. *Somerset.* Hodder & Stoughton Queen's England Series
Norway, A.H. *Highways and Byways in Devon and Cornwall.* Chapman & Hall
Peel, J.H.B. *Portrait of Exmoor.* Hale
Pevsner, N. *North Devon.* Penguin Buildings of England Series
Pevsner, N. *South Devon.* Penguin Buildings of England Series
Pevsner, N. *South & West Somerset.* Penguin Buildings of England Series.
Waite, V. *Portrait of the Quantocks.* Hale
Webber, R. *The Devon and Somerset Blackdowns.* Hale
Whitlock, R. *Somerset.* Batsford

Art, Architecture & History

Acland, A. *A Devon Family: The Story of the Aclands.* Phillimore
Ayres, J. (Ed.) *Paupers and Pig Killers. The Diary of William Holland (Vicar of Over Stowey) 1799-1818.* Alan Sutton
Clifton-Taylor, A. *English Parish Churches as Works of Art.* Batsford
Dunning, R. *A History of Somerset.* Phillimore
Dyer, J. *Prehistoric England & Wales.* Penguin
Grinsell, L.V. *The Archaeology of Exmoor.* David & Charles
Hawkes, J. *Guide to Prehistoric & Roman Monuments in England and Wales.* Cardinal
Jones, S. *Legends of Devon.* Bossiney Books
Jones, S. *Legends of Somerset.* Bossiney Books
Lamplugh, L. *Barnstaple: Town on the Taw.* Phillimore
Lamplugh, L. *A History of Ilfracombe.* Phillimore
Morris, J. (Ed) *Domesday Book: Devon.* Phillimore
Morris, J. (Ed) *Domesday Book: Somerset.* Phillimore
Staines, R. *A History of Devon.* Phillimore
Tooley, R.V. *Maps and Map-Makers.* Batsford

Canals

Hadfield, C. *The Canals of South West England.* David & Charles
Harris, H. *The Grand Western Canal.* David & Charles
Rolt, L.T.C. *Inland Waterways of England.* Batsford
Russell, R. *Lost Canals & Waterways of Britain.* Sphere

Fiction, Literary Interest, and Early Travellers

Blackmore, R.D. *Lorna Doone.* Pan
Burton, S.H. *The Lorna Doone Trail.* Exmoor Press
Defoe, D. *A Tour Through England and Wales.* Penguin
Dunn, W.H. *The Author of Lorna Doone.* Hale
Kingsley, C. *Westward Ho!* Heron
Lawrence, B. *Coleridge and Wordsworth in Somerset.* David & Charles
Moorman, M. *Journal of Dorothy Wordsworth.* Oxford
Morris, C. *The Journeys of Celia Fiennes.* Macdonald
Williamson, H. *The Lone Swallows.* Alan Sutton
Williamson, H. *Tarka the Otter.* Bodley Head

Railways

Brown, Prideaux & Ratcliffe *The Lynton & Barnstaple Railway.* David & Charles
MacDermot, E.T. *History of the Great Western Railway.* Ian Allan
Sellick, R. *The West Somerset Mineral Railway.* David & Charles

Ships and Harbours

Burton, S.H. *The North Devon Coast.* Werner Laurie
Farr, G. *Ships and Harbours of Exmoor.* Exmoor Press
Hodges, C.W. *The Overland Launch.* (See Countisbury.) Heinemann

Walks and Walking

Exmoor National Park *Waymarked Walks, Vols 1,2 & 3*
Gunnell, C. *Somerset and North Devon Coastal Path.* H.M.S.O.
Rowett, H. *The Two Moors Way.* Ramblers Association
S.W.W.Association. *The South West Way.* S.W.W.Association